RELIGION AND
THE PUBLIC ORDER

THE INSTITUTE OF CHURCH AND STATE
VILLANOVA UNIVERSITY SCHOOL OF LAW

RELIGION AND
THE PUBLIC ORDER

NUMBER FIVE

An Annual Review of Church and State,
  and of Religion, Law, and Society

Edited by DONALD A. GIANNELLA

The Institute of Church and State
  Villanova University School of Law

CORNELL UNIVERSITY PRESS

Ithaca and London

First published 1969

Standard Book Number 8014–0527–0

Library of Congress Catalog Number 79–87016

PRINTED IN THE UNITED STATES OF AMERICA
BY CAYUGA PRESS, INC.

Contents

ARTICLES

MARTIN E. MARTY

Secularization in the American Public Order

In recent years the term "secularization" has come into common usage in historical, sociological, and theological analyses of culture. While it has taken on many shadings of meaning—some of them contradictory—in general it refers to a process by which, progressively, God has been edged out of the affairs of man. As symbol or reality, God does not have to be reckoned with as he once was in both social and personal life. The natural replaces the supernatural, the immanent stands in the place of the transcendent, concern is for the physical, not the metaphysical. Human history is the only horizon; the world "rounds itself out." No sacral symbols or religious or quasi-religious symbols are necessary for interpreting man's world. While no one speaks of the world as wholly secularized, an impressive number of analysts have seen the West and, by inference and indirection, the world itself moving "beyond religion."

More recently the concept of secularization has begun to be called into question.[1] Is it adequate to describe what we need to know about

Martin E. Marty is Professor of Church History at the University of Chicago Divinity School.

Author's note: In this essay, conceived as a survey, I discuss the literature on secularization from 1950 to 1967, with particular emphasis on American historical development. Rather than concentrating on one or two illuminating events, I have dealt with wholes, surmising this approach may be most useful to the broadest variety of readers.

[1] See, e.g., Ch. I, HERBERT W. RICHARDSON, TOWARD AN AMERICAN THEOLOGY (1967).

[3]

the West and especially about America? Does it refer to a single, mono-dimensional, mono-directional process, or do manifest contradictions in historical tendencies limit its analytical usefulness? How should we account for the astonishing varieties of religions, the impressive durability of the religious response, the evident spiritual hungers among our contemporaries? Historians and sociologists were the first to complain about the misleading character of the word secularization when it is used to suggest the all-embracing life-style and spiritual substance of an epoch. Theologians, too, have begun to question the appropriateness of the category as an all-inclusive term.

At first glance, how men decide about the term may seem to be nothing more than an analytic and academic matter, but it will none the less have an impact on the future. How men perceive contemporary reality and how they envision the future has important consequences for practical action. The task of describing the "mental universe"—the sacred canopy [2] or secular cosmos—which contemporaries inhabit should be a major item on the scholars' agendas. People of reflective capacity should seek understanding of the sources of this contemporary universe, whether they be located five hundred years ago in the Renaissance [3] or two centuries ago with the Enlightenment or ten years ago with Sputnik.

Out of such understanding come practical decisions. Several examples should illustrate. In the public order the religious and the secular constantly come into each other's spheres and personal fates are involved. If it is true in any sense that the courts read and count the ballots, these courts must be able to discern secular tendencies in religious America and religious tendencies in secular America. Political leaders must be mindful not only of the state of religious institutions to the extent that they may represent voting blocs, but must also respect the distinct beliefs and the prejudices of the voters themselves on vital issues like peace and race, and take into account other

[2] The term is from PETER BERGER, THE SACRED CANOPY (1967); THOMAS LUCKMAN speaks of "the sacred cosmos" in THE INVISIBLE RELIGION (1967); from his book I also draw the distinction between secularization in institutions, the sacred cosmos, and the basic myth or world view.

[3] ERICH KAHLER, THE MEANING OF HISTORY (1964) pushes the inquiry into roots of secularization back many centuries, at least to the time of St. Augustine.

similar opinions often based on the voters' relations to that which concerns them ultimately, whether this be God or non-God or anti-God. Communicators through the public media have to reckon constantly with their responsibility as shapers of values, morals, and attitudes; they have preempted positions historically occupied by priestly figures and ecclesiastical forces.[4] Educators are busy trying to make provision for inculcating and developing beliefs, opinions, notions, and attitudes in students of all ages. Since public education has so many of its roots in religious tradition there is no possibility that the educational establishment can permanently evade questions of religious and nonreligious commitment.

We have seen again and again in the 1960's that a slight misreading of the public temper can be disastrous for politicians' careers, complicating for the lives of judges, and embarrassing to communicators or educators who have not been mindful of the religious views of their clienteles. Since few of the people making public decisions touching on ultimate values are professionally involved or vocationally equipped to locate such decisions in theology or in philosophy, those responsible for theological and antitheological heritages have found it necessary to concentrate on and contend for differing positions on the subject of secularization and to explain these to the public.

No one comes to the task of explanation without assumptions, whether they be implicit or explicit. How one defines sacred and secular, how he relates to them, how he remembers childhood experiences with both and in the many-man's-land between them—all these will color his exposition. Sometimes these assumptions and presuppositions are so confusing that they lead to mischief among people who do not recognize them but who do read the results of analysis by people who hold them.

David Martin has shown,[5] for instance, how a hidden metaphysic lurks behind much analysis of the development of secularization.

---

[4] WILLIAM STEPHENSON, THE PLAY THEORY OF MASS COMMUNICATION (1967) discusses the areas of life which media reach easily and those ("belief," etc.) where they meet some resistance.

[5] Martin, *Towards Eliminating the Concept of Secularization*, PENGUIN SURVEY OF THE SOCIAL SCIENCES 1965 (J. Gould ed. 1965); I have slightly revised some of his emphases.

Sometimes it rests on an unexamined and insubstantial distinction between otherworldliness and thisworldliness. In such terms all trends to thisworldliness represent a tendency toward or a fulfillment of secularization. Is the distinction useful? How does one classify those Eastern religions which have never been regarded as otherworldly, or a Texas Baptist millionaire who is seen by all the world as a materialist, but who genuinely yearns for and adheres to an explicitly otherworldly Gospel?

Beyond these questions, Martin asks, are there not Rationalist, Marxist, or Existentialist biases in most cases? The Rationalist philosophy of history and program of action has, since the eighteenth century, seen religion and supernaturalism as superstitious barriers to the development or fulfillment of reason and freedom, and has envisaged the progressive elimination of religion from the human scene. The Marxist version has, since the nineteenth century, described religion as an opiate, a deterrent to the unfolding of the future that the Marxists have foreseen and that they have tried to help bring into being. Even more self-confidently and with an almost metaphysical passion, classic Marxism has uttered the prophecy of the death of God, the assured base of what would look like a secular possibility in personal life and society. In the twentieth century, the Existentialist interpretation has characteristically tried to account for an absurd universe in which man acts. The reflective Existentialist finds little of the meaning which God or other elements in the religious continuity have imposed upon understanding.

Neither David Martin nor others who have sensed the disguised metaphysical commitments behind such interpretations would try to suggest that they are employed mindlessly by people to block out views of reality which conflict with their assumptions. Marxists, Existentialists, and Rationalists come with various presuppositions and exhibit a wild pluralism. Many of them give due credit to the complexity of the human venture and give an accounting of the durability of religion. Others who are more simplistic are serenely certain about the outcome of history; they write off the survival of religion as a problematic element in the time table of secularization. Still others use the residual (and sometimes increasing) religious elements as bogeys to inspire half-hearted sharers of their vision to actively oppose religion as "bad faith," or as enslaving or narcotic in its effects.

A relatively new element in the analyses of secularization showed up in theological circles a third of a century ago and came near to styling a school of "secular theology" in the early 1960's.[6] Whereas preachers and theologians in the Christian tradition at least had long scorned the secular and equated it with opposition to the sacral in general and the faith in particular, now—first in German Protestantism and then across the Christian West, including Roman Catholicism—a main line of interpretation saw secularization as a positive working out of Biblical motifs.

This movement derived in part from the polemic against "religion as unbelief" in the writings of Karl Barth, from the idea of Friedrich Gogarten that the Bible gave the impulse to Western secularization, and from the vision of Dietrich Bonhoeffer that the world was coming of age and that man was moving beyond religion. It is more difficult to trace this movement in Eastern Christianity, although some Russian Orthodox theologians have regularly pointed out that they are

---

[6] This list is restricted to books which make "religionlessness" or "secularization" a fundamental category; it is not an attempt at an exhaustive introduction to "new theology," "radical theology," "death of God theology," etc.: K. BARTH, CHURCH DOGMATICS (1936); D. BONHOEFFER, PRISONER FOR GOD (1953); D. CALLAHAN, THE SECULAR CITY DEBATE (1966); H. COX, THE SECULAR CITY (1965); C. DUQUOC, SPIRITUALITY IN THE SECULAR CITY (1966); G. EBELING, WORD AND FAITH (1963); F. GOGARTEN, DER MENSCH ZWISCHEN GOTT UND WELT (1956); M. JARRETT-KERR, THE SECULAR PROMISE (1964); D. JENKINS, BEYOND RELIGION (1962); W. HAMILTON, THE NEW ESSENCE OF CHRISTIANITY (1961); A. MACINTYRE, SECULARIZATION AND MORAL CHANGE (1967); MacIntyre has disassociated himself from Christianity and is not part of a "movement"; C. MICHALSON, WORLDLY THEOLOGY (1967); D. MUNBY, THE IDEA OF A SECULAR SOCIETY (1963); L. NEWBIGIN, HONEST RELIGION FOR SECULAR MAN (1966); J. A. PHILLIPS, CHRIST FOR US IN THE THEOLOGY OF DIETRICH BONHOEFFER (1967); J. A. T. ROBINSON, HONEST TO GOD (1963); L. SHINER, THE SECULARIZATION OF HISTORY (1966); R. G. SMITH, THE NEW MAN: CHRISTIANITY AND MAN'S COMING OF AGE (1956) and SECULAR CHRISTIANITY (1966); P. VAN BUREN, THE SECULAR MEANING OF THE GOSPEL (1963); A. T. VAN LEEUWEN, CHRISTIANITY AND WORLD HISTORY (1965); G. WILMORE, THE SECULAR RELEVANCE OF THE CHURCH (1962); C. WILLIAMS, FAITH FOR A SECULAR AGE (1966); G. WINTER, THE NEW CREATION AS METROPOLIS (1963). For highly critical works in this category, see: A. E. LOEN, SECULARIZATION: SCIENCE WITHOUT GOD? (1967); E. MASCALL, THE SECULARIZATION OF CHRISTIANITY (1966).

really the experts at living with and effecting syntheses with secularizers! But it is hard to picture the positive view of secularization disappearing wholly from Catholic and Protestant thought in the West, however much the theologians may qualify their earlier unguarded enthusiasm for the process.

The problems raised for theological work by such a point of view need not be detailed here. Suffice it to say that some have seen secular theology as a betrayal of the faith itself;[7] others have seen it as a problem that must be faced and a possibility with which Christians or other religious people may work; still others, perhaps a waning minority, have made it the be-all and end-all of religious reflection and have suggested that all theological themes must be embraced under it.

We note the theologians' affirmations only to underscore the complexity of the topic and to anticipate an element of public misunderstanding in the field of action in society. For now it is possible to summarize the secular thinkers' brief and almost canonical view of Western development over half a millennium. Astronomy first led man to see that he was not at the center of the universe. Philosophy taught him to doubt. History and sociology taught him to see the relativity of all positions and institutions, including religious ones. Science robbed him of his uniqueness in separation from nature. Personal experience led him to question the presence of God, and practically he learned to live the same way whether God and the priests existed or not. The result was a widespread "public atheism," often disguised under myriad religious symbols.

To be more specific: the American environment has provided a special case for the student of secularization in the legal and constitutional sphere. One should never underestimate the impact of secularization in this context; "church" and "state" have always been potent entities in the lives of Western man. The forces which have served to symbolize or enact his relationship to the ultimate on the one hand and those which have led him to war and through peace naturally play a great part in his destiny and daily life. The sacral sanctions for

---

[7] *See* MASCALL, *supra* n. 6.

kingship, the state, and the governmental order have been consistently vivid.

Any change in the fundamental relationships between sacred and secular in the realm of government and the state will influence many aspects of peoples' lives. Such change comes through legal and constitutional alterations. When the United States of America made changes it went further than any other nation before it (and perhaps since) in carefully demarking the legal zones of influence. The lines have not been perfectly neat, of course; the "wall" of separation has always had fissures and cracks,[8] and church and state have intruded upon each other formally and informally in countless ways throughout national history. But a novel element introduced into the United States Constitution differentiated it from previous constitutional and covenantal experience in the West.

The heart of this novelty lay in the fact that the Constitution was metaphysically silent. It simply did not and does not commit people to specific views of transcendence, of the ultimate, of God. Dennis Munby has suggested that among other elements these two at least must be present in the base of a secular society: it must not coerce people to a specific faith, and it must not lend its weight to the support of one or several. It is noncommittal.[9] The late Father John Courtney Murray, S.J.,[10] never tired of pointing out that Americans throughout their history have regularly brought private metaphysical interpretations to the Constitution and our institutional history; thus for many a strictly separationist Baptist theological interpretation of the relation between church and state has predominated. But these exegeses did not have and could not have had official endorsement.

Starting with Virginia in the late eighteenth century and continuing up through the first third of the nineteenth century in New England, the states undertook the disestablishment of religion. The ensuing revolution in the administrative life of the church altered it more profoundly than anything else which had occurred since the

---

[8] The most comprehensive gathering of material on separation and nonseparation remains ANSON PHELPS STOKES, CHURCH AND STATE IN THE UNITED STATES (3 vols. 1950).

[9] *See* MUNBY, *supra* n. 6, at 14 ff.

[10] *See, e.g.,* J. C. MURRAY, WE HOLD THESE TRUTHS (1960).

beginning of the Constantinian era in the early fourth century. This adjustment produced freedom of religion and effected what have come to be called "voluntary churches"; it also had political consequences: the public realm could not invoke a specific religious sanction or depend on a particular religious interpretation.

So the Constitution, while it allows all kinds of religions in the nation, is fundamentally secular in most understandable uses of the term. And the early national experience of separation of church and state saw the ecclesiastical forces willingly accepting the secular terms as basis for their own mission and competition. To Christopher Dawson the presence of hundreds of competitive denominational groups contributed further to American-style secularization, for the self-defeating divisions made clear to all that there was no single vivifying and interpenetrative interpretive scheme of the kind he imagined must have existed in fourteen centuries of "Christendom." In such an interpretation pluralism is equivalent to secularism. Pluralism represents a "nothing" term, a vacuum, an empty concept, a ground rule to be filled by ideology, and in the American instance this situation bred secularism. (One could also stress the opposite: that this most pluralist of societies forced people to find a consensus; in Perry Miller's term, Americanization was not an inheritance but an achievement for each person and group.[11] Out of their striving something like a general national religiousness served to compete against denominational particularity.)

The secularization of the state on a legal basis has meant that other fundamental institutions have had to be formally secular, too, in so far as they were under state control. For almost two hundred years the logic of the Constitution has been worked out in various ways, and one would not look for neatness in adaptations. Yet American public school education has moved steadily toward the secular and away from ecclesiastical auspices. The numbers of religiously based colleges and universities have been reduced as the sphere of public higher education has increased. Self-chosen secularization also ap-

---

[11] P. MILLER, NATURE'S NATION, Ch. I (1967).

peared on this level of education.[12] Just before the beginning of the twentieth century, many church-related schools which were free to remain churchly chose to sequester, to reduce, or to eliminate theological studies and to enlarge and enhance practical and scientific areas in the curriculum.

When Gertrude Stein called America "the first new nation" she was referring to its head start in the processes of mass production, but she might have pointed out that it was the first to "go secular" in the legal sense. Many have seen this anticipation of a post-Christian constitutional context as the base for a pervasive secularity which has often been shrouded or obscured by Americans as they keep up their habits of church-going or giving reverence to God and being religious in other ways in their private, familial, and ecclesiastical spheres. Since America has also set a pace in industrialization, science, and technology—other realms commonly seen to be "secular" and not in need of the God-hypothesis—America is placed high on the scale of advanced Western secular societies.

Here is the place to call a halt to such generalizations and to comment, in the fashion of David S. Martin, on the limits of the concept "secularization" and on the complexity and ambiguity of the American development. To do so involves one in some necessary criticism of the linear interpreters of secularization as an all-embracing style and an inevitable force.

One must ask such interpreters to be more secular than they seem to be in practice, or in other words, to be more empirical, pragmatic, analytical, and in a way agnostic. Those who speak of a fulfilled secularization as an inevitable in national history are dealing with the future as if it had already occurred, as if they knew its outcome and could bounce it back into history. One must ask them how do they "know" the future, the outcome, the end of the story. Is there a disguised metaphysic in their inevitabilist view? [13]

---

[12] L. Veysey, The Emergence of the American University (1965). *See especially* Ch. I.

[13] For a full development of the analytic aproach to history, see Arthur Danto, Analytical Philosophy of History (1965).

One could turn this around and ask what makes them so sure that they can extrapolate from the trends of Western technology and constitutional history and discern a line of human development normative for all societies in the future; in which case the only interesting element in the future history of secularization would be the observance of how and when people follow the timetable of secularization. At other moments of epochal change in culture something like the contemporary "public atheism" has emerged and has inspired prophecies of a secular future. But after the change it became clear that the earlier secular age (certain moments in the Greco-Roman world; the Renaissance; the Enlightenment) had harbored and nurtured symbols and myths which later periods saw to be religious in character; and the ensuing age, instead of moving to a more consistent secularity, turned out to have significant religious elements as well. Only if we are of low imagination or high metaphysical wisdom is it possible for us to be sure that no new "rude beast slouches to Bethlehem to be born."

The secular interpretation has to do violence to the residual religious elements inherited from the old covenant or dispensation. It must overlook world religions attracting hundreds of millions of people; the numerous sacred cosmoses which exist in various cultures; the astrologers, haruspicators, and soothsayers who find employment in popular and sophisticated culture; the serious philosophical striving for ultimate meanings. The vast majority of the people in the "free world" and the developing nations would certainly denominate themselves religious, and this self-chosen appellation, one would think, should count for something. If theologians wish to issue critiques of these religions from certain normative points of view or to call them disguised kinds of secularity, they do so at hazard to the appropriate use of terms and language. This is particularly true in the United States, where almost all people on a percentage scale (97 percent to 99 percent, depending on how the question is phrased)[14] respond to poll-takers with the affirmation that they believe in God, and where a clear majority affiliate with religious institutions.

[14] As, for example, in the Gallup poll of autumn, 1965.

At this point it might be well to issue some warnings. Note that I am not saying that no radical assault on inherited religions has occurred. Perhaps the religio-secular mixture is more devastating to inherited "true" religion than would be pure-form secularity; some theologians, at least, are clear in their contention for such a secularity as a better basis for Christian life and mission. Nor am I able to make comment on "the essential nature of man and society" in this mixed cultural framework. One can do so on the basis of a particular revelation or by philosophical speculation; but if he restricts himself to empirical tools of historians and sociologists he must report that until now the development of secular man and society, especially in America, has been at best partial. With Nietzsche one may well say that "man is an indeterminate being" or, better, in the secular use of language, man has ordinarily been so up to the present moment. It is entirely possible that his religious tendencies may eventually wither and be repressed. It may also be creative to envision purely secular futures so that men may know how to make choice. But such envisioning is game-playing and it does not license one to predict the future. Will there be more or less religion of particular kinds in the future? We do not know. We can chart trends and project on the basis of curves; we may "feel something in our bones" and have intuitions in our hearts and minds, but a chaste secular understanding would limit observation to what has occurred and not to what man and society will be in the future.

If one cannot look to the future, then, he will look first to the present. Here the social sciences and particularly sociology have served well to help define American secularization. They have noted the segmentation and specialization of life that happens in complex societies, and few are more complex than the American. They have recognized the radical religious change that America has certainly undergone. But few sociologists who observe the religious factor in American life would be able to come up with evidence that the nation has become secularized in the theologians' use of that term.[15]

---

[15] Among sociologists who stress "radical religious change" as opposed to simple secularization are J. Milton Yinger, Gerhard Lenski, Andrew Greeley, John

As with the present, so with the past: if one wishes to account on a scholarly basis for how things are he does well to see how they have come to be, and historical research can help account for much in America's particular case that will help explain a situation so baffling to ideological advocates or observers of secularization. Such research does not "prove" the truth about the essential nature of man or his future, but more modestly it helps explain his present. Such explanation may be of more use to jurists, educators, businessmen, shapers of opinion, and communicators than is speculation over the secular not-yet.

The thesis implied in what has gone before is simple: secularization is a historical process or set of events and it will necessarily take on a different character in different environments. It may well have common features around the world, as Donald E. Smith has shown in the instance of India when compared to the West.[16] But the differences command attention, too, differences arising from the historical developments of the various specific religions, including not only the distinctions between East and West but those within the West. Where there have been established churches and anticlericalism one may expect to see and indeed does see a different kind of secularization from that where there has been disestablishment and but minor anticlericalism. The records may well differ where there have been heterogeneous religions as opposed to areas of homogeneity, or coercive contexts over against persuasive ones from the religious point of view—in short, there are differences between the European nations and the United States.

In recent years the gap between Europe and America may be closing on this front, too. America "rejoined the world" after a century of relative isolation, and strong intercultural forces, particularly in the age of the public media, draw people together also in spiritual matters. Americans read Nietzsche and Marx, Darwin and Camus, and come somehow under their spell; Europeans adopt American fashions and fads and inherit some of the United States' history. David Martin

Thomas, Thomas Luckmann, Peter Berger, Seymour Lipset, Charles Y. Glock, and Rodney Stark.

[16] D. E. SMITH, INDIA AS A SECULAR STATE (1963).

has shown that there are religious survivals in England which reasonably match American practices.[17] But differences remain, reflecting a disparate historical development of institutions, of the cosmos of citizens' perceptions, and of the myths to accompany their world views.

If secularization takes meaning not as an inevitable dogma or a determinist sociological process but as a multifaceted motif among others in history, it is reasonable to ask how the history is acquired by contemporaries. G. J. Renier, in a brilliant discussion of historical method,[18] points out that, unlike individuals, society has no memory; it must achieve one. Although formal historians are more or less the official custodians of the lore and gatekeepers to the past, Renier would not overestimate their direct impact; the past speaks in many quieter and more indirect ways.

In America young people acquire their peculiar religio-secular blend of history through education. Ruth Miller Elson in *Guardians of Tradition* (1964) has set forth in impressive detail how religious ideals were fused with national lore in the textbooks of the nineteenth century. A certain official and accepted history tended to well up and this has survived into the present through many transformations and sophistications to help shape national attitudes. There are other means; public ceremonies accompanying military life, holidays, the public liturgy, and the accepted rites of passage [19] unify people around certain sacral versions of national and personal history. Symbols of the fusion can be seen on coins, seals, and flags, and can be heard in music.[20] Literary and oral tradition provide the young from generation to generation with pervasive and complex if sometimes understandably inaccurate versions of the past.

The past may not be wholly determinative; Americans are often described as present-minded "now" people. Cosmic generalizers see them as ahistorical or even antihistorical, devoting themselves to Adamic myths of nature and innocence. Insofar as this is true, however, there is a further irony to be reflected toward those who see

17 D. MARTIN, A SOCIOLOGY OF ENGLISH RELIGION (1967).
18 G. J. RENIER, HISTORY: ITS PURPOSE AND METHOD, Ch. I (1950).
19 W. L. WARNER, THE FAMILY OF GOD (1961) details many of these.
20 *See* I STOKES, *supra* n. 8, at 467.

pure-form secularization as the major trend. The "innocence" which has repeatedly been promulgated as a national characteristic regularly takes on mythic and symbolic cast and is itself curiously religious. Thus R. W. B. Lewis in his *The American Adam* (1955) has reached into ecclesiastical (Bushnell, Parker, Brownson) and nonecclesiastical (Parkman, Thoreau, Melville) orbits to present a picture of a quasi-religious cult of innocence among present-minded and futuristic Americans in the past. And David W. Noble in *Historians against History* (1965) supplements this ironic version by showing that it was precisely the historical fraternity which was the keeper of the antihistorical covenant. The historians have regularly yearned for nature over history, America over Europe, simplicity over complexity, the farm over the city—and in the process have contributed to a new history full of religious regard for a national covenant. They have been, in his reading, anything but secularizers! Even "the new left" [21] of radical and Marxist historians has found itself unable to evade the religious substratum in American life. Repudiating the consensus-stressed reading of American history in vogue among post-World War II circles (a vogue which would naturally accent the homogenizing religions and symbols of national life), they stress the conflict in the past. But that conflict has also more often than not taken on a religious dimension, as in the case of the Negro in a white world, or of abolitionism, millennialism, and the founding of utopias which violate national consensus.

Thus, the various strands of the American tradition, even conflicting ones, blend religious elements with secular trends in an inextricable whole up to the present moment. This leads to a second thesis or summary statement: just as "secularization" is historically colored by the experience of various societies (e.g., America and its subcultures), so in the American circumstance it represents part of a very mixed quasi-religious history that shows few signs of dissipation.

Often this religious cast will appear to be submerged. Thus if one

---

[21] Unger, *The "New Left" and American History: Some Recent Trends in United States Historiography*, 72 THE AMERICAN HISTORICAL REVIEW 1227 (1967).

compares source books [22] of documents on American history in the colonial and the national period, the "secularization" of the latter period will be evident. The colonial era is full of theocratic elements, religious establishment, covenants, and other marks which show up in documents no matter how few people in the society may have been formally religious. In the national period, democratic society, disestablishment, and nontheological informal covenants of an industrial society press a different set of concerns on those who collect documents. One deals with the rise of factories, the changes in tariffs, the prosecution of wars, the question of taxes; the elusive mythic elements of culture are submerged.

This is not to say that democratic and industrial revolutions do not produce profound changes. E. J. Hobsbawm speaks of the industrial period as a time of "the secularization of the males" [23] by which he cannot simply mean that all women stayed godly and all men became godless. Rather, "women" may represent the home, privacy, leisure, personal spirituality; "males" may mean work- and production-orientations, the practical and problem-solving parts of the world. If so, "female" and "male" characteristics have been intertwined and are coexistent. The secularization of the males (legislature, laboratory, factory, etc.) is as radical as all-embracing secularization could be imagined to be. But ths process never preempted all of national history and does not do so now.

In an impressive passage Ernest Gellner [24] tries to account for the survival of Marxism in the modern world and sees in its persistence something parallel to survival of Judaeo-Christian elements in the West. He allows that "original" Marxism and classical Biblical faiths may remain only nominal doctrines, may lose their full-fledged cognitive character, may see a transformation of their symbols; they may be largely displaced; they may seem to be nothing more than the moraine left by a moving glacier. But they are part of the landscape

[22] One may take, for example, A HISTORY OF THE UNITED STATES (H. T. Lefler ed. 1960) and compare the number of documents specifically relating to religion in Vol. I with the few in Vol. II, which covers the nineteenth century.

[23] E. J. HOBSBAWM, THE AGE OF REVOLUTION 218 (1962).

[24] E. GELLNER, THOUGHT AND CHANGE 123 (1964).

and have to be reckoned with. He suggests that this is so because they were part of the two societies' ideology at the (century-long?) "moment" when the societies passed over "the hump of transition" to new approved social contracts.

If this kind of religious survival is the case in the United States, we may expect for some time that issues dealing with religion and secularity are not in range of being settled. We can cite several examples of what happens whenever someone tampers with the approved social contract or sets out to rearrange elements in the landscape. The public reaction (running as high as 80 percent in public opinion polls) against the Supreme Court decisions *Engel v. Vitale* and *School District of Abington Township v. Schempp* demonstrates that "religious" America did not understand any adjustment in what it believed to be the unwritten contract for devotional elements in public education. Significantly, "secular" America teamed up with a minority of ecclesiastical leaders, lay and clerical, to show that the Supreme Court acted on the logic of the Constitution and not out of harmony with American institutional life, and suggested that ritual and devotion belonged elsewhere, not in the liturgy of public institutions.

Similarly, in what might be called the "politics of pulpit and pew" there has been much confusion in the recent past. A new breed of clerical and lay leadership has become discontent with privatization of religion and has sought to make the religious impulse a pervasive force in social and public affairs. This has led many in that group to take unpopular stands on social issues such as war and peace, race, housing, and urban conditions. "Religious" America, schooled in an individualistic religion that prevailed at the moment America went "over the hump of transition," is puzzled as it faces the coalition of "secular" America with that new articulate social-minded leadership. Whether or not the Jewish and Christian faiths in their long histories would have found the momentary individualism that has surfaced from time to time in the American past cogenial, since it is seen to have been present in national myth, it is recognized as part of the social contract now being tested and potentially violated.

To speak of *the* hump of transition does not do justice to the number of formative developments in the American past; to demonstrate the complexity of this history it is necessary to illustrate several major moments and movements in which "religious" and "secular" elements were united. I shall refer to colonization, revolution, the frontier experience, urbanization-industrialization, and contemporary issues.

1. No major nation has been made up of so many diverse elements as has the United States. These came from many nations over a period of three and a half centuries and they still are coming. The latecomers, those who arrived after the middle third of the nineteenth century (from almost everywhere except England and Scotland), found themselves making their way as "guests" in a "host" culture. They are usually spoken of as "immigrants" and not colonists, for the latter group have the right of priority. (Franklin Delano Roosevelt showed profound insight and rare humor when he referred to the Daughters of the American Revolution in a speech at their solemn assembly as "fellow immigrants.") While the majority of citizens are heirs of the immigrants and not the colonists, they find themselves adopting the colonizing ancestors. Their citizenship and Americanization courses provide them with the myth which "the guardians of tradition" have stewarded. Even among the colonizers there often seems to be particular stress on New Englanders, though one need not labor the point. In many senses, all Americans now are Puritans or Colonists.

Colonization, the movement from Europe to America, from settled to experimental life, represents the primal or matricial experience. It is the first "hump of transition" of people on the way to an approved new social contract. Whoever revisits this moment finds a tangle of motivations, half-religious, half-secular. In the southern colonies, in the Carolinas and earlier and in particular in Virginia, there was joint concern for making money *and* for spreading Christian religion among "the savages" and for perpetuating it. In the middle colonies, William Penn was the most articulate man of dual motives as he set out to provide for a Bible commonwealth on Quaker patterns. The good Dutchmen of New Amsterdam who were less explicit about religious experiment and more casual about religious provision were balanced by the continental groups which found the middle colonies places of religious refuge. In New England the religious movement was characteristically dominant, though it takes no muck-raker to see the practicality and prudence that went into Puritan and Pilgrim schemes for "the wilderness." The Puritans came to "complete the positive part of church reformation," to go on an "errand into the wilderness," to be a "cittie set upon a hill," and to provide a Zion in the new world.

John Adams, looking back on the Revolution of 1776, liked to say that the real revolution occurred earlier—before the military hostilities. True; it began whenever Old World foot first stepped on New World shore. The move involved some sort of cutting off from Europe and some hope for a new world and a new contract or covenant. Colonists brought little along with them, but they did bring various religious constructs in need of a new environment.

At different times over the years, vogues of interpretation have caused historians to stress religious or secular motifs. After one school has emphasized the economic motives for colonization, another school will take the religious profession of "the fathers" seriously and will stress their theological ideas and ecclesiastical intentions. For all but extremists this cannot be an either/or, it must be a both/and history. Whoever appeals to the migrating fathers as fathers of us all will be discovering that the primal experience of America was a blend of religion and secularity. To deny one or another violates the historical documents and the integrity of historical reporting; to neglect the event and the myth itself deprives one of the first element in the development of American memory.

2. In the middle and toward the end of the eighteenth century a constellation of events provides a second opportunity for seeing why as America passed over the "hump of transition" it carried religious and secular elements along to predetermine later life. These events include the religious First Great Awakening, the celebrated issues leading up to the American Revolution, the development of the Constitution, and the rise of nationalism, as thirteen nations became one nation.

This period is consistently alluded to by people who set out to define what is normative about America. In this it plays a role analogous to the Biblical period for Christian faith, and its documents—the Declaration of Independence and the Constitution—are "the scriptures" by which later events are measured through many transformations. Here again the blending of elements is obvious. When an American late in the twentieth century appeals to "the founding fathers," it is not immediately clear whether he is referring to the Winthrops and Bradfords and Penns, or the Washingtons and Franklins and Jeffersons; whether he has in mind the armed forefathers trudging off to Thanksgiving Day services (as he saw them in the classroom-painting) or the unarmed scribes heading for Constitutional Convention. They are both sets of "fathers" and in surprisingly similar ways.

The First Great Awakening of the 1730's is one of the less well-known among the events that gave the nation its second set of fathers. (Perhaps its absence from many histories helps substantiate the secularist interpretation of the American past; this event is seen as "purely" religious and therefore does not make its way into texts and folklore.) This Awakening was "the first mass movement in American life" and is regarded by historians as doing much to provide the American colonies with a common purpose, language, and mission. In a recent quantitative symbol analysis, a statistics-minded historian has observed that the rise of uniting symbols between 1735–1775 cannot be comprehended apart from the fact of prior conditioning in intercolonial experience; the only such experience he can think of is the Great Awakening or religious revival.[25] Whether or not later Americans know the chronology or the details of that event, they have profited both from its effect and from the ways in which it contributed to the view that in America one "gets" or acquires religion and makes a choice about it.

The pre-revolutionary rhetoric which helped foster common purpose and later nationhood was largely religious in origin. "The Pulpit of the American Revolution" has deserved and received full credit, but it may be well to note that its impact was made despite the fact that the churches in America were at that time weak and ineffective,

[25] R. L. MERRITT, SYMBOLS OF AMERICAN COMMUNITY, 1735–1775 173 (1966); he does not bother to document his assertion; for a good general accounting of this Awakening see EDWIN SCOTT GAUSTAD, THE GREAT AWAKENING IN NEW ENGLAND (1957). Unfortunately no major work on the whole colonial Awakening exists.

lower in popular support than they have been before or since; and, one might add, we are learning that different sets of pulpit "fathers" were involved than we had thought previously. John Adams and a century of Unitarian New England historians stamped into the public imagery the role that New England liberal Congregationalist preachers like Jonathan Mayhew had played; now a retracing of the steps shows that "backwoods" conservative Calvinist evangelists were at least not less successful in anticipating Revolution and nationhood.[26]

The more one wishes to untangle the events that went into Revolution the more he sees religion intertwined. The Stamp Act crisis evoked many a sermon on independence and freedom from tyranny, but the opposition by non-Anglicans to the establishment of a resident Bishop of the Church of England in the Colonies was an equally effective unifying agent in colonial affairs.[27]

After the Revolution religious ideas came from two sources—from Calvinist and other colonial religious residues, and from the tradition of the Enlightenment, with its devotion to The Supreme Being, The Divine Governor, Providence, and "our most holy religion" of nature and reason and nation. The former may have worked its way in accidentally and unobtrusively through occasional bits of remembered theology just as much as it came through the pragmatic recognition of "the dark side of life" and the assertion of what Reinhold Niebuhr called the only empirically verifiable Christian doctrine, that of "original sin." The Constitution was a compromise based on the fathers' common recognition that power in the hands of rulers or people was a problem, and that only a system of checks and balances could check men's grasping tendencies and balance their interests.[28]

The mixture of evangelism and enlightenment that characterized the period has survived and been transformed as an element of national memory and experience. Later evangelicals like Robert Baird were able to draw the "arch-infidel" Thomas Jefferson into the orbit of respectability for the favor he had done the voluntary churches

---

[26] *See* A. HEIMERT, RELIGION AND THE AMERICAN MIND (1966).

[27] C. BRIDENBAUGH, MITRE AND SCEPTRE (1962).

[28] This story is told in full in FORREST MCDONALD, E PLURIBUS UNUM (1955); note the theme in the first two lines of the book.

and even he, the enemy of so much in the sects, became a "founding father of us all." And George Washington, who seemed to make a studied attempt to be noncommittal on particular sectarian doctrines and classic Christian practices turns out to be the Father of His Country, covered with a sacral mantle, in Unitarian and Fundamentalist churches alike. The American "Enlightenment" may have been pagan from the point of view of traditional Christian supernaturalism, but it became easy to baptize and appropriate.

3. When issues of West and South appear in the third grand strophe of the American experience the situation does not change; indeed, the religious element is more overt again. "The West" symbolizes the frontier which for a century inspired and attracted missionary-evangelists, activists, and church-building revivalists. The folklore of the West is given over no less to these preachers than it is to saloon-keepers, and the countless little churches came to be as much a part of archetypal frontier towns as did commercial buildings. Revivals, camp meetings, shall-we-gather-at-the-river-events are associated with these years and places and the vast American majority which has not shared small town life or rural Western experience finds itself adopting visions of culture gained from it. By the 1840's a generation of major historians and literary figures was on hand to reflect on the new nation which now had a history and in the West an open frontier; Hawthorne, Melville, Emerson, Parker, Thoreau and others all wanted to be "post-Christian" as they looked at the long past and the new opportunity. But in the age of Over-Soul, Transcendentalism, and the new religions of democracy they neither were post-religious nor capable of outgrowing reflection on the colonial religious past as it was being reenacted in the Western present of community-building and symbol-evocation.

Meanwhile during the nineteenth century North-South issues had a religious undertone. John Kenneth Galbraith says that the Civil War (along with the Depression of the 1930's) is the event of the past with which practical Americans—from legislators on down, or over—have to reckon daily. When they do, they come across a history of religious and antireligious abolitionists, theological ideologues who defended slavery, a President who dealt with the Union as religious mysticism, one who spoke of God's "almost chosen people" and whose whole rhetoric was marked by Biblical cadence, and Confederate armies experiencing religious revival. There is little possibility that recourse to Civil War themes will move people beyond the religious aura surrounding much of the national past. In the Civil War the nation "stayed together" and kept an identity; it moved over this hump of transition again with a mixture of Judeo-Christian and independent motifs.

4. The fourth major change came with urbanization and industrialization. The plot is less clear here and there are reasons why those who stress secular interpretation find more to work with when they come to it. The contemporary city seems to militate against unifying imagery; it is pluralist and competitive by nature. The ancient hieroglyph for the city (a cross in a circle) has little to do with the plotless, unwalled, unprotected modern city which lacks crossroads and sacral center or *axis mundi*. Much of the American religious myth was associated with agrarian and village imagery, and the city presents problems not only for the religious institutions (one phase of secularization) but also for the symbols and myths in the public's "sacred cosmos" and world-view.

Despite these problems, the merchant city was certainly marked by durable religious elements; it was heavily churched and the elites of its power structure played prominent parts in religious development. The ethic of aspiration and production had a Protestant Christian base. The self-made man was only a semi-secular model of one kind of Protestant, and even in the industrial city, much of the ethos and ethic was developed as "a gospel of wealth." "Social Darwinism" fitted in well with many kinds of religions from the past and became an obvious new kind of religion.

Urbanization greatly complicated the pattern of American pluralism. The "ghetto experience" of Jews, Catholics, and Negroes deprived them of some elements belonging to the past of the evangelicals and other long-established mainliners. Yet examination of these subcultures reveals that they nurtured parallel combinations of religious and secular idea patterns and institutions. For many a third- or fourth-generation heir of the ghettoes, the quest for roots and identity leads to a moment of vital fusion between specific religious visions and folk experiences.

These four sets of events or moments of transition belong to the past, and the advocate of a straight secular version of American culture could reasonably argue that they are not at issue. How are things today? By shifting the debate there would in even these terms be an acquiescence to the point that America has at least been on a later timetable of secularization, since most chroniclers would say that the modern West had passed over its "hump" long before the early twentieth century. But even if the story is brought to the present, the fusion remains. Were one to add a third volume to our mythical two-volume (colonial/national) source book of documents, would pure secularity appear?

A new source book would have to do justice to the peace movement, with the coalition of clerics, academicians, and journalists in the forefront. It would relate to the Civil Rights and later Black Power struggles, both of which attract endless "Reverends" and "Rabbis" and "Sisters" to leadership roles and to the ranks, where they are joined by motivated religious laymen. The documents would include debates about urban culture, about pop art, about the world of "hippies," about conscientious objection—and in all of these matters a religious dimension is again fused with the secular. A study of the *New York Times Index* would reveal that, if anything, religion is more frequently on the front page in "secular" America than it had been in recent decades.

Today the nation may very well be heading over a hump of transition toward a new social contract, toward . . . what? Men do not know; impatient with the old, desiring to be *avant-garde,* hesitant to label the new and the not-yet, they reach for the prefix "post": they head for post-historic life, for post-industrial man, for post-modernity, post-civilization, post-Christendom, post-ecumenism, post-linearity: the list is as nearly endless as are complaints against the exhausted traditions which have survived into this time. It would be foolish to make quantitative or qualitative predictions about the relationship of religion to secularity in the future; it is slightly less hazardous to foresee an interplay which will rob us of simplicity.

In review, we have not cast this critical glance at the ideological use of the concept "secularity" in order to present a conservative or static view of secure religiousness in America. Radical religious change may be a bigger problem for religionist and secularist than would be either static religion or clarified secularity. It causes revision of historic claims of truth on the part of the religious and provides moving targets for secularists; it suggests an unnerving ability on the part of laymen to adapt and improvise right under the noses of clergy and theologians; for the secularist it provides bewildering evidence of the durability of religion in some form or other. For all, it ought to eliminate boredom from history.

Historical scholarship is less concerned with telling people in a culture what to do than with trying to portray how things have been. In that spirit we have offered these mixed comments on a mixed experiment in religious culture in a secular age and on secular life in a culture that often thinks of itself as religious.

ARTHUR SUTHERLAND

Historians, Lawyers, and "Establishment of Religion"

I

Mark DeWolfe Howe, Charles Warren Professor of American Legal History at Harvard, died on February 28, 1967. His sudden death grieved the entire Harvard community, brought a deep sense of loss which has no parallel in the present university generation. Mark Howe would have been a rare man in any time. He combined the courage of advocacy when advocacy was needed, with "the competence to use our problems to determine the questions we ask of the past, without twisting the past to the present purpose." [1] He was a thorough lawyer; he was a conscientious, talented historian. The Villanova Institute of Church and State, inviting an essay on Mark Howe's work, leads me to wonder, a little, about the supposed qualities of historians and of lawyers. I ask myself, with as much self-severity as I can muster, whether the lawyer who ventures to write of the past, recent or remote, is characteristically an advocate of some disputed cause, selecting for his comment only those past records which favor his side. Do professional historians characteristically detach themselves from causes, and so turn up more reliable accounts of what happened last Tuesday twelvemonth?

Arthur Sutherland is Professor of Law at the Harvard Law School.
[1] The words are those of Willard Hurst, in *Mark Howe: Legal Historian,* 80 HARV. L. REV. 1638, 1640 (1967).

This is a difficult question to answer wisely, for oddly enough the harshest criticism of each profession comes from within its own membership. Charles and Mary Beard, in their *Rise of American Civilization* take Sir Thomas Erskine May to task as a "Whig historian." He showed his Whig bias, they say, in his *Constitutional History*, by asserting that George III himself fixed English policy toward America in 1775 and the succeeding war years; and they chide Sir George Otto Trevelyan as an "English Liberal . . . a nephew of the great Whig apologist, Macaulay" [2] for his attempted demonstration in *The American Revolution* that the War of Independence was disliked by the British nation. But Charles Beard himself has recently been chidden by one of his fellows. A 1963 historian critic finds that Beard erred in attributing to the founding fathers of the American Constitution "petty human motives, especially those of personal aggrandizement" in shaping that Constitution.[3]

Ironically, one finds in a lawyer's book the most conspicuous recent criticism of lawyers as historians. Mark Howe, in *The Garden and the Wilderness*, chides Justices of the Supreme Court for "reading prohibitions of establishment into the due process clause of the Fourteenth Amendment that simply are not there." [4]

He writes:

In recent years the Court has decided a number of important cases relating to church and state and, in each of the cases, has alleged that the command of history, not the preference of the justices, has brought the Court to its decision. . . . When however, the Court endeavors to write an authoritative chapter in the intellectual history of the American people, as it does when it lays historical foundations beneath its readings of the First Amendment, then any distortion becomes a matter of consequence. The misreading is of moment not because it has led the Court to a mistaken decision—for the decision may well be right and wise—but because it has woven synthetic strands into the tapestry

---

[2] Vol. I, at 279 ff. (1928).

[3] Murphy, *Time to Reclaim: The Current Challenge of American Constitutional History*, 69 AMERICAN HISTORICAL REVIEW 64, 68–69 (1963). Professor Murphy probably referred to CHARLES BEARD, AN ECONOMIC INTERPRETATION OF THE CONSTITUTION OF THE UNITED STATES (1913).

[4] M. HOWE, THE GARDEN AND THE WILDERNESS 146 (1965).

of American history. It may be that as a lawyer I take the Court's distorting lessons in American intellectual history too seriously. I must remind you, however, that a great many Americans—lawyers and non-lawyers alike—tend to think that because a majority of the justices have the power to bind us by their law they are also empowered to bind us by their history. Happily that is not the case. Each of us is entirely free to find his history in other places than the pages of the *United States Reports*.[5]

Indeed all of us—lawyers, professors, or politicians—are prone to arrange our data so as most convincingly to persuade. But Howe's character as a dispassionate lawyer-critic is demonstrated by his double life; for he was an academician and a historian as well as a lawyer. In both his intellectual lives Mark Howe lived strictly and fairly.

Oddly enough, the lawyers he was criticizing in *The Garden and the Wilderness* are members of that group within the legal profession one would suppose least of all tempted to untenable demonstration of dogma by selective use of historical materials—the Justices of the Supreme Court of the United States. But the Justices, when they decide original constitutional questions on the featureless generalities of substantive due process, necessarily, and properly, and with reasonable explicitness, rely on grounds of social wellbeing, on the "felt necessities of the time, the prevalent moral and political theories, intuitions of public policy, avowed or unconscious." [6] Having so decided something, they must feel the desire of all mankind to demonstrate that they decided rightly, and like all the rest of us seek supporting testimony in man's past experience. In that shadowy land, even wise men may lose their way.

Howe was a scrupulous man, and did not indict all justices as inevitably bad historians. He was right in this. Neither Brandeis's history of the presidential power of removal in his dissenting opinion in *Myers v. United States*,[7] nor Jackson's historical analysis of the Presi-

[5] *Id.* at 4–5.

[6] O. W. HOLMES, THE COMMON LAW 1 (1881).

[7] 272 U.S. 52, 240 (1926) (dissenting opinion). Compare the critique of Taft's *Myers* opinion in Charles Allen Miller's Ph.D. thesis at Harvard, "The Supreme Court and the Uses of History" (1967).

dent's power of seizure in his *Youngstown Sheet & Tube* concurrence,[8] has drawn the volume of fire which Charles Fairman, an impeccable lawyer-scholar, directed at the dissenting opinion in *Adamson v. California*,[9] in which Mr. Justice Black expounded what he thought was the intent of the Fourteenth Amendment's congressional proponents to "incorporate," literatim, the Bill of Rights in the Fourteenth. Some judicial writings, that is to say, contain better history than others.

Perhaps in judging any account of the past, a presumption in favor of, or against the story, depending on the titular profession of the author, is less useful than an analysis of the story itself. There is more than one way to learn the art of a historian of politics, or a historian of constitutionalism. Scrupulous search for all relevant records; evaluation with informed care; re-creation of the past by selection of material not to prove an a priori point, but to exclude irrelevant detail;[10] all these in order to bring alive again action or thought which has ceased to exist; success in these ideals is the proper standard by which to judge the historian's achievement. He is not justly evaluated simply by scrutinizing the institutional process in which he labored to attain the requisite self-discipline, knowledge, and experience to tell the story rightly.

Of course the man who attempts this re-creation undertakes an exacting task. Miss C. V. Wedgewood called on her own distinguished experience when she wrote of the historian's problem:

He gains his knowledge through evidence which, at the very best, is incomplete; which is always contradictory; which raises as many questions as it solves; which breaks off tormentingly just where he needs it most, or, yet more tormentingly, becomes ambiguous and dark. He can never establish the truth. He can only grope towards it; he gropes, moreover, with an intellect which, being furnished in the twentieth century,

[8] Youngstown Sheet & Tube v. Sawyer, 343 U.S. 579, 634 (1952) (concurring opinion).

[9] 332 U.S. 46, 68 (1947); *see* Fairman, *Does the Fourteenth Amendment Incorporate the Bill of Rights? The Original Understanding*, 2 STAN. L. REV. 5 (1949); THE GARDEN AND THE WILDERNESS at 136.

[10] Some selection of relevant from irrelevant material is necessary in telling any story accurately but effectively. Mistress Quickly, nearly four centuries ago, demonstrated that some details are best omitted in an account of past events. *See* HENRY IV, Pt. II, Act III Scene 1.

finds it extremely difficult to understand any other, which is over-confident, apt to leap to wrong conclusions, unaware of its own shortcomings or, if aware, then unable to make allowances for them. The greatest scholar can never reach more than some kind of partial and personal version of truth as it once was. All the efforts of historical scholarship are ultimately reduced to a mere matter of human opinion.[11]

This hazardous enterprise of re-creating the past Mark Howe undertook in his life as a scholar of the law. He carried it out with a rare combination of high intelligence, deep learning, and detachment from conventional attitudes, without condemning any opinion as hackneyed error simply because of its wide acceptance. His biographical studies of Justice Holmes, and his editions of the Justice's correspondence with his family during the Civil War, and later with Sir Frederick Pollock and Harold Laski, are probably his best-known works.[12] Howe contributed wisely and unselfishly to student literature of constitutional law, and of the law of church and state in the United States.[13] He put much of himself into all of these books; none was a mere aggregation of material originating elsewhere. But in *The Garden and the Wilderness,* published in 1965, he wrote his own political philosophy; he set forth his own opinions of American policy and precedent in church-state relations, of political and social as well as legal precedent. This short book is quite unlike any of his other works.

II

The discipline required to select and shape a series of public lectures can produce great literature. Holmes' Lowell Lectures published in 1881 as *The Common Law,* furnish an early example.[14] One tends

[11] In her charming book of historical essays, TRUTH AND OPINION 101 (1960).

[12] HOLMES-POLLOCK LETTERS, THE CORRESPONDENCE OF MR. JUSTICE HOLMES AND SIR FREDERICK POLLOCK, 1874–1932 (1941); TOUCHED WITH FIRE; THE CIVIL WAR LETTERS AND DIARY OF OLIVER WENDELL HOLMES, JR., 1861–1864 (1946); HOLMES–LASKI LETTERS; THE CORRESPONDENCE OF MR. JUSTICE HOLMES AND HAROLD J. LASKI, 1916–1936 (1953); JUSTICE OLIVER WENDELL HOLMES (1957–1962); Vol. I. THE SHAPING YEARS, 1841–1870 (1957).

[13] P. FREUND, A. SUTHERLAND, M. HOWE & E. BROWN, CONSTITUTIONAL LAW, CASES AND OTHER PROBLEMS (3d ed. 1967); M. HOWE, CASES ON CHURCH AND STATE IN THE UNITED STATES (1952).

[14] Boston, Little, Brown. In 1963 Mark Howe edited a new edition for the

to forget that Blackstone's *Commentaries,* published two centuries ago, had a similar origin. Yale's Storrs Lectures have brought into being a series of distinguished books, among them Pound's *Introduction to the Philosophy of Law,* Cardozo's *Nature of the Judicial Process,* Holdworth's *Charles Dickens as a Legal Historian,* and Becker's *Heavenly City of the Eighteenth Century Philosophers.*

The Garden and the Wilderness originated as a series of six lectures, delivered in November and December 1964 at the Hebrew Union College-Jewish Institute of Religion in New York City on the invitation of the Frank L. Weil Institute for Studies in Religion and the Humanities. In his Foreword, Howe tells of "the uneasiness which accompanies the rendition of spoken into printed words," which "suddenly seem to need the sustaining apparatus of learning—the footnotes that establish industry and intimate wisdom, the cautious phrasings that authenticate judgment and suggest vision." His pages, he says, were put in print as they were spoken. He need not have deprecated their form. This book is the most clear, scholarly, and authoritative statement now in print of the need to revise some judicial pronouncements concerning the "establishment clause" of the First Amendment, and to revise statements of its prohibitory effect against the states by way of the vaguely-contoured clauses of the Fourteenth.

The title Howe takes from a statement of Roger Williams:

The faithful labors of many witnesses of Jesus Christ, extant to the world, abundantly proving that the church of the Jews under the Old Testament in the type, and the church of the Christians under the New Testament in the antitype, were both separate from the world; and that when they have opened a gap in the hedge or wall of separation between the garden of the church and the wilderness of the world, God hath ever broke down the wall itself, removed the candlestick, and made His garden a wilderness, as at this day. And that therefore if He will ever please to restore His garden and paradise again, it must of necessity be walled in peculiarly unto Himself from the world; and that all shall

Belknap Press of the Harvard University Press; in 1964 Little, Brown by arrangement with the Harvard Press, brought the book out in a paperback print. The 1963 edition and the paperback contain a valuable introduction by Professor Howe.

be saved out of the world are to be transplanted out of the wilderness of the world and added unto his church or garden.[15]

This early use of the "wall of separation" metaphor Howe contrasts with Jefferson's letter of January 1, 1802, written in reply to an "address" of esteem and approbation sent him by a Baptist association of Danbury, Connecticut. Here I quote from Jefferson's letter more fully than Howe did:

> Believing with you that religion is a matter which lies solely between man and his God, that he owes account to none other for his faith or his worship, that the legislative powers of government reach actions only, and not opinions, I contemplate with sovereign reverence that act of the whole American people which declared that their legislature should "make no law respecting an establishment of religion, or prohibiting the free exercise thereof," thus building a wall of separation between church and State. Adhering to this expression of the supreme will of the nation in behalf of the rights of conscience, I shall see with sincere satisfaction the progress of those sentiments which tend to restore to man all his natural rights, convinced he has no natural right in opposition to his social duties.[16]

Professor Howe opened his first lecture with a quotation from Mr. Justice Reed, "A rule of law should not be drawn from a figure of speech." [17] Jefferson and Madison, both of Virginia, professed an article of political faith then current among the intellectuals of that state, that no man should be taxed to support some religious sect. Jefferson's preamble to Virginia's Act for Establishing Religious Freedom reflects the eighteenth-century rationalism which made him a child of Europe's Enlightenment. It bespoke a fear of "the impious presumption" of ecclesiastical rulers which might establish and maintain false religion throughout the land.[18] Jefferson used the "wall"

---

[15] THE GARDEN AND THE WILDERNESS at 5–6, quoted from PERRY MILLER, ROGER WILLIAMS: HIS CONTRIBUTION TO THE AMERICAN TRADITION 89, 98 (1953).

[16] 16 JEFFERSON'S WORKS 281 (Monticello ed. 1903).

[17] Illinois *ex rel.* McCollum v. Board of Educ., 333 U.S. 203, 247 (1948) (dissenting opinion).

[18] Through this interpretation of the Jeffersonian tradition, Howe writes, the

figure of speech to advocate protection of the individual against "ecclesiastical rulers" of the state; he was expounding an anticlerical political theory.

Roger Williams, on the other hand, had used the metaphor differently. His concern, Howe tells us, was to protect the garden of religion; his principle of separation was predominantly theological. A century after Williams died, his urge to foster religion was still alive among the New Englanders who participated in the drafting of the First Amendment. Massachusetts men, using the device of the federal structure, Howe tells us, would watch over the garden Massachusetts, for beyond "lay the wilderness, America." [19] But from Jefferson's and Madison's writings the Supreme Court has distilled a legal doctrine primarily negative. Attributing Jeffersonian eighteenth-century anticlericalism to all the makers of the First Amendment, the Court's majority have aspired (so their opinions suggest) to protect the nation against the dangers of creeping clericalism.

The difference between Williams and Jefferson, like other differences in constitutional theory, is one of degree, of differing stress. Mr. Justice Black's much-quoted *Everson* dictum expresses the Jeffersonian view:

Neither a state nor the Federal Government can set up a church. Neither can pass laws which aid one religion, aid all religions, or prefer one religion over another. Neither can force or influence a person to go to or to remain away from church against his will or force him to profess a belief or disbelief in any religion. No person can be punished for entertaining or professing religious beliefs or disbeliefs, for church attendance or non-attendance. No tax in any amount, large or small, can be levied to support any religious activities or institutions, whatever they may be called, or whatever form they may adopt to teach or practice religion. Neither a state nor the Federal Government can, openly or secretly, participate in the affairs of any religious organizations or groups and vice versa. In the words of Jefferson, the clause against establishment

---

Virginia Court of Appeals in 1832 once held that no trust for a religious purpose was enforceable in Virginia courts in the case of Gallego's Executors v. Attorney General, 3 Leigh 487 (1832). THE GARDEN AND THE WILDERNESS at 2.

[19] *Id.* at 26.

of religion by law was intended to erect a wall of separation between Church and State.[20]

Perhaps the most extreme statement of this constitutional tendency is that of Mr. Justice Douglas, concurring in *Engel v. Vitale*,[21] the New York Regent's Prayer case. He wrote:

It is customary in deciding a constitutional question to treat it in its narrowest form. Yet at times the setting of the question gives it a form and content which no abstract treatment could give. The point for decision is whether the Government can constitutionally finance a religious exercise. Our system at the federal and state levels is presently honeycombed with such financing.[22]

Nevertheless I think it is an unconstitutional undertaking whatever form it takes. First a word as to what this case does not involve. Plainly, our Bill of Rights would not permit a State or the Federal Government to adopt an official prayer and penalize anyone who would not utter it. This, however, is not that case, for there is no element of compulsion or coercion in New York's regulation requiring that public schools be opened each day with the following prayer:

"Almighty God, we acknowledge our dependence upon Thee, and we

[20] Everson v. Board of Educ., 330 U.S. 1, 15–16 (1947).

[21] 370 U.S. 421, 437 (1962) (concurring opinion).

[22] In an illustrative footnote at the outset of his opinion, Mr. Justice Douglas cites chaplains in the armed forces and the Congress, set up (he reminds us) by the First Congress which proposed the First Amendment. He cites compulsory chapel at service Academies, religious services in federal hospitals and prisons, presidential religious proclamations, use of the Bible to administer oaths, availability of N.Y.A. and W.P.A. funds for parochial schools in depression years, G.I. Bill of Rights payments to denominational schools for veterans' tuition, federal payments to denominational schools for nurses' training, benefits of the National School Lunch Act for parochial pupils. The Justice quotes from a scholarly authority to point out that " 'the Hospital Survey and Construction Act of 1946 . . . specifically made money available to non-public hospitals. The slogan "In God We Trust" is used by the Treasury Department, and Congress recently added God to the pledge of allegiance. . . . [R]eligious instruction is given in the District's National Training School for Boys. Religious organizations are exempt from the federal income tax and are granted postal privileges. Up to defined limits, . . . contributions to religious organizations are deductible for federal income tax purposes. There are no limits to the deductibility of gifts and bequests to religious institutions made under the federal gift and estate tax laws. This list of federal "aids" could easily be expanded [the Justice notes] and of course there is a long list in each state.' FELLMAN, THE LIMITS OF FREEDOM (1959), pp. 40–41." *Id.* at 437.

beg Thy blessings upon us, our parents, our teachers and our Country." . . .

I cannot say that to authorize this prayer is to establish a religion in the strictly historic meaning of those words. A religion is not established in the usual sense merely by letting those who choose to do so say the prayer that the public school teacher leads. Yet once government finances a religious exercise it inserts a divisive influence into our communities. . . .

Public money devoted to payment of religious costs, educational or other, brings the quest for more. It brings too the struggle of sect against sect for the larger share or for any. Here one by numbers alone will benefit most, there another. That is precisely the history of societies which have had an established religion and dissident groups. [Citing Madison's Remonstrance] Par. 8, 11. It is the very thing Jefferson and Madison experienced and sought to guard against, whether in its blunt or in its more screened forms. Ibid. The end of such strife cannot be other than to destroy the cherished liberty. The dominating group will achieve the dominant benefit; or all will embroil the state in their dissensions. Id., Par. 11.

What New York does with this prayer is a break with that tradition. I therefore join the Court in reversing the judgment below." [23]

The actual decision in *Engel v. Vitale* is not untenable. The school children formed a captive audience. The school prayer, pallid and brief as it was, still aggravated some of their parents. The children had to participate by passive presence, or make themselves conspicuous by departure or protest. *Engel* is a sort of anaemic *McCollum*,[24] the earlier decision of the Court prohibiting use of public school premises for classes in religious instruction during the school day even though the student participation was optional. But the Douglas language in *Engel* is tendentious. It moves toward the argument that public provision of standard secular textbooks for parochial pupils is unconstitutional, even though such governmental action puts no pressure on any pupil.

[23] 370 U.S. at 437-44.
[24] Illinois *ex rel.* McCollum v. Board of Educ. 333 U.S. 203 (1948). Here religious education went on in Illinois public school classrooms (by unpaid guest teachers). The McCollum boy was subject to classmate pressure when he withdrew.

The sorts of governmental action Mr. Justice Douglas enumerated have a long history in America. In 1789 the public power in one way or another gave support to churches in many of the states—perhaps in all, if all the evidence were available. Massachusetts, for example, supported her Congregational churches by tax power. Howe points out that a respectable school of thought asserts that the First Amendment's establishment clause was intended to prevent the Congress from meddling with such state establishments as existed in 1789 [25] and that the literal wording of the First Amendment would support that intention; but he thinks that the debate in the Congress in the summer of 1789 suggests a somewhat different impulse for the establishment clause.[26]

I here shall quote from the records of congressional debate, and from proposals in state ratifying conventions in 1788 a little more extensively than Howe could, limited as he was in the time for each lecture. These records bear out his thesis.

In the House of Representatives on June 8, 1789, Madison proposed, among other amendments:

The civil rights of none shall be abridged on account of religious belief or worship, nor shall any national religion be established, nor shall the full and equal rights of conscience be in any manner, or on any pretext, infringed.[27]

and also proposed:

[N]o State shall violate the equal rights of conscience, the freedom of the press, or trial by jury in criminal cases.[28]

On July 21 the House sent Madison's proposed amendments

together with the amendments to the said Constitution, as proposed by

[25] He cites Snee, *Religious Disestablishment and the Fourteenth Amendment*, 1954 WASH. U.L.Q. 371 and W. KATZ, RELIGION AND AMERICAN CONSTITUTIONS 8–10 (1964).

[26] THE GARDEN AND THE WILDERNESS at 20.

[27] 1 ANNALS OF CONGRESS 434.

[28] *Id.* at 440–41. Madison would have added this restriction on the states, he explained, because, as in the prohibitions of bills of attainder, and ex post facto laws he said, "I think there is more danger of those powers being abused by the State Governments than by the Government of the United States." *Id.* at 440.

the several States . . . to a committee, to consist of a member from each
State, with instruction to take the subject of amendments to the Constitution of the United States generally into their consideration, and to report thereupon to the House.[29]

Madison represented Virginia on this select committee. As the House
submitted to the committee the various state proposals for amendments, made in their resolutions of ratification and rejection, some
account of the state wishes as to establishment and free exercise of
religion is here relevant.

Of the eleven states which had ratified the Constitution before the
House debates on the Bill of Rights in the summer of 1789, five asked
for or recommended amendments. The Massachusetts convention ratified,

acknowledging with grateful hearts, the goodness of the Supreme Ruler
of the Universe in affording the People of the United States in the course
of his providence an opportunity deliberately & peaceably without fraud
or surprize of entering into an explicit & solemn Compact with each
other by assenting to & ratifying a New Constitution in order to form a
more perfect Union, establish Justice, insure Domestic tranquility, provide for the common defense, promote the general welfare & secure the
blessings of Liberty to themselves & their posterity,[30]

but "recommended" various amendments, none of which concerned establishment or free exercise of religion. South Carolina ratified with certain proposals, of which the only one concerning religion
suggested adding "other" in the clause of Article VI which follows
the requirement of an "Oath or affirmation" to support the Constitution, so that it would read "but no other religious test shall ever be
required." New Hampshire recommended among divers matters that

Congress shall make no Laws touching Religion, or to infringe the rights
of conscience.[31]

[29] *Id.* at 665. Two States, Rhode Island and North Carolina, had not then ratified the Constitution. Hence the committee had only eleven members instead of
thirteen.
[30] DOCUMENTS ILLUSTRATIVE OF THE FORMATION OF THE UNION OF THE
AMERICAN STATES, H. DOC. 398, 69th CONG. 1ST SESS. 1018 (1927).
[31] *Id.* at 1026.

Virginia declared on June 26, 1788

that among other essential rights the liberty of Conscience and of the Press cannot be cancelled abridged restrained or modified by any authority of the United States[32]

and went on to propose a Declaration or Bill of Rights in some such manner as the following:

Nineteenth, That any person religiously scrupulous of bearing arms ought to be exempted upon payment of an equivalent to employ another to bear arms in his stead. Twentieth, That religion or the duty which we owe to our Creator, and the manner of discharging it can be directed only by reason and conviction, not by force or violence, and therefore all men have an equal, natural and unalienable right to the free exercise of religion according to the dictates of conscience, and that no particular religious sect or society ought to be favored or established by Law in preference to others.[33]

The delegates of New York, the last state of the eleven to ratify before the debates in Congress in 1789, recited on July 26, 1788 that they "did declare and make known," among other matters

that the People have an equal, natural and unalienable right, freely and peaceably to Exercise their Religion according to the dictates of Conscience, and that no religious Sect or Society ought to be favoured or established by Law in preference of others.[34]

North Carolina rejected the Constitution on August 1, 1788. Her convention resolved that a Declaration of Rights should first be laid before Congress and the state conventions. Her proposals, in that resolution were, however, before Congress during the 1789 debates. She proposed affirmations for those who are "religiously scrupulous" in place of oaths to procure search-warrants; she proposed that conscientious objectors to military service might hire substitutes, and added

that religion, or the duty which we owe to our Creator, and the manner

---

[32] *Id.* at 1027.   [33] *Id.* at 1030.   [34] *Id.* at 1035.

of discharging it, can be directed only by reason and conviction, not by force or violence, and therefore all men have an equal, natural and unalienable right to the free exercise of religion according to the dictates of conscience, and that no particular religious sect or society ought to be favoured or established by law in preference to others.[35]

Rhode Island did not ratify until May 29, 1790. Then her Delegates did "declare and make known" a statement indistinguishable from the Virginia "Twentieth" clause, and from the similar clause in North Carolina. Thus Virginia, New York, North Carolina, and the tardy Rhode Islanders declared for free exercise, and urged that "no religious sect be favored or established by law in preference of others." [36] New Hampshire came out for freedom of conscience and recommended that Congress make "no law touching religion." South Carolina merely opposed any religious test for officeholding. In Massachusetts the descendants of the Puritans thanked God and did nothing more about establishment. Equal treatment for religious sects was asked by four states, Virginia, New York, North Carolina, and Rhode Island. Only New Hampshire asked Congress to keep its hands off religion.

The wishes of all these states except Rhode Island concerning church and state were submitted to the select committee of the House on July 21, 1789, together with Madison's proposals of June 8. The select committee having reported, the House debated the proposals in committee of the whole beginning on August 13. On the fifteenth the committee of the whole took up the establishment question. The select committee had proposed to insert in Article I, Section 9, of the Constitution, among its other prohibitions on the national government, that

no religion shall be established by law, nor shall the equal rights of conscience be infringed.[37]

Various members objected to the phrasing. Mr. Sherman of Connecti-

---

[35] *Id.* at 1047.

[36] The Rhode Island resolution is found *id.* at 1053.

[37] Accustomed as one is to finding the Amendments seriatim following the end of the original Constitution, the extent of the debate, in 1789, about distributing them in the text, like modern statutory amendments, still comes as a surprise.

cut thought the amendment unnecessary because no such power had been delegated to the Congress.[38]

Mr. Madison said, he apprehended the meaning of the words to be, that Congress should not establish a religion, and enforce the legal observation of it by law, nor compel men to worship God in any manner contrary to their conscience. Whether the words are necessary or not, he did not mean to say, but they had been required by some of the State Conventions, who seemed to entertain an opinion that . . . the clause of the Constitution, which gave power to Congress to make all laws necessary and proper to carry into execution the Constitution, and the laws made under it, enabled them to make laws of such a nature as might infringe the rights of conscience, and establish a national religion; to prevent these effects he presumed the amendment was intended, and he thought it as well expressed as the nature of the language would admit.

Mr. Huntington [of Connnecticut] said that he feared, with the gentleman first up on this subject, that the words might be taken in such latitude as to be extremely hurtful to the cause of religion. He understood the amendment to mean what had been expressed by the gentleman from Virginia; but others might find it convenient to put another construction upon it. The ministers of their congregations to the Eastward were maintained by the contributions of those who belonged to their society; the expense of building meeting-houses was contributed in the same manner. These things were regulated by by-laws. If an action was brought before a Federal Court on any of these cases, the person who had neglected to perform his engagements could not be compelled to do it; for a support of ministers or building of places of worship might be construed into a religious establishment.

By the charter of Rhode Island, no religion could be established by law; he could give a history of the effects of such a regulation; indeed the people were now enjoying the blessed fruits of it. He hoped, therefore, the amendment would be made in such a way as to secure the rights of conscience, and a free exercise of the rights of religion, but not to patronize those who professed no religion at all.

Mr. Madison thought, if the word "national" was inserted before religion, it would satisfy the minds of honorable gentlemen. He believed

[38] This debate begins at 1 ANNALS OF CONGRESS 729.

that the people feared one sect might obtain a pre-eminence, or two combine together, and establish a religion to which they would compel others to conform. He thought if the word "national" was introduced, it would point the amendment directly to the object it was intended to prevent.

Mr. Livermore [of New Hampshire] was not satisfied with that amendment; but he did not wish them to dwell long on the subject. He thought it would be better if it were altered, and made to read in this manner, that Congress shall make no laws touching religion, or infringing the rights of conscience.[39]

Here Mr. Gerry of Massachusetts objected to the word "national" in Madison's proposals.

Mr. Madison withdrew his motion, but observed that the words "no national religion shall be established by law," did not imply that the Government was a national one; the question was then taken on Mr. Livermore's motion, and passed in the affirmative, thirty-one for, and twenty against it.

As the debate on amendments straggled ahead, Madison arose again, to urge the members to recall what constituents had demanded.

Have not the people been told that the rights of conscience, the freedom of speech, the liberty of the press, and trial by jury, were in jeopardy? That they ought not to adopt the Constitution until those important rights were secured to them?

On August 17 the committee of the whole approved Madison's proposal to add to Article I, Section 10, a provision that "no State shall infringe the equal rights of conscience, nor the freedom of speech, or of the press, nor of the right of trial by jury in criminal cases." On August 20, the House on motion of Fisher Ames of Massachusetts approved still another version of what are now the religion clauses of the First Amendment.

Congress shall make no law establishing religion, or to prevent the free exercise thereof, or to infringe the rights of conscience.

[39] Livermore's proposal contained precisely the same words the New Hampshire ratifying convention had used when demanding amendments to the Constitution.

The language was getting close to the form finally adopted. On August 24 the House ordered a fair copy of the Amendments engrossed and sent to the Senate. As the Senate then sat with "closed doors," its debates are not recorded in the Annals of that period, which only note that on September 9 the Senate agreed to some of the House proposals and disagreed with some, and that the Senate so informed the House. On September 21 the House proposed a committee of conference on the disagreements. On the twenty-fourth the House considered that committee's report, and agreed with the Senate in everything except the wording of what are now the First and the Sixth Amendments, and a change in the Senate proposal for Article I.[40] The House recommended the First as it now stands.[41] On the following day the Senate concurred in the revisions proposed by the House.

On the same day the House proposed to request the President to "recommend to the people of the United States a day of public thanksgiving and prayer, to be observed by acknowledging, with grateful hearts, the many signal favors of Almighty God, especially by affording them an opportunity peaceably to establish a Constitution of government for their safety and happiness." On the twenty-sixth of September the Senate concurred in this religious action of the United States Congress.

On December 15, 1791, Virginia approved the Amendments now numbered I to X.[42] She was the eleventh state to do so; and thus three-quarters of the then fourteen states had ratified,[43] as Article V

[40] Never ratified. See n. 42 infra.

[41] Save for "a" in place of "the" before "free exercise." Probably a copyist's error. It is not significant.

[42] Lest I be taken to task for an omission, though one not relevant, I should explain that the Congress on September 25, 1789, submitted twelve, not ten, proposed Articles of Amendments to the states. They can be found in the STATUTES AT LARGE, Vol. 1, at pages 97 and 98. The original Article I of those twelve regulated the number of members of the House; Article II made ineffective any Act of Congress changing the pay of Senators and Congressmen until after a subsequent election of Congressmen. Virginia ratified all twelve, but the original Articles I and II never achieved ratification by three-quarters of the States. Thus the present First Amendment was the third of the original twelve Articles submitted by the Congress.

[43] Vermont had become the fourteenth state on March 4, 1791. Three-quarters

of the Constitution required, and the First Amendment was in force.

Where did this leave the United States as respects church-state relations? By its specific terms the First Amendment, whatever its limits might be, limited only the Congress. States remained free to give direct support to churches.[44] Howe suggested that the First Amendment freed the states from any fear that in a developing federal common law the national courts might include the then rather familiar doctrine that Christianity is part and parcel of the common law, and might enforce a national decisional law of religion. He is probably correct in expanding the 1789 understanding of "Congress shall make no law" to include a similar prohibition against any other form of national action, judicial or executive.[45] Thus what Mark Howe calls "the *de facto* establishment," so familiar in American life and American institutions, gained in the First Amendment a safeguard against possible federal intrusion. And Madison himself recognized that "no law respecting an establishment of religion" was not an all-inclusive prohibition. Less than two months after the legislature of his state had made the First Amendment effective, Madison voted to set the pay of an Army chaplain at $50 per month, the pay of a major.[46]

III

Some disputations among historians concern matters having modest importance, if any. In his *Heavenly City*, Carl Becker wrote of "time spent by historians in determining 'whether Charles the Fat was at Ingelheim or Lustnau on July 1, 887.' "[47] But Howe pointed out that our Supreme Court lays down the law, that the "Court's current in-

---

of fourteen states is a difficult piece of political arithmetic; but assuredly ten states do not make the requisite three-quarters. Eleven makes it, with a fraction over.

[44] *See* THE GARDEN AND THE WILDERNESS at 37, and the Declaration of Rights of the Massachusetts Constitution of 1780, Article III. And states could penalize unlawful religious exercises. *See* Permoli v. Municipality No. 1, 4 U.S. (3 How.) 589 (1845).

[45] THE GARDEN AND THE WILDERNESS at 31.

[46] *See* 3 ANNALS OF CONGRESS 355 (1792).

[47] P. 89. Becker was quoting from, and echoing, a gibe by James Harvey Robinson twenty years earlier, in THE NEW HISTORY at 22, 79 ff, 81.

clination to extract a few homespun absolutes from the complexities of a pluralistic tradition" has a direct relation to our achieving a national educational program with dimensions adequate to the times.[48] He saw with dismay an argument that the First Amendment, intended to prevent unwelcome national intrusion into state religious arrangements, should instead inhibit national aid to such educational projects as state remedial-reading programs, available alike to the pupil in a parochial school and the pupil in a public school. We need, he told us, "a reminder of the part which the unanalyzed, perhaps even the unrecognized, concept of equality played in the constitutional history of the first half of the nineteenth century." [49]

Howe might have added a reminder that by May 1790 four states whose ratifying conventions called for a clause concerning establishments—Virginia, New York, North Carolina and Rhode Island— had all urged in identical words that no "religious sect or society ought to be favored or established by law in preference to others." This is an egalitarian, not an exclusionary, concept. Three of these identical demands must have been in the minds of the congressmen who shaped the First Amendment in the summer of 1789. All four may have been read by the Virginian legislators whose ratification in December 1791 made the First Amendment effective. Those four states contained about a million and a half of the three million six hundred thousand people who inhabited the United States at the time of the 1790 census.

Maitland wrote in 1897 with his customary wisdom:

The history of law must be a history of ideas. It must represent not merely what men have done and said, but what men thought in bygone ages. The task of reconstructing ancient ideas is hazardous, and can only be accomplished little by little. If we are in a hurry to get to the beginning we shall miss the path.[50]

Constitutional clauses are rarely self-defining. At best, men in 1969 can make only a half-educated guess at precisely what a "law respecting

---

[48] THE GARDEN AND THE WILDERNESS at 174. See in this connection the Elementary and Secondary Act of 1965, Pub.L.No. 89–10, 79 Stat. 27 and Flast v. Cohen, 392 U.S. 83 (1968) *reversing* 271 F.Supp.1 S.D.N.Y.(1967)

[49] THE GARDEN AND THE WILDERNESS at 32.

[50] F. MAITLAND, DOMESDAY BOOK AND BEYOND 356 (1897).

an establishment of religion" meant to Madison of Virginia and Huntington of Connecticut and the other congressmen and senators in the summer of 1789, and to the legislators of the eleven ratifying states in the next two years. Certainly few if any of the eighteenth-century legislators would have tolerated any national interference with the religious exercises permitted in the states. Probably none of them would have tolerated a "Church of the United States" on the model of the Church of England. Probably few if any of them would have tolerated a federal distribution of funds to, say, Episcopal churches in exclusionary preference to other sects. But from here on the guessing becomes more difficult, the light is dimmer. And only sheer guess-work, supported by anachronism and contrary to the indication of eighteenth-century opinion, could lead to a conclusion that the First Amendment's establishment clause would in 1791 have invalidated nonpreferential federal instructional benefits to pupils of parochial and public schools alike if the Congress had then set up such a program.

The effect of what Mark Howe found to be a mistaken history of the First Amendment and its restrictions on the national government becomes compounded when the same principles are applied to limit the states. Howe demonstrates with vigor that when Justices speak of applying the First Amendment's establishment clause against states by means of the Fourteenth, of applying it even where there is no restriction of religious free exercise, the historical uncertainty becomes deeper, the unstated premises are still more obscure. The Justices have not told us exactly which words of the Fourteenth Amendment mean, or how they mean, that "no State shall make a law respecting an establishment of religion." [51] The due process and equal protection clauses are probably what they had in mind; the Court has allowed the privileges and immunities clause to go into a coma; due process and equal protection are all that are left. These phrases are well suited to protect all persons against state tyranny, but they can not be made to mean "no State shall make any law respecting an

---

[51] THE GARDEN AND THE WILDERNESS at 136.

establishment of religion" where no one is oppressed or hampered or embarrassed in his beliefs or in his religious exercise.

Here I should stop complaining about what some of the Justices have said, and pay some attention to what the Court has actually done. For it has decided in a rational and just manner a series of cases involving state interference with free exercise of religion. It has never held unconstitutional state or federal benefits which have no elements of oppression of individuals, or interference with free exercise of religion.[52] With the Court's decisions I take no issue. One might start with *Cochran* in 1930.[53] There the Court upheld, against the complaint of a Louisiana taxpayer, a state statute providing free secular textbooks for school children in both public and parochial schools. The unsuccessful taxpayer had not contended that the textbook aid created an "establishment of religion." His constitutional argument was based on the Fourteenth Amendment, which, he said, forbade taxation for a "private" purpose. Chief Justice Hughes wrote for the unanimous Court:

[W]e can not doubt that the taxing power of the state is exerted for a public purpose. . . . [The legislation's] interest is education, broadly; its method, comprehensive. Individual interests are aided only as the common interest is safeguarded.[54]

Recently some comment (not by the Supreme Court) has suggested that when that Court decided *Cochran*, it had not yet become aware that the Fourteenth Amendment "incorporated" the entire first; hence that *Cochran* is now discarded. But five years before *Cochran*, Mr.

---

[52] There have been such decisions in State Courts. *See, e.g.,* Horace Mann League v. Board of Public Works, 242 Md. 645 (1966), *appeal dismissed* 385 U.S. 97 (1966); *contra,* Bowerman v. O'Connor, 247 A. 2d 82 (R.I. 1968). After this paper had been sent to the Institute of Church and State I was retained as one of counsel on appeal in the Rhode Island case; I was one of counsel for the Maryland colleges in the Horace Mann litigation; these matters I here state to make clear my professional involvement in the subject-matter of this paper. As a delegate to the New York Constitutional Convention of 1938 I voted for a provision to permit parochial pupils to use public school buses. And, like Mark Howe's paternal grandfather, mine was a Protestant minister.

[53] Cochran v. Louisiana State Bd. of Educ. 281 U.S. 370 (1930).

[54] *Id.* at 375.

Justice Sanford had written for the majority in *Gitlow v. New York*: [55]

For present purposes we may and do assume that freedom of speech and of the press—which are protected by the First Amendment from abridgment by Congress—are among the fundamental rights and "liberties" protected by the due process clause of the Fourteenth Amendment from impairment by the states.[56]

And only four years after *Cochran* Mr. Justice Cardozo wrote in a concurring opinion for himself and Justices Brandeis and Stone in *Hamilton v. Regents*:

I assume for present purposes that the religious liberty protected by the First Amendment against invasion by the nation is protected by the Fourteenth Amendment against invasion by the states. . . . The First Amendment, if it be read into the Fourteenth, makes invalid any state law "respecting an establishment of religion or prohibiting the free exercise thereof." [57]

The Court knew what it was about when it decided *Cochran,* a few years after *Gitlow,* a few before *Hamilton.* And in 1947 Mr. Justice Black, in his *Everson* opinion for the Court, wrote "It is much too late to argue that legislation intended to facilitate the opportunity of children to get a secular education serves no public purpose," demonstrating the point by citing *Cochran,* with no suggestion that it was a worn-out precedent.[58]

In 1940 the Supreme Court, in *Cantwell v. Connecticut,*[59] reversed a state court conviction of some Jehovah's Witnesses; they had been evangelizing in New Haven streets, and were found guilty of a statutory crime, soliciting money without a license, and of a common-law offense, inciting a breach of the peace. Mr. Justice Roberts wrote for the Court:

---

[55] 268 U.S. 652 (1925).   [56] *Id.* at 666.

[57] 293 U.S. 245, 265–267. The year after *Cochran,* the Court in Near v. Minnesota 283 U.S. 697 (1931), citing *Gitlow,* had held that the Fourteenth Amendment contained the same guarantees of free speech and press as the First. *Id.* at 707. I find it difficult to believe that the Justices in 1931 were unaware that freedom of religion was constitutionally on a par with freedom of expression.

[58] Everson v. Board of Education, 330 U.S. 1, 7 (1947).

[59] 310 U.S. 296 (1940).

The fundamental concept of liberty embraced in that [Fourteenth] Amendment embraces the liberties guaranteed by the First Amendment. The First Amendment declares that Congress shall make no law respecting an establishment of religion or prohibiting the free exercise thereof. The Fourteenth Amendment has rendered the legislatures of the states as incompetent as Congress to enact such laws.[60]

But he added a statement that the constitutional inhibition of legislation on religion has a double aspect:

. . . it forestalls compulsion by law of the acceptance of any creed or the practice of any form of worship. Freedom of conscience and freedom to adhere to such religious organization or form of worship as the individual may choose cannot be restricted by law. On the other hand, it safeguards the free exercise of the chosen form of religion. Thus the Amendment embraces two concepts,—freedom to believe and freedom to act.[61]

In 1943 came *West Virginia v. Barnette,*[62] which held unconstitutional a state board of education regulation punishing a public-school pupil and his parents for his refusal to salute the national flag on grounds of conscience. In 1947 the Court upheld transportation at public expense for parochial school children in the *Everson* case.[63] That decision was followed recently in the *Allen* case,[64] which upheld the public loan of textbooks to parochial school students and removed the doubts concerning the scope of the *Cochran* case as precedent. In three cases, *McCollum* in 1948, *Engel* in 1962, and *Schempp,* in 1963,[65] the Court held unconstitutional religious exercises in public schools which the pupil had to attend or get an excuse, though in *Zorach v. Clauson* in 1952 the Court upheld the release of pupils who wished to attend religious gatherings off the School grounds.[66]

I suggest that in no case has the Supreme Court decided that a

---

[60] *Id.* at 303   [61] *Ibid.*   [62] 319 U.S. 624 (1945).
[63] Everson v. Board, 330 U.S. 1 (1947).   [64] 392 U.S. 236 (1968).
[65] Illinois *ex rel.* McCollum v. Board of Educ. 333 U.S. 203 (1948); Engel v. Vitale, 370 U.S. 421 (1962); School Dist. of Abington v. Schempp, 374 U.S. 203 (1963).
[66] Zorach v. Clauson, 343 U.S. 306 (1952). For a recent scholarly review of the cases see Giannella, *Religious Liberty, Nonestablishment and Doctrinal Development, Part II. The Nonestablishment Principle,* 81 HARV. L. REV. 513 (1968).

nonpreferential governmental activity, with a secular objective, and with no element of religious compulsion on the individual, is nevertheless unconstitutional because some incidental advantage may accrue to some religious group. That is to say the Court, I think, has decided wisely even when some of its Justices wrote somewhat questionable history. As usual, I end up by concluding that the Supreme Court of the United States is a very valuable organ of government.

In 1923 Charles Warren, the lawyer-historian for whom Howe's Chair was named, wrote a history of the Judiciary Act of 1789 which helped persuade the Supreme Court to set aside a precedent it had followed for 96 years.[67] Howe's *The Garden and the Wilderness* will not have to overturn any precedent; but that remarkable little book may well bring some revision in judicial historiography. Few scholars leave such a monument.

---

[67] *See* Warren, *New Light on the History of the Federal Judiciary Act of* 1789, 37 HARV. L. REV. 49 (1923) and *Erie. R. Co. v. Tompkins,* 304 U.S. 64 (1938).

ROBERT C. CASAD

Compulsory Education
and Individual Rights

The opposition of the Old Order Amish to compulsory secondary education, as contrary to their religious beliefs, raises some important questions concerning the limits of state power and the scope of religious liberty. Does a child have a religious-freedom interest that can be asserted in seeking exemption from a compulsory secondary education law? If he does not, does his parent have a right in the name of religious freedom to keep the child out of high school? Does a closed, separated folk culture that rejects as sinful the value system of the larger society have a constitutional right to exist in America today? Or can the state force it to become assimilated by compelling its participation in our chief integrative institution—the public school? [1]

There is a special need to ask these questions now. Certain states with sizable Amish populations have recently enacted laws that seem, to the Amish, to pose a mortal threat to their existence as a separate people. These are laws pertaining to the certification of teachers, the

Robert C. Casad is Professor of Law at the University of Kansas School of Law.
[1] A. INGLIS, PRINCIPLES OF SECONDARY EDUCATION (1918) (Reprinted, 1953) is cited as one of the first significant treatments of the "integrating" function of our common schools. *See also* W. FRENCH, BEHAVIORAL GOALS OF GENERAL EDUCATION IN HIGH SCHOOL 21–29 (1957); J. CONANT, THE CHILD, THE PARENT AND THE STATE 91 (1959).

[51]

consolidation of rural schools into urban ones, and the increase in the number of years of required school attendance.[2]

When the Amish have asked to be exempted from such laws, they have been ignored or misunderstood by the legislators who have gone ahead and enacted the laws in the sincere, but probably mistaken belief that they are thereby benefitting all the people, Amish included.[3]

A recent Kansas case squarely presenting the Amish position with respect to compulsory secondary education has received considerable national attention.[4] Unfortunately, the Amish had no more success making their case understood in the courts than they had in the legislature. The Kansas Supreme Court which decided against them apparently did not see the problem,[5] and when, with considerable difficulty, appeal to the United States Supreme Court was sought,

---

[2] *See* IOWA CODE ANN. §257.25 (1966) (educational standards); §299.1 (1966) (compulsory attendance at school taught by a certified teacher). Before 1965 the compulsory attendance law called for a "competent" rather than a "certified" teacher. *See also* KAN. STAT. ANN. §72–4801 (1967 Supp.), deleting the exemption for students who complete the eighth grade. The Iowa Legislature later recanted and provided for the exemption of Amish children from the requirements of IOWA CODE ANN. §299.1 (1966). *See* Iowa Leg. Serv. (No. 3), p. 476–477 (Senate File 785) (1967). For a commentary on the Iowa struggle see Littell, *State of Iowa vs. The Amish*, 83 CHRIST. CENT. 234 (1966) and Mather, *That Amish Thing, id.* at 245.

After this article was written, the Kansas Legislature, too, recanted to accommodate the Amish. KAN. STAT. ANN. § 72–1111 (1968 Supp.) See n. 120 *infra*.

[3] *Cf.* statement of Rep. John B. Unruh, sponsor of the 1965 Kansas law, *infra* notes 30, 31. For an excellent account of the struggles of the Amish against school consolidation and compulsory secondary education, see Note, *The Right Not to be Modern Men: The Amish and Compulsory Education*, 53 VA. L. REV. 925, 937–948 (1967). *See also,* Scalise, *The Amish in Iowa and Teacher Certification*, 31 ALBANY L. REV. 1 (1967); Comment, *The Amish School Controversy in Iowa*, 10 ST. LOUIS *U.L.J.* 555 (1966); Erickson, *The Plain People and the Public Schools,* SATURDAY REVIEW, Nov. 19, 1966, at 85.

[4] State v. Garber, 197 Kan. 567, 419 P. 2d 896 (1966). The prosecution of Garber followed soon after the *Borntrager* case in Buchanan County, Iowa, which resulted in Amish parents being fined $10,000 for refusing to send their children to a school taught by a certified teacher. (*See* Scalise, *supra* n. 3, at 31.) Events surrounding the *Borntrager* case resulted in the widely circulated picture of Amish children fleeing to the tall corn to escape the sheriff's deputies. (See NEWSWEEK, Dec. 6, 1965, at 38.) These incidents led to the formation of the National Committee for Amish Religious Freedom for the purpose, among other things, of securing judicial review of the *Garber* case.

[5] See discussion of the Kansas Supreme Court's decision, *infra* nn. 34–39.

jurisdiction was denied without comment (three justices dissenting).[6]

The Amish deserve a better hearing than they have received. In view of their fears, it would seem that the state should be extremely cautious in this matter. It ought to be very clear that the state can constitutionally subject the Amish youth to public high school before we go too far. The Amish fears may turn out to be justified, and we may find, too late, that we have inadvertently "exterminated" a harmless folk society.[7]

The most difficult barrier to understanding the Amish position in this matter is the natural tendency to apply standard American values in evaluating their case. The first step must be to try to see the Amish as they see themselves.

WHO ARE THE AMISH?

The Old Order Amish Mennonite Church [8] is a small religious sect that has stubbornly maintained a closed, separate society, with its own internal institutions of control,[9] all based on an antique value system.

[6] Garber v. Kansas, 389 U.S. 81 (1967). Chief Justice Warren and Justices Douglas and Fortas thought probable jurisdiction should be noted. Because Garber's religion disapproves litigation, the case was carried for him by the National Committee For Amish Religious Freedom and the American Civil Liberties Union.

[7] See Erickson, How to Exterminate the Amish Without Really Trying, in THE AMISH AND THEIR SCHOOLS 6 (1967) (circulated by the National Committee for Amish Religious Freedom).

[8] General sources on the Amish society upon which the text relies heavily include J. HOSTETLER, AMISH SOCIETY (1963); W. KOLLMORGEN, CULTURE OF A CONTEMPORARY RURAL COMMUNITY: THE OLD ORDER AMISH OF LANCASTER COUNTY, PENNSYLVANIA 82 (U.S. Dept. of Ag. Rural Life Studies, No. 4 1942); W. SCHREIBER, OUR AMISH NEIGHBORS (1962); E. SMITH, THE AMISH PEOPLE, 1958; THE MENNONITE ENCYCLOPEDIA (1955–1959).

[9] The distinctive character of the Amish folk society is developed in HOSTETLER, supra n. 8, at 3–22. The rules of conduct are incorporated in the Ordnung of each community. These rules are specific taboos and commands, and normally are not written. For a sample Ordnung see id. at 59–61. Compliance with the Ordnung is enforced by the sanctions of Bann (excommunication) and Meidung (shunning). "Meidung requires that members receive no favors from the excommunicated person, that they do not buy from or sell to an excommunicated person, that no member shall eat at the same table with an excommunicated person, and if the case involves husband or wife, they are to suspend their usual marital relations." Id. at 63. For an account of a dramatic case in which an ex-Amishman sought a court injunction against the imposition of Meidung against him, see Yoder, Caesar and the Meidung, 23 MENNONITE Q. REV. 76–98 (1949).

Although they are few in number,[10] the Amish have attracted a great deal of attention. Their quaint dress and the ancient buggies they use for transportation are natural curiosities to tourists and sightseers, and the phenomenon of an eighteenth-century society in the midst of twentieth-century America has intrigued many students of anthropology and sociology. Although they live within the borders of a larger, alien society, they can be readily identified not only by their peculiar dress and tonsorial standards, but also by their language.[11] Their separateness is inspired by their religious belief as to what God's will is for them, and so all of the devices by which they maintain their separateness have religious significance.

Sometimes the existence of unassimilated groups like the Amish can cause problems, but the Amish, at least, seem to pose no real threat to American society. They are content to let non-Amish people go their own ways and make no attempt to proselytize. They are ordinarily obedient to the commands of civil government; they pay their taxes and their creditors and rarely are involved in civil disturbances. It has been said that since the first Amishman came to America in about 1720, not one has been imprisoned for a felony.[12] There are no Amishmen on relief rolls. In many ways they are model, law-abiding citizens. But when the commands of government encroach into an area they consider to be within the exclusive jurisdiction of their separated society, the Amish will refuse to cooperate and may even resist actively, although nonviolently. They will not bear arms in the armed forces. They commonly refuse governmental assistance in agricultural matters,[13] and have resisted the imposition of

---

[10] The 1967 Yearbook of American Churches, p. 63, gives 20,416 as the total membership of the Old Order Amish Mennonite Church. This figure includes only baptized members, however. If children are included, the total may be near 50,000. *See* Gehman, *Plainest of Pennsylvania's Plain People: Amish Folk,* 128 NATL. GEOG. 227, 228 (1965).

[11] The language, Pennsylvania Dutch, a German dialect, is also spoken by some non-Amish groups. HOSTETLER, *supra* n. 8, at 139.

[12] Address by Franklin H. Littell, President of Iowa Wesleyan College, at the National Conference on "Freedom and Control in Education," University of Chicago, March 28, 1967.

[13] HOSTETLER, *supra* n. 8, at 99.

crop controls and inclusion in the federal social security system.[14]

But it is their opposition to compulsory education laws that is the most persistent and dramatic cause of tension between the Amish and governmental authority representing the larger society, for the schools not only teach a repugnant value system, but also seek to integrate ethnic groups into a standardized mass society. This produces a direct conflict with the most basic tenet of the Amish religion—separation from the world.[15]

Be not conformed to this world, but be ye transformed by the renewing of your mind that ye may prove what is that good and acceptable and perfect will of God.[16]

From this scriptural command they have developed a dualistic conception of reality.

To the Amish there is a divine spiritual reality, the Kingdom of God, and a Satanic Kingdom that dominates the present world. It is the duty of a Christian to keep himself "unspotted from the world" and separate from the desires, intent, and goals of the worldly person. . . . This to the Amishman means among other things that one should not dress and behave like the world.[17]

A second Biblical passage is nearly as important:

Be ye not unequally yoked together with unbelievers; for what fellowship hath righteousness with unrighteousness? and what communion hath light with darkness? [18]

The Amish interpret this passage as forbidding too close association with outsiders. To the Amish these beliefs are not mere social philosophy: they are fundamental to the whole question of their existence on earth. They regard themselves as a chosen pilgrim people, merely sojourning in this evil world while proving their worthiness for salva-

---

[14] SEE INT. REV. CODE of 1954, §1402(h), *as amended* by Act of July 30, 1965; Pub. L. No. 89–97, §319 (c), 79 Stat. 391.

[15] HOSTETLER, *supra* n. 8, at 49.

[16] Romans 12:1.

[17] HOSTETLER, *supra* n. 8, at 48.

[18] II Corinthians 6:14.

tion. Salvation is not assured; it is gained through works—principally compliance with the commands and taboos of the church, no matter how irrational they may seem.[19] Specific taboos vary from community to community but generally the Old Order Amish refuse to own electrical appliances, telephones, radios, automobiles, etc.[20]

Pride is sin, so the Amish avoid activities that exalt the individual ego. They do not seek to make themselves or their homes more beautiful. Amassing wealth, which the larger American society regards as a high-order value, is prideful and sinful, except to the extent necessary to provide for the family and to share the costs of the Amish community. Agriculture as a way of life has religious importance for the Amish, since it seems to them to bring them nearer to God and His immediate handiwork—the earth, animals, weather, etc.—and since their separate society could scarcely exist in an urban setting.[21] They do not distinguish between their society and their religious community; they are the same.

The preparation of people for life in the Amish society involves inculcation of the value system of that society and training in the skills necessary for successful farming and homemaking—about the only acceptable vocations. Through the years the Amish have developed educational patterns and practices to accomplish this end.

The advent of compulsory education laws has posed serious problems which the Amish have met as best they could. Where permitted they have set up separate parochial elementary schools which comply generally with the state's requirements while retaining the basic Amish educational system.

Sometimes, however, specific regulations—such as the requirement of "certification" for all teachers—prevent this. The Amish want teachers of their own faith, and very few Amishmen can meet the educational and professional standards necessary for certification. If they cannot have their own teachers, the Amish are usually willing to send their children to public elementary schools, which, after all, do concentrate on basic skills the Amish consider valuable: the traditional "three R's." [22] Before the movement to school consolidation

---

[19] HOSTETLER, *supra* n. 8, at 50.   [20] *Id.* at 61.   [21] *Id.* at 66.
[22] *See generally,* F. STOLL, WHO SHALL EDUCATE OUR CHILDREN? (1965). The

this meant usually one-room country schools where most of the pupils were Amish children anyway.

But high school presents a serious problem. The Amish are opposed to formal education as such beyond the elementary grades. Even if the school were composed only of Amishmen and taught by an Amish teacher, for reasons that are both religious and practical they could not accept the curriculum prescribed by most states. Practically, they see little or no value in it as compared to the on-the-farm training they traditionally have provided for their young people. Time spent in learning about art, literature, and science is time lost from learning how to farm, cook, and sew. From the standpoint of their religion, art and literature are conducive to pride and worldly pleasure. Science teaches ideas about nature that conflict with their literal interpretation of scripture. And while they object to secondary school training generally, they object doubly to the public secondary school for their children. Too much formal learning tends to make children dissatisfied with the simple farm life of the Amish community regardless of the school attended. Moreover, in view of the pressures for conformity to which teenagers in school are subjected, the Amish fear that in the public school their children might internalize the values of the larger society.

Legislators and public officials have often mistaken the intensity of the Amish commitment in their opposition to compulsory secular education. Amish parents have suffered severe fines and even imprisonment for their refusal to require their children to attend school.[23] Sometimes desperate truant officers have had to seek the help of sheriffs to drag the children bodily to school.[24]

Pathway Publishing Corp., Aylmer, Ontario, publisher of the Stoll book, also publishes a periodical, *The Blackboard Bulletin,* which deals with educational questions "in the interests of Amish schools and homes."

[23] *See,* State v. Hershberger, 103 Ohio App. 188, 144 N.E.2d 693 (1955); 77 Ohio L. Abs. 487, 150 N.E.2d 671 (1958); 83 Ohio L. Abs. 63, 168 N.E.2d 12 (1959); *In re* Miller, an Iowa District Court decision as cited in Note, *The Right Not to be Modern Men: The Amish and Compulsory Education,* 53 VA. L. REV. 925, 939 (1967).

[24] See account of the Oelwein, Iowa, controversy in NEWSWEEK, Dec. 6, 1965, at 38. For a more complete treatment of the same, see Erickson, Showdown at an

An important point to bear in mind concerning the Amish attitude toward secondary school is that the Amish consider the years from fifteen to nineteen as the time for young people to decide whether or not they are going to join the Amish church and society.[25] Baptism symbolizes their acceptance of the faith and their admittance to full membership in the separated community, with all the burdens that entails. People are not ready for baptism until late adolescence, when they are considered mature enough to decide for themselves that they will turn their backs on the outside world.[26]

While the Amish believe this decision must be voluntary, they naturally want their children to choose to join the Amish church and community. They feel that if their children are to choose well, and wisely, they must spend these adolescent years participating in the regular routine life which will prepare them for the life of an Amish-man. If a child attends high school for any length of time, they feel he is effectively lost to Amish society. Facts are scarce on the question of how many who go to high school are able to return to the Amish community.[27] It seems hardly deniable, however, that a general requirement of secondary education will make it more difficult for the Amish to maintain their separate society, as more and more youth are subjected to the integrating influences of the public high school.

Amish Schoolhouse, Background Paper No. 3, National Conference on Freedom and Control in Education, University of Chicago, March 28–29, 1967.

[25] HOSTETLER, *supra* n. 8, at 51–52.

[26] "Great emphasis is placed upon the difficulty of walking the 'straight and narrow way.' The applicants are told it is better not to make a vow than to vow and later break it; on a Saturday prior to baptism they are asked to meet with the ministers where they are given opportunity to 'turn back' if they so desire." *Id.* at 52.

[27] Hostetler gives a number of illuminating examples, but no aggregate figures. Some groups will allow children who feel they do want to go on with their education to take correspondence courses. One ex-Amishman, now a college senior, told me that roughly half the children of his age group left the community he was associated with. He felt the proportion of defectors would be considerably higher if children were forced to go to high school. It should be noted, however, that he was referring to a marginal Amish community that was on the verge of leaving the Old Order (which it since has done) to affiliate with the slightly less conservative Beachy Amish Church. The rate of defection in stable Old Order communities is not so high. *Cf.* n. 117 *infra*.

The Kansas Law and the Garber Case

Before 1965 the Kansas Compulsory Education Law required that children attend an approved school until age sixteen or until completion of the eighth grade.[28] In 1965 the legislature undertook a major revision of the statutes pertaining to the unification of school districts and the financing of public schools. At the same session the compulsory attendance law was amended to delete the exemption for students who had completed the eighth grade.[29] This amendment was not a part of the reform legislation urged by the State Superintendent of Public Instruction. It was not sponsored by the Kansas State Teachers Association or the state PTA, nor did those organizations ever declare themselves either for or against the amendment. The bill embodying the amendment was introduced by an individual legislator who was in no way related to the educational "establishment." After the bill was introduced the State Superintendent did record his approval of the change, but his office did not work actively for its passage.

No statistical surveys were made by or presented to the legislature to show the potential impact of the change. There apparently were no data even indicating how many children would be affected: i.e., how many there were who complete the eighth grade before reaching sixteen but do not go on to high school voluntarily.

To discover what motivated the legislature to enact such a law under such circumstances, the author made inquiry of the bill's sponsor, Representative John B. Unruh. Mr. Unruh responded, "I did not have any help from the Department of Education. The bill was my own idea, firmly believing it is good for all the youth of Kansas." [30] He had two objectives in introducing the bill: one was to combat the dropout problem (which his original bill sought to do by raising the age of required attendance to eighteen) by a sanction directed not at the parents, but at the dropout himself—loss of his driver's license

[28] 5 KAN. STAT. ANN. §72–4801 (1964).
[29] Ibid., §72–4801 (1967 Supp.).
[30] Letter dated Oct. 15, 1967.

until age eighteen. This part of his bill failed to pass. The other objective "was to give the children of certain religious groups an opportunity to attend high school." He noted that there were a large number of conservative Mennonites in his district, whose practices and attitudes are similar to those the Amish.

Most of the younger parents wanted to send their children on to High
School but because of the criticism from some of the older members
would keep them at home. . . . One of my main objectives was to stop
the criticism the younger parents were getting and to give the Mennonite youth the same opportunity to attend high school as his neighbor.
Yes, we did think of what this bill would do to certain religious groups.
An amendment was offered on the floor of the House to exclude children for religious purposes. I told the House at that time, and I still
maintain I am correct, that it is not against their religion, it is against
only their customs and perhaps their principles.[31]

Mr. Unruh himself had been raised in the conservative Church of
God in Christ, Mennonite, and his testimony before the House was
very persuasive.

Of course, none of this background appears in the statute. The
law appears to be a general enactment, and it may be that most of
the legislators who supported it did not share the sponsor's particular
interest in its passage. The effect of the amendment on religious
groups who oppose compulsory secondary education was considered,
but that consideration apparently was directed at the position of the
conservative Mennonites described by Representative Unruh. That
group, while extremely conservative, is considerably different from the
Old Order Amish. The representative from the district which includes the main concentration of Amish in Kansas opposed the bill,
and it was he who introduced the amendment for a religious exemption alluded to in Unruh's letter, quoted above.

After the adoption of the 1965 amendment to the compulsory attendance law, the Amish community in Yoder, Kansas, created the
Amish Parochial School Vocational Plan in an attempt to comply

[31] *Ibid.*

with the law. Under the plan, children who had completed the eighth grade of public school but who had not reached age sixteen could continue their education by means of a combination of formal classroom schooling and home study and vocational training. The formal classes were held one morning each week under the direction of an Amish farmer whose own formal education consisted of eight years of public school. Instruction was in English, except for a German reading course. On the remaining days of the school week the students were required to spend one hour in study at home and five hours in vocational training on and about the farm. Written reports of the home study and vocational work were submitted to the teacher.[32]

Sharon Garber had completed the eighth grade of public school at age thirteen in May of 1964, before the amendment of the compulsory attendance law. She did not go on to high school, but continued her education through a correspondence school which had the approval of the United States Office of Education.[33] In the fall of 1965, after the effective date of the amendment to the compulsory education law, she enrolled in the Amish school described above.

On October 18, 1965, Sharon's father, LeRoy Garber, was formally charged with failing to require his daughter to attend school as required by law. He defended on the grounds that he had complied with the law in sending Sharon to the Amish school, but that if the court should find that did not fulfill the law's requirements, he nevertheless could not be convicted since to apply the statute to him would infringe religious liberty. The case was tried without jury on an agreed statement of facts. Garber was found guilty and was fined the statutory minimum of five dollars.

Garber himself was reluctant to press his defense further. The Amish religion does not approve of litigation. He somehow was persuaded, however, to permit his attorney to appeal to the Kansas Supreme

---

[32] The Kansas statutes require attendance at school "continuously" "for such period as the public school of the district . . . is in session," 5 KAN. STAT ANN. §72–1111 (1968 Supp.). They also provide that students must be under direct supervision by a teacher. 5 KAN. STAT. ANN. §72–1106 (1964). The Amish school clearly did not meet these requirements.

[33] See n. 27 supra.

Court. On November 6, 1966, that court handed down its decision affirming the conviction.[34] The opinion in the case recited the facts, including something of the history and tenets of the Old Order Amish Mennonite church as well as the facts relating to the particular positions of defendant and his daughter. The court first considered the question of whether the Amish parochial school met the requirements of the statute [35] as a substitute for public school attendance. Agreeing with the trial court that it did not, the court then turned to the constitutional question. Its decision on this point is epitomized in the following passage:

> In accommodating between the competing right of the state to compel action in the public welfare and the right of the individual to his constitutional religious freedom the courts have distinguished between religious beliefs and religious practices. Failure to comply with reasonable requirements in the exercise of the police power for the general welfare has never been condoned in the name of religious freedom. As stated in *Commonwealth v. Beiler,* "religious liberty includes an absolute right to believe but only a limited right to act." [36]

The court did not elaborate on the distinction between "religious beliefs and religious practices," nor did it attempt to fix any boundary between the "right to believe" and the "right to act." Instead of examining what the limits of the "right to act" might be, or what requirements in the exercise of the police power might be "reasonable," the court simply recited a number of seemingly unrelated cases in which regulations were upheld over religious objections, taking all verbatim from the *Beiler* case. It also quoted from *Prince v. Massachusetts*[37] a passage indicating that parental rights could be restricted

---

[34] State v. Garber, 197 Kan. 567, 419 P.2d 896 (1966).

[35] See n. 32 *supra.*

[36] 197 Kan. at 573, 419 P. 2d at 901. Commonwealth v. Beiler, 168 Pa. Super. 462, 79 A. 2d 134 (1951), the case referred to by the court, had upheld the conviction of an Amish parent for failing to send his child to high school.

[37] 321 U.S. 158 (1944), in which defendant had been convicted of violating the child labor law in permitting her nine-year-old niece to sell religious publications on the street. It should be noted that most commentators consider the *Prince* case seriously weakened, or perhaps even tacitly overruled as an authority by Sherbert v. Verner, 374 U.S. 398 (1963). *See e.g.,* Giannella, *Religious Liberty,*

in the public interest. The court then said it was unable to see how religious freedom was abridged. Assuming that the quotations from *Beiler* and *Prince* had established that the state could restrict defendant's religious "practice," the court said:

There is no infringement upon the right to worship or to believe insofar as either defendant or his daughter is concerned. Their freedom to worship and to believe remain absolute and are not affected by our compulsory school attendance law. Defendant may instruct his daughter in religious beliefs as he desires. It can scarcely be doubted that defendant is sincere when he says his religious convictions are violated if his daughter receives a secular type of education found in the secondary public schools, but it is apparent he does not object to secular education per se since his daughter has attended the elementary public schools eight years. We are not called upon to attempt to prescribe any permissible degree of secularity in education beyond which religious freedom is infringed. The question of how long a child should attend school is not a religious one.[38]

Of course, for the vast majority of people in the larger society the question of how long a child should attend school is not a religious one. To them school attendance does not pose any conflict in values. But in religious freedom cases it is the claimant's definition of what is and what is not religious that should be considered.[39] To the defendant Garber, who had to choose between the commands of the state and those of his church, that question was *primarily* a religious one. And contrary to the court's statement, the determination of the "permissible degree of secularity in education beyond which religious freedom is infringed" was precisely the issue it *was* called upon to decide. At this point the Kansas court's complete disregard of the United States Supreme Court's ruling in *Sherbert v. Verner*[40] appears as a crucial factor, for reference to the doctrine of that case would have led directly to a consideration of that question.

Nonestablishment, and Doctrinal Development: Part I. The Religious Liberty Guarantee, 80 HARV. L. REV. 1381 at 1395 (1967).

[38] 197 Kan. at 574, 419 P. 2d at 902.

[39] See n. 68 *infra.*

[40] 374 U.S. 398 (1963).

The Sherbert Doctrine

It has been said that the *Sherbert* decision signals "the dawn of a new day for religious freedom claims." [41] Whether or not this is true remains to be seen, but clearly that decision goes further than any other to require the state to be more accommodating to the claims of radical religious groups. In that case the court considered an appeal by a Seventh Day Adventist from a decision of the Supreme Court of South Carolina which had upheld a ruling disqualifying her for unemployment compensation benefits because in refusing a Saturday job she had failed without good cause to accept suitable work when offered. She had contended that she had religious scruples against working on Saturday, the Sabbath Day of her faith, and that the South Carolina ruling put a burden on her because of her religion. The Supreme Court agreed with her position and reversed, saying:

If, therefore, the decision of the South Carolina Supreme Court is to withstand appellant's constitutional challenge, it must be either because her disqualification as a beneficiary represents no infringement by the State of her constitutional rights of free exercise, or because any incidental burden on the free exercise of appellant's religion may be justified by a "compelling state interest in the regulation of a subject within the State's constitutional power to regulate." [42]

In holding that the Saturday work condition could not be constitutionally applied to Mrs. Sherbert, the Court in effect held that South Carolina must allow an exception for Sabbatarians from a rule that is perfectly valid insofar as everyone else is concerned.

The language of Mr. Justice Brennan's majority opinion is replete with relative terms. The question was whether some "compelling" state interest justified a "substantial" infringement.

It is basic that no showing merely of a rational relationship to some colorable state interest would suffice; in this highly sensitive constitutional

---

[41] Galanter, *Religious Freedoms in the United States: A Turning Point?*, 1966 Wisc. L. Rev. 217, 241.

[42] 374 U.S. at 403 (1963).

area "[o]nly the gravest abuses, endangering paramount interests, give occasion for permissible limitation." [43]

The earlier case of *Braunfeld v. Brown*,[44] where a Sunday closing law was applied to a Jewish merchant whose religion required that he be closed Saturday, was distinguished by noting that the burden of the closing law on the Jewish merchant was "less direct" than that involved in the *Sherbert* case, and that the secular purpose of the law— providing a uniform day of rest—could not be achieved if Sabbatarians were to be exempted. Exemption would pose administrative problems of such a magnitude as to render the entire statutory scheme unworkable.[45]

The clear implication of the *Sherbert* opinion is that there must be a weighing of conflicting interests: the states' interest in uniform application of the law and the individual's claim of religious freedom. Unless the state's interest in requiring compliance without exception outweighs the individual's claim to be free of the duty to comply, an exception must be made. It is not enough for the state to show that the challenged regulation has a direct relation to some important policy goal. To justify the sacrifice of free exercise rights "it would be plainly incumbent upon the [party representing the states' interest] to demonstrate that no alternative forms of regulation would combat such abuses without infringing First Amendment rights." [46]

The decision in *Sherbert v. Verner* was important in clarifying the scope of free exercise rights and the proper relation between the free exercise and establishment clauses of the First Amendment. It seemed to lay the ghost of the "strict neutrality" theory,[47] which had found support in some prior pronouncements of the Supreme Court.[48]

[43] *Id.* at 406.   [44] 366 U.S. 599 (1961).

[45] Sherbert v. Verner, 374 U.S. 398, 408–409 (1963).

[46] *Id.* at 407.

[47] See Kauper, *Schempp and Sherbert: Studies in Neutrality and Accommodation*, 1963 RELIGION AND THE PUBLIC ORDER 3, 29 (1964).

[48] And even in the language of Justice Clark's chief opinion in School Dist. v. Schempp, 374 U.S. 203, 222 (1963), decided the same day as Sherbert v. Verner. The "strict neutrality" theory would hold that the state cannot use religion as a basis for classification either for conference of a privilege or imposition of a burden.

But the weighing and balancing of state interests and individual interests, of the requirements of separation of church and state implicit in the establishment clause and the requirements of effective religious liberty under the free exercise clause, that *Sherbert* calls for is by no means a simple process. About the only direct guidance the Court itself gives on how to strike the balance is its attempt to distinguish the case from *Braunfeld v. Brown*,[49] and *Abington School District v. Schempp*.[50] The value of this guidance is lessened by the fact that four of the justices were not persuaded that the *Braunfeld* case was distinguishable.[51]

A short time after the *Sherbert* ruling the Court, apparently unanimously, in *In re Jenison*,[52] extended the protection of the free exercise clause to a litigant who sought exemption from jury duty on the ground that her religious scruples forbade her to sit in judgment on others. In a brief *per curiam* decision the Court granted certiorari and summarily reversed and remanded the case to the state court that had denied the exemption, "for further consideration in the light of *Sherbert v. Verner*." [53] The decision of the Supreme Court does not go far to relieve uncertainties left by *Sherbert*, but it does suggest that the Justices who dissented in *Sherbert* were at least sufficiently reconciled to that decision to refrain from dissenting in *Jenison*.

While the Supreme Court itself has not done anything more with the *Sherbert* principle, certain state courts have. The Minnesota court, on remand in *Jenison*, found that the state had not sufficiently shown that its interest in obtaining competent jurors would be so threatened by an exemption for those who opposed jury service on religious grounds as to warrant the real imposition on their religious freedom.[54]

Under this theory Mrs. Sherbert's religion would not be a valid basis for exempting her from the criterion of "availability for work" applied to all others. *See* P. KURLAND, RELIGION AND THE LAW 17–18, 111–112 (1962).

[49] 366 U.S. 599 (1961).   [50] 374 U.S. 203 (1963).

[51] Justice Douglas and Justice Stewart, who each concurred separately, and Justices Harlan and White who dissented.

[52] 375 U.S. 14 (1963).   [53] *Ibid.*

[54] *In re* Jenison, 267 Minn. 136 at 137, 125 N.W.2d 588 at 589 (1963).

The California Supreme Court in *People v. Woody*[55] held that a general criminal prohibition against the use of peyote, a nonaddictive hallucinatory narcotic, could not constitutionally be applied against a member of the Native American Church, an Indian religious organization. The use of peyote was a central feature of the ritual of the church, and the peyote was itself an object of worship. The California court sought to apply the "two-fold analysis" which the majority opinion in *Sherbert* called for, examining first whether the statute in fact imposed a substantial burden on the defendant's free exercise of religion, and second whether the burden was justified by some compelling state interest. Finding that the direct prohibition against the use of peyote "removed the theological heart of Peyotism," [56] the court directed most of its attention to the question of the "compelling state interest." The state's opposition to exempting the defendant rested on two main grounds: the deleterious effects of Peyotism on the Indian community itself, and the difficulties that exemption would pose for the enforcement of the narcotics law because of the likelihood of fraudulent claims. The court found no evidence that the use of peyote caused any permanent physical injury to the Indians, nor that it made them more likely to become users of other more harmful drugs. The court also noted that the moral standards of members of the Native American Church were generally higher than those of Indians outside the Church.

The state also urged that it had a duty to eliminate the use of peyote among the Indians because of its "symbolic" significance in "obstructing enlightenment" and its tendency to shackle the Indians to primitive conditions. The response of the Court to this contention could be as relevant to the case of the Amishman Garber as to the Indian Woody:

We know of no doctrine that the state, in its asserted omniscience, should undertake to deny to defendants the observance of their religion in order to free them from the suppositious "shackles" of their "unenlightened" and "primitive condition." [57]

---

[55] 61 Cal.2d 716, 394 P.2d 813, 40 Cal. Rptr. 69 (1964).

[56] *Id* at 722, 394 P.2d at 818, 40 Cal. Rptr. at 74.

[57] *Id*. at 723, 394 P.2d at 818, 40 Cal. Rptr. at 75.

The court likewise rejected the state's second contention: the threat
to effective enforcement of the narcotics laws. Drawing again from
Justice Brennan's majority opinion in *Sherbert v. Verner,* the court
found no indication that the limited exemption would cause such
difficulties, and that even if there were a possibility of spurious claims,
the state would have to show that "no alternative forms of regulation
would combat such abuses without infringing first amendment
rights." [58] The court noted that other states had excepted the sac-
ramental use of peyote from their narcotics laws without causing any
apparent enforcement problems.[59] Among the enforcement difficulties
urged by the state was the fact that the exemption would require an
inquiry in each case into the bona fides of any defendant's religious
beliefs. The court, however, did not regard this as especially troublesome, noting that the relevant inquiry was simply the sincerity of the
defendant's claim, not the truth or validity of the belief he professed.[60]

The Federal Commissioner of Food and Drugs endorsed the California court's decision in *Woody* by authorizing an exemption from
the federal narcotics laws for the bona fide use of peyote in the ceremonies of the Native American Church.[61] Attempts by members of
other sects[62] to gain exemption from state and federal narcotics laws,
however, have been unsuccessful. In *State v. Bullard*[63] defendant
sought exemption from the state narcotics laws, which he was charged

[58] *Id.* at 723, 394 P.2d 819, 40 Cal. Rptr. at 75.

[59] The court cited New Mexico Statutes (1959) 54–5–16, and Montana Statutes
(1959) 94–35–123 as examples of specific statutory exemptions, and an Arizona
trial court judgment that reached the same result without the aid of a statute.

[60] Citing United States v. Ballard, 322 U.S. 78 (1944).

[61] 21 C.F.R. §166.3(c) (1966).

[62] In *In re* Grady, 61 Cal. 2d 887, 394 P.2d 728, 39 Cal. Rptr. 912 (1964),
the California court granted habeas corpus to one who had been convicted of
possession of peyote before the *Woody* ruling. Grady had claimed the peyote was
for religious uses, and so the court ordered him released from custody pending
retrial on the issue of whether his use of peyote was in the bona fide practice of religion. Grady was not a member of the Native American Church, but was leader of
a small unaffiliated group of peyote worshippers. To the extent that the Grady case
suggests that exemption can be required on the basis of individual sincerity of
belief alone, unrelated to the tenets of any organized religious body, it must be
compared to *Leary v. United States, infra* note 65.

[63] 267 N.C. 599, 148 S.E.2d 565 (1966).

with violating by possessing peyote and marijuana, on the ground that he was a member of the Neo-American Church, whose tenets were described in words virtually identical to those the California court used in *People v. Woody* to describe the Native American Church. Defendant claimed peyote was essential and marijuana "most advisable" in the practices of the church. In affirming his conviction the North Carolina court did not apply the *Sherbert* interest-balancing analysis, but simply ruled that the exercise of religion provided no excuse for acts that constituted "threats to the public safety, morals, peace and order." [64] The court did note that the sincerity of defendant's belief was questionable, and so the *Sherbert* approach might well have yielded the same result.

In *Leary v. United States*[65] the Court of Appeals for the Fifth Circuit was faced with a Hindu's contention that application of the federal narcotics control laws to him infringed his free exercise of religion. Leary sought reversal of his conviction for unlawful possession of marijuana on the ground that the government had shown no such compelling interest as would be required by the *Sherbert* principle to warrant applying the law to one who sincerely believed the use of marijuana was important to his religion. He had introduced evidence that marijuana was relatively harmless to individuals, and he contended that unless the government refuted this evidence, no compelling interest could be shown. The court rejected this contention, however, finding a compelling interest in the need to regulate the traffic in marijuana, which Congress had found a serious threat to public safety, peace, and order. The court also found no evidence that the use of marijuana, unlike the use of peyote in the Native American Church, was essential to the practice of Hinduism. In view of these conclusions, and considering the enforcement difficulties that exemption of persons in Leary's position would pose, the court held that Leary's personal sincerity of belief did not entitle him to exceptional treatment.

Some scholars have seen in the *Sherbert* decision an occasion for a

[64] *Id* at 603, 148 S.E.2d at 569.   [65] 383 F.2d 851 (5th Cir. 1967).

re-examination of religious liberty cases and principles in the light of the attitude of "accommodation" and "benevolent neutrality" [66] revealed in that case. Commendable studies have been made by Professor Galanter [67] and Professor Giannella [68] analyzing the religious liberty cases from the new vistas opened up by *Sherbert* and seeking to identify and supply a basis for weighing the various state and individual interests. These writers basically agree on the factors that must be considered on the religious side of the scale:

(1) Sincerity of the individual. This concerns the claimant's own commitment to the religious position he is maintaining.[69]

(2) The importance or "centrality" of the religious factor involved. This determination normally requires some assessment of the particular religious practice or commands in the light of the tenets and teachings of the religious sect of which the claimant is a member.[70]

(3) The extent to which the governmental regulation interferes with religious practices or commands: i.e., how direct, and how heavy is the burden imposed upon the individual's free exercise of religion.[71]

Both would agree that in cases concerning the protection of religious liberty, what is and is not "religious" must be determined in accordance with the criteria appropriate to the claimant's religion, at least if it is a theistic one,[72] not by reference to the standards of the majority, as the Kansas Court did in the *Garber* case.

These commentators differ, however, in their analysis of the factors on the "public interest" side of the scale. Both recognize that the "compelling interest" that must appear is an interest in applying the challenged regulation without exception—not just a general interest in the matter regulated.

---

[66] *See* Kauper, *Schempp and Sherbert: Studies in Neutrality and Accommodation,* 1963 RELIGION AND THE PUBLIC ORDER 3, 16 (1963).

[67] Galanter, *Religious Freedoms in the United States: A Turning Point?* 1966 WISC. L. REV. 217 (1966). [Hereinafter cited as Galanter.]

[68] Giannella, *Religious Liberty, Nonestablishment, and Doctrinal Development. Part I. The Religious Liberty Guarantee,* 80 HARV. L. REV. 1381 (1967). [Hereinafter cited as Giannella.]

[69] Galanter at 271–274; Giannella at 1417–18.

[70] Galanter at 274–278; Giannella at 1419–1421.

[71] Galanter at 278–280; Giannella at 1421–1423.

[72] Galanter at 264; Giannella at 1423.

Giannella organizes the cases around the public goal sought by the regulation. From his examination of the cases decided since 1940, he found that the courts have tended to regard some public goals as more compelling than others in comparison to religious liberty claims.[73] Thus regulations which promote public health and safety, such as requirements of compulsory vaccination, are more compelling than welfare regulations, such as prohibitions of door-to-door distribution of literature, which merely promote public comfort and convenience. Deviations from rules of basic morality, the kinds of rules that underlie crimes that are *mala in se,* are not to be justified by claims of religious freedom. Economic regulations may be weighted very strongly in comparison to religious liberty claims, or not so strongly, depending upon whether or not uniformity of application is essential to the regulatory scheme, and whether exemption would create an unwarranted advantage for the claimant. General civic duties are accorded varying weights, depending upon the type of duty. The duty to pay taxes is similar to economic regulations where uniformity of application is important and definite preferences could result from exemption. Jury duty, on the other hand, does not rank as so compelling. Military service represents a compelling interest of great importance, although our nation has always recognized some sort of exemption from it in deference to religious scruples.

Giannella does not treat compulsory school attendance laws, and so it is not certain where in his analytical framework the Amish claim for exemption would lie.

Galanter's approach is quite different. Since under *Sherbert* the "compelling interest" that must be considered in these cases is not the interest in the subject matter regulated, but the interest in avoiding the religious exemption or in not providing an alternative scheme of regulation, he identifies two not clearly distinguishable types of interest: avoiding expense and administrative inconvenience; and avoiding interference with the implementation of policy.[74] In analyzing the state's interest in policy implementation, Galanter classifies the cases not according to the type of activity regulated, but according to the

[73] Giannella at 1390–1416.   [74] Galanter at 281.

relation of the actor to the persons whom the policy seeks to protect. He finds four categories: [75]

(1) Where the state's asserted interest is primarily in the welfare of the party who makes the claim for religious exemption (e.g., the blood transfusion cases).

(2) Where the asserted state interest is in the welfare of those who are voluntarily consorting with the one who makes the claim for religious exemption (e.g., the snake-handling, polygamy and faith-healing cases).

(3) Where the religious exemption would have some possible effect on unconsenting others, but in a gross and diffuse way (e.g., refusal of jury duty and military service, crop limitations, and compulsory union membership).

(4) Where the exemption could affect specifiable nonconsenting others in a tangible way (e.g., door-to-door purveyors of religious literature).

Galanter regards these categories as reflecting increasing degrees of state interest, from the least in category one to the greatest in category four.[76] He feels a "compelling state interest" can only be shown where the religious exception would pose some tangible threat to unconsenting others.[77] Limitations other than compelling interest inhibit recognition of religious exceptions, however, notably the restrictions on official preference of religion that derive from the establishment clause.[78]

Since he defines "compelling interest" in terms of how the exemption affects "unconsenting others," Galanter is led to consider the quality of the consent.[79] And this leads squarely to what he feels may be the "ultimate dilemma of the First Amendment." [80] Where does the religious freedom of children fit in the scheme of balancing that the *Sherbert* doctrine seems to call for? Are compulsory education laws designed to promote the welfare of the children themselves

---

[75] *Id.* at 282–83.

[76] Inconveniently, however, not all laws fit neatly in the pattern. The same law may seek to protect more than one of these categories of people.

[77] Galanter at 283.   [78] *Id.* at 288.   [79] *Id.* at 284.   [80] *Ibid.*

against their claim for a religious exemption? If so, such regulations would appear to reflect a "category one" state interest, and would be regarded as not too "compelling." Or do such laws have as their object the protection of children as "unconsenting (since they lack the capacity to consent) others" from the activities of the claimant (their parents)? If so, such laws would appear to reflect a state interest of the most compelling (category four) type.

BALANCING THE INTERESTS

In applying the insights provided by Giannella and Galanter to the problem presented by such a case as *State v. Garber*,[81] it is important to bear in mind that we are dealing here with a *secondary* education requirement. The children who are affected have completed eight grades of school and are usually over thirteen years old. The alternative to formal secondary education is not that the children will be loosed unprepared upon society. These children, for the most part, will simply disappear from the larger society, to become integrated in a closed subsociety with its own devices to prevent crime and poverty and to see that all members are productive.

It is also important to bear in mind that these statutes aim at producing a definite action on the part of one person, the child, but enforce compliance by requiring action of a different sort by another, the parent, under threat of penal sanction. Thus, in evaluating the interests on the religious liberty side of the question, we must be concerned with two different kinds of interests: the interest in avoiding the obligation of school attendance, and the interest in avoiding the obligation to see that one's child goes to school.

It is not clear to whom the interest in avoiding school attendance "belongs": the child, or the parent. Is it an aspect of the child's own religious freedom? Or is it part of the parent's right as natural guardian to direct the destiny of the child? Or is it an element of the parent's own free exercise of religion, as would be the case where his religion imposes an obligation on him to bring his child up in the

[81] 197 Kan 567, 419 P. 2d 896 (1966).

"true way," which for some reason cannot be done if the child is sent to high school? [82]

Insofar as the parent's general right of control is concerned, it has been held that the state can displace that by legislation that has a "reasonable relation to some purpose within the competency of the state." [83] But insofar as the interest in avoiding school attendance rests on a religious freedom claim, whether it "belongs" to child or parent, the *Sherbert* balancing test would apply. If the infringement of religious freedom is substantial, a compelling state interest, not just a reasonable relation to a valid state purpose, would be necessary to override the claim for exemption. The question of whether the religious freedom claim "belongs" to the child or to the parent would have little practical relevance if the religious beliefs of the parent and child were identical, but if they were different it would be necessary to decide whose interest is to be used in the balancing process. Since the law ultimately seeks to compel the child's attendance at school, it would seem that the child's interest should be considered, *if* the child is recognized as having a religious liberty interest in his own right. If the child is recognized as having such an interest, and if he has no sincere religious conviction that would be violated by high school attendance, he could be required to attend despite strong religious objections on the part of the parent.

Does a child who has completed the eighth grade but who has not yet reached age sixteen have any claim to religious freedom in his own right? The compulsory education cases have ignored this question, but it would seem to be important in cases such as *Garber*, especially when one of the presuppositions of the law may be, as Representative Unruh proposed, that the children's interests are potentially different from those of the parents. Cases arising in other contexts have suggested that twelve- and thirteen-year-old children can determine im-

---

[82] The Supreme Court, in Prince v. Massachusetts, 321 U.S. 158 (1944) noted the distinction of these interests, but did not refine them. "The rights of children to exercise their religion, and of parents to give them religious training and to encourage them in the practice of religious belief, as against preponderant sentiment and assertion of state power voicing it, have had recognition here." *Id.* at 165.

[83] Pierce v. Society of Sisters, 268 U.S. 510, 535 (1925).

portant religious questions for themselves.[84] It might be appropriate to consider Amish children at that stage of development as having a capacity to choose not to follow their parents' religious objections to high school attendance. Since we lack dependable criteria for determining when a mature religious conscience develops in an individual, such a rule would be subject to some uncertainty, but the child who has decided not to follow his parents' beliefs has at least indicated some capacity for independent decision.

Of course, even if the child is regarded as having this capacity, and his obligation to attend school is regarded as referable to his religious liberty claim, the other obligation—that of seeing to it that the child attends—must still be determined by reference to the parent's own religious liberty interest. The state interest may be sufficiently compelling when weighed against the child's religious liberty claim to require that the child attend high school, but it does not necessarily follow that the state's interest will be sufficiently compelling to require the parent to violate his own religious convictions and force the child into school if the child, for some reason, does not go. It is one thing to say that the child must attend school despite the risk that may pose to his immortal soul. It is something else to say that the parent must play an active role in what he conceives to be his own child's damnation, thereby jeopardizing his own hopes for eternity. Alternative measures to enforce school attendance without subjecting the parent to the choice of hell or jail are surely available. The power of the state to fine or imprison the parent thus would seem to depend on some different considerations from those that support the state's power to force the child into school.

[84] *See, e.g.,* Hehman v. Hehman, 13 Misc.2d 318, 178 N.Y.S.2d 328 (1958) (13-year-old); and Martin v. Martin, 308 N.Y. 136, 123 N.E.2d 812, 127 N.Y.S.2d 851 (1954) (12-year-old). In these cases children were given the choice of whether they were to be trained in accordance with their mother's or their father's religion. Of course, whether Amish children at that age are capable of making such a profound decision, in view of the very close familial relation that characterizes the Amish, is conjectural. If an Amish child does have a determination to go on in school in spite of parental objections, however, it probably indicates such a breakdown of parental control as to make it virtually certain the child will leave the Amish fold when he can.

The Religious Liberty Interest

Sincerity. In weighing the religious liberty and state interests in a case like *State v. Garber,* the religious liberty claim appears quite strong. Insofar as the element of sincerity is concerned, it was never doubted in the *Garber* case. The Supreme Court of Kansas specifically noted that factor in the following words:

It can scarcely be doubted that defendant is sincere when he says his religious convictions are violated if his daughter receives a secular type of education found in the secondary public schools.[85]

The court did not really consider whether the daughter was old enough to have a claim to religious liberty in her own right, although it did say "There is no infringement upon the right to worship and to believe insofar as either defendant or his daughter are concerned."[86] The court seems to have assumed that if the daughter did have religious freedom, she had chosen to follow her father's beliefs.

Importance of the Religious Belief or Practice. In this aspect, too, the religious interest weighs heavily in the *Garber* case. The doctrine of separation from the world, which is the main basis for the Amish resistance to secondary school, is the heart of all that is distinctive about the Old Order Amish. It is a direct command that colors their whole conception of their relation to the Creator. That doctrine is as central to the Amish religion as the use of peyote to the Native American Church.

And, of course, the idea of separation is also essential to the very existence of the Amish as a separate culture. The Supreme Court of Kansas acknowledged the importance of this principle to the Amish.

A cardinal tenet in the Amish faith is the Biblical injunction, "Be not conformed to this world," adherence to which, under their rigid interpretation, has doubtless contributed to their survival as a cultural group. Opposition to public secondary schools derives from their feeling that eventually this exposure of their children to that secular influence will erode the Amish way of life.[87]

[85] 197 Kan. 567, 574, 419 P.2d 986, 902.   [86] *Ibid.*
[87] *Id.* at 569, 419 P.2d at 898.

COMPULSORY EDUCATION   [77]

In Europe, where they lacked the protection of religious freedoms that they have enjoyed in America, the Amish have long since disappeared as a separate subculture.[88] So there is some historical basis for their fears.

Extent of the Governmental Interference. In this respect too, the religious liberty claim of the Amish appears to have great weight. The law commands that the child do something the religion specifically prohibits. It directly orders the father to disregard the command of his religion—that he raise his child to live in the Amish society as the only way to salvation. The interference with religious freedom is obviously substantial and direct.

The interference here is more serious than that which the Supreme Court condemned in *Sherbert v. Verner.*[89] There it was indirect. The South Carolina unemployment compensation law did not require Mrs. Sherbert to work on Saturday in contravention of her religious scruples; it merely made it economically disadvantageous if she refused to do so. In *Garber,* however, the interference of the compulsory attendance law with both the child's and the parent's asserted religious freedom is direct.

Likewise the interference in *Garber* appears more onerous than that presented in the peyote case, *People v. Woody.*[90] There public law prohibited what the religion encouraged, but it did not appear that failure to consume peyote was a positive sin. The Indians could have obeyed the law and still not have risked damnation. The Mormon polygamy case [91] and *Prince v. Massachusetts,*[92] both cases that the Pennsylvania court in *Commonwealth v. Beiler* [93] and therefore the

---

[88] HOSTETLER, AMISH SOCIETY 38–44 (1963): "The Amish in Europe . . . were too mobile, too scattered, and too persecuted to constitute a folk culture, . . . when the Amish came to America in the eighteenth century they found conditions favorable for growth and development. They could live adjacent to each other on family farms and maintain relatively self-sufficient and closely knit communities. Under these conditions, an integrated folk culture could develop and maintain its identity. Thus the Amish survived in the New World, emerging as distinctive, small, homogeneous, and self-governing communities." *Id.* at 44.

[89] 374 U.S. 398 (1963).

[90] 61 Cal.2d 716, 394 P.2d 813, 40 Cal. Rptr. 9. (1964).

[91] Reynolds v. United States, 98 U.S. 145 (1878).

[92] 321 U.S. 158 (1944). See n. 37 *supra.*

[93] 168 Pa. Super. 462, 79 A.2d 134 (1951).

Kansas court in *State v. Garber*[94] relied upon heavily, were cases in which the state sought to prohibit activity the church encouraged but did not require.[95] In *Garber,* on the other hand, the state required what the church forbade. A distinction like that between the prevention of a desirable act and the requiring of a prohibited act may be too tenuous to be significant in some areas, but in situations concerning religious requirements and prohibitions of an ultimate, eternal importance, it would seem that a distinction should be drawn. In other situations wherein the law has required the performance of acts forbidden by religious beliefs, the courts have seen the need for an exception to accommodate the religious liberty interest. Most notable in this respect are the flag salute case[96] and *In re Jenison,*[97] where the doctrine of *Sherbert v. Verner* was invoked to protect the religious scruples of a woman who refused to perform jury service. The few cases in which the courts have upheld the power of the state to require without exception what the religion prohibits—notably the compulsory vaccination[98] and the blood transfusion[99] cases—are probably distinguishable on the ground of the character of the state interest. They admittedly involve a direct and substantial interference insofar as the religious freedom interest is concerned.

The State Interest

There is little ground for arguing that the state's interest in avoiding administrative expense and inconvenience is sufficiently "compelling" to warrant denying an exception to the Amish. On the contrary, exempting them would save the state the expense of educating a number of children. Administration of the exemption would be

[94] 197 Kan. 567, 419 P.2d 896 (1966).

[95] Although in *Prince* the nine–year-old girl apparently believed she would be condemned if she did not sell the tracts 321 U.S. 158, 163 (1944).

[96] West Virginia State Bd. of Educ. v. Barnette, 319 U.S. 624 (1943).

[97] 375 U.S. 14 (1963); *on remand* 267 Minn. 136, 125 N.W.2d 588 (1963).

[98] See especially Wright v. DeWitt School District, 238 Ark. 906, 385 S.W.2d 644 (1965), in which the court did consider the *Sherbert* doctrine, but found it inapplicable.

[99] *See, e.g.,* Application of the President and Directors of Georgetown College, Inc. 331 F.2d 1000 (D.C. Cir.), *rehearing denied,* 321 F.2d 1010, *cert. den.,* 377 U.S. 978 (1964). *But cf. In re* Brook's Estate, 32 Ill.2d 361, 205 N.E. 2d 435 (1965). *See also* 42 IND. L. J. 386 (1967).

simple, for the Amish are readily identifiable. There is virtually no possibility of spurious claims being asserted.

Whether exempting the Amish would be subversive of the policy underlying the compulsory education law is more difficult to determine because it is not clear just what the public interest served by this law is. Compulsory education actually seems to partake of several of the public interest functions identified by Giannella. In some respects the obligation to attend school resembles the "Civic Duties": [100] paying taxes, serving on juries, performing military service. An informed people is advantageous for our society, and to that end the state imposes on everyone a duty to submit to education. But the relation between the public purpose and the acts required in compulsory school attendance is somewhat more remote than is true of the other civic duties. Every exemption from the duty to pay taxes has a direct effect on public revenue. Every exemption from jury or military service reduces by one the fund of available jurors or military personnel. But exemption of a person from school attendance does not necessarily mean the reservoir of informed persons has been reduced. Nor does attendance necessarily mean that the reservoir is increased.

The Minnesota court, which granted exemption from compulsory jury service to Mrs. Jenison, regarded the state's interest as insufficient to override the religious liberty claim:

[U]ntil and unless further experience indicates that the indiscriminate invoking of the First Amendment poses a serious threat to the effective functioning of the jury system, any person whose religious convictions prohibit compulsory jury duty shall henceforth be exempt.[101]

Insofar as compulsory education rests upon a general civic duty, the same approach to exemption would surely be justified.

Exemption on religious liberty grounds has not been allowed in the case of the general duty to pay taxes,[102] and the *Sherbert* doctrine probably does not indicate any different result. But that duty is clear-

---

[100] *See* Giannella at 1409.

[101] *In re* Jenison 267 Minn. 136, 137, 125 N.W.2d 588, 589 (1963).

[102] *See e.g.,* Abraham J. Muste, 35 T.C. 913 (1961); *cf.* Giannella at 1410.

ly distinguishable from the duty of school attendance, both in the more direct relation to the public purpose and in the potential economic preference (and consequent "establishment" problems) exemption would entail.

The compulsory education laws also have some attributes like those regulations described by Giannella under the classification of "Public Health and Safety." [103] Those are regulations which serve to protect people in general against certain specific hazards. Compulsory vaccination requirements which serve to protect not only the individual inoculated but others as well are notable examples of regulations of this type which have withstood challenges on religious liberty grounds.[104] Giannella also would include in this category regulations which prohibit certain kinds of conduct that may be harmful only to those who engage in it, or those who consort with such persons, such as laws relating to snake-handling [105] and the use of narcotics.[106] Ignorance and poverty are recognized as major contributing causes of a number of evils which not only affect the individuals suffering from them, but also threaten the health and safety of others and the society as a whole. The public interest in preventing these evils is strong, and in our society education appears as the only effective antidote. But if exemption would be unlikely to lead to the kind of conditions the public interest seeks to guard against, the policy goals of the law would not be subverted. In *Wright v. DeWitt School Dist.*[107] plaintiff argued that smallpox was no longer the threat it once was, that there had not been a case of it in the county for over fifty years, and that therefore the danger was so remote that there was no compelling state interest in refusing an exemption on religious freedom grounds to the compulsory vaccination law. The Arkansas Court, however, thinking mainly in "clear and present danger" terms, rejected this contention, taking judicial notice that smallpox was an ever-

[103] Giannella at 1390.

[104] *See, e.g.,* Wright v. DeWitt School Dist., 238 Ark. 906, 385 S.W.2d 644 (1965).

[105] *See, e.g.,* Kirk v. Commonwealth, 186 Va. 839, 44 S.E.2d 409 (1947).

[106] Narcotics laws may also be considered under the category of rules relating to "Public Morality." *See* Giannella at 1406–1408.

[107] Wright v. DeWitt School Dist., 238 Ark. 906, 385 S.W.2d 644 (1965).

present hazard. The result might have been different if instead of basing his argument on statistical improbability, the claimant could have shown that some alternative measures acceptable to him could have been taken which would provide as great assurance as vaccination that he or his children would not fall victim to smallpox, and would not become carriers of that disease.

In the case of a compulsory high school attendance law, if a claimant could prove not only the statistical improbability that a child would fall into poverty and degradation if exempted but also that alternative arrangements applicable to the child would provide at least as much assurance as school attendance that the child would not fall victim to the hazards the schools guard against, the state seemingly would have no justifiable interest in imposing the requirement on him in the face of a strong religious liberty claim for exemption. Of course, the "alternative arrangement" should probably be something other than individual wealth, to avoid invidious distinctions based on economic circumstance. But if an "alternative arrangement" applicable to all persons in the same position as the claimant with respect to the religious and public interests could be shown, it would seem that exemption should be allowed.

The majority opinion in the *Sherbert* case indicates that the state must bear the burden of showing that there is no practical alternative to the general regulation, but if the claimant wants to predicate his claim to the religious exemption on the independent existence of some alternative arrangement applicable to him, it seems most proper that he should bear the burden of proof on that issue. An Amishman would have little difficulty proving that such an alternative existed, and that exempting him and all other Amishmen would pose no threat to the public health and safety. The Amish provide safeguards against poverty, crime, and unhealthful physical conditions within the framework of their separated society. They are thrifty and industrious, religiously so in the literal sense of the word. They are well known as very good and productive farmers in spite of their refusal to use modern machinery. All are employed. Elderly people are cared for. Although their religious scruples prevent them from buying insurance, they have institutional means of loss-sharing to prevent economic ruin to any member from natural hazards and crop failure. Because they "take care of their own" and have little impact on the larger society, Congress has seen fit to exempt them from the Social Security tax,[108] in deference to their religious objections. States surely could exempt them from the secondary education requirement without violating the establishment clause. Insofar, then, as the interest served by the compulsory secondary school attendance law is that of protecting the public health and safety, exemption for the Amish would seem to be constitutionally required by the *Sherbert* principle.

The compulsory education laws likewise partake to some degree of "Public Welfare Regulations,"[109] as defined by Giannella, especially those he calls "Economic Regulations." The schools serve both to prepare persons for effective economic roles and to control entry into the labor market. But in this aspect of the public interest too there appears no "compelling interest" in denying exception for the Amish. They are not really in the labor market of the larger society. Unless we assume the children are going to abandon the Amish society, they have no need for the formal education provided in secondary school to become productive workers. They are carefully trained in agriculture and homemaking arts and skills within the separated community. Their early entry into the labor market will have no impact on the overall economy, for they will not be displacing others from jobs. Amish farmers do not hire non-Amish farm workers if they can possibly avoid it. It seems clear, then, that the imperceptible economic consequences of allowing the Amish to avoid high school would not be a sufficient "compelling interest" to warrant denying them an exemption.

Again, to some extent the compulsory school attendance laws serve to protect a vulnerable group of people—children under a certain age—from unwise decisions by themselves or their parents that can have far reaching and undesirable consequences. The state can act to protect the interests of persons who through immaturity or incapacity are unable to protect themselves. Blood transfusions can be ordered, in

[108] *See* INT. REV. CODE of 1954 § 1402(h), *as amended by* Act. of July 30, 1965, Pub. L. No. 89–97, § 319(c), 79 Stat. 391.
[109] Giannella at 1397.

spite of religious objections, to save children and even adults who, in view of the extremity of their situation, are regarded as not wholly capable of deciding for themselves.[110] Religious objections have not been allowed as a basis for avoiding the duty to provide medical care for children.[111] While the lack of education may not have so direct and final an effect on the child's welfare as the lack of medical attention, it does ordinarily subject the child to a real and permanent handicap in the life-long struggle to wrest a decent living from our technology-oriented society. A person of mature judgment who decides, for religious or other reasons, to live a life of poverty should be free to do so, if he does not thereby cause injury to others. But a child should be shielded against premature decisions that might condemn him to such a life. Compulsory education laws provide this sort of shield. The state's interest in not allowing a religious exemption here, where the state's concern is with protecting an immature individual rather than the public health, safety, welfare, or economy, appears more compelling since the consequences of exemption would be more directly subversive of that purpose.

This reasoning, however, rests on the assumption that the child would in fact be likely to encounter the evils associated with inadequate schooling if the state did not force him to attend. In the case of children who must make their way in the larger society the assumption may well be warranted. But if the child is to make his way in the Amish society, he has no need for secondary education to protect him against privation. Moreover, prolonged exposure to secondary education may in fact impair his chances of living a happy and successful life as an Amishman.[112] No compelling interest in seeing that he is prepared for life in the larger society is apparent insofar as those who will become Amishmen are concerned.

But what of those who will not become Amishmen? Some may

---

110 See n. 99 *supra*.

111 *See, e.g.,* Morrison v. State, 252 S.W.2d 97 (Mo. App. 1952); Mitchell v. Davis, 205 S.W.2d 812 (Tex. Civ. App. 1947).

112 See Erickson, *Storm Front: State Regulation of Nonpublic Schools,* 62 LIBERTY Nov.–Dec., 1967 at 20. "When individuals are alienated from their origins and close-knit communities are disrupted, psychological malfunctions usually ensue."

want to become assimilated into the larger society. Unless their parents are forced to send them to school, the chances are they will not do so, and the children will be deprived of their right to preparation for life in the outer world. These are the individuals Representative Unruh was trying to help when he proposed the bill that became the new Kansas Compulsory Education Law.[113] Probably the state does have an interest in protecting those who choose to reject the Amish society. But are children at that age, when they are still under their parents' general authority, to be regarded as capable of making such a decision for themselves? The Amish church does not consider them so, but as suggested above [114] the state probably could accord recognition to their determination to reject their parent's religion for this purpose. This would provide a convenient means of identifying those the state needs to protect from those who need no such protection. Of course, there are undoubtedly some who will ultimately leave the Amish society who are not yet ready at that age to make such a choice. Does the state have an interest in anticipating that decision for them? And if it does, would that interest support, as a means of prior protection against that decision, a requirement that could influence the decision itself, not only for those who would otherwise decide to reject Amish life, but others as well? The burden the state must bear, under the *Sherbert* doctrine, to justify nonexemption in such a case would seem to be a heavy one indeed.

If the children are not regarded as having religious freedom in their own right, then the question becomes one of whether the state interest is sufficiently compelling to warrant displacing the parents' claim as natural guardians and their religious liberty claim deriving from their obligation to raise their children in the "true way." To warrant that, there would have to be some basis for concluding that the state's guidance would be superior to that of the parents.[115] Such superiority could be shown in the case of those children who are going to leave the Amish society, but not for the others. The problem comes in distinguishing the two groups when credence cannot be given to the child's own choice. If all are kept out of school, the lack

---

[113] See nn. 30 and 31 *supra*.   [114] See *supra*, text at note 84.
[115] See Erickson, *supra* n. 112.

of secular education could discourage some who would otherwise choose to leave the Amish society. But if all are sent to school, that could encourage some to defect who would otherwise remain in the Amish fold. The determination of the kind of education they are to receive is likely to affect their ultimate decision.

If the fact that the two groups are indistinguishable is thought to justify treating all alike, it next needs to be shown why that justifies taking the power of decision of all parents away (and forcing all children to attend two or three extra years of school) rather than leaving the power of decision in all parents (with the consequent risk that some children who do or will want to leave the Amish society will be unable to convince their parents to let them go on in school). In some of the blood transfusion cases [116] courts have sought to explain overriding the parent's right by saying that that right does not allow the parent to prevent the child from forming his own religious beliefs, and so the child must be kept alive by the state till he is able to make that religious decision for himself. That kind of argument could be used to support the power of the state, in the interest of all children, to keep alive their freedom to choose for themselves, without having that decision to some extent determined for them by their lack of adequate schooling to make their way in the outside world. But this argument cuts both ways: the additional schooling also acts to some extent to determine their decision by making it more difficult for them to adjust to Amish life. And in any event, the argument is not nearly so persuasive in a case where the matter at stake is not life or death. Depriving all parents of the power of decision and forcing all children to attend high school as a means of protecting those who will reject Amish life could only be justified if the defecting group were relatively larger than the others, or if they posed a really serious social problem. Neither seems to be the case at present,[117] but if all children

---

[116] *See, e.g., In re* Clark, 90 Ohio L. Abs. 21, 185 N.E.2d 128 (1962). The cases often quote the familiar passage from Prince v. Massachusetts, 321 U.S. 158, 170 (1944): "Parents may be free to become martyrs themselves. But it does not follow they are free, in identical circumstances, to make martyrs of their children before they have reached the age of full and legal discretion when they can make that choice for themselves."

[117] Hostetler notes that "the loss of members is very limited in some Amish dis-

are forced into high school the number of defections may increase to the point where they are a social problem. The occasion for the state's interference here has some of the appearance of a self-fulfilling prophecy.

It is not at all clear that prior protection of this sort against a later decision to leave the Amish society is necessary. There may be feasible alternatives, such as special training courses tailored specifically to the needs of defecting Amishmen.[118] Moreover, some assessment should be made of the effect of enforced high school attendance on the mental health of those who will remain Amishmen. This problem deserves serious study before the legislature decides to force adolescents into a situation that all their prior experience, their parents, and their church tells them is of the Devil's own creation.[119]

In summary, from any point of view the state's interest in imposing standard secondary education on Amish children seems rather weak. And when this interest is weighed against the religious liberty claim of the children or their parents, the balance seems even more favorable to the Amish than that observed in the cases of *Sherbert v. Verner, In re Jenison,* and *People v. Woody.* Exemption of the Amish would pose no hazards to others or to society at large. The only apparent justification for state interference is to insure that those Amish children who later will drop out of the Amish society to join the larger one are adequately prepared, for their own protection and to prevent their becoming a burden to the larger society. But this does not seem to justify imposing the requirement to be prepared for life in the larger society on all Amish children. There is nothing to indicate that the problem of defecting Amishmen is so acute as to warrant taking the power of decision away from parents and children in this

---

tricts and considerable in others." In one Pennsylvania Church he found that 30 percent of the children did not join the parents' church. J. HOSTETLER, AMISH SOCIETY, 210 (1963). *Cf.* n. 27 *supra.*

[118] *See* Erickson, *supra* n. 112, at 31. Erickson notes that the same idea has been advanced by Dean Kelley, who refers to it as a "Half-way House for Escaping Amishmen." Kelley, *Is There Room For the Amish?* TOWN AND COUNTRY CHURCH, May–June, 1966 at 7–9, 30.

[119] See Erickson, *supra* n. 112.

matter. Alternative solutions to the problem of runaway Amishmen, such as special training programs, are certainly possible.

The most the state can justifiably do in this regard, it would seem, would be to take away the parents' power of decision with respect to those few children who do have at an early age an intention to leave the Old Order society. The state could recognize that children who have reached teen-age and who have completed eight grades are capable of deciding to reject their parents' religion. Since their own claim would take precedence over that of their parents in this matter, the law could justifiably require their parents to send them to school. To neutralize to some extent the parents' position of dominance, the law could prescribe exemption only for those who specifically apply for it. This would lend some strength to the child's position: if he does not apply, the parents must send him to school. The intrusion of the state thus would be limited to cases where parental authority had already broken down (admittedly a rare case among Amish families). The state would not be disrupting an otherwise stable family situation, as it would if all children were forced into high school.

It would be preferable, of course, for the problem of secondary school attendance by the Amish to be settled by the legislature. The legislative process is capable of developing and weighing the kinds of data necessary for a sound solution. The Iowa Legislature found it necessary to reconsider its attempt to force all Amish children into standard grade schools, and the Kansas Legislature has now changed its mind about imposing the secondary school requirement on them.[120]

120 An exemption was provided by the 1968 Kansas Legislature. KAN STAT. ANN. §72–1111 (1968 Supp). Parents who are "members" of a "recognized church or religious denomination that objects to a regular public high school education" now can satisfy the compulsory attendance law by enrolling their children in a special educational program which the law permits the church or denomination to establish. The exemption is not specifically limited to churches or denominations that are identified with separated sub-societies, nor is there any express requirement that the church's or denomination's "objection" to "regular public high school education" be based on religious beliefs or principles. To qualify for the exemption the program must include a weekly total of at least five hours of classroom instruction by an officially certified teacher, but the rest of the students' time may be devoted to parent-supervised projects in agriculture or homemaking, to

The courts are not really appropriate institutions for the formulation of solutions to social problems as perplexing as the relation of the larger society to separated subsocieties. Until the legislatures produce some justifiable solution, however, the courts, under the *Sherbert* doctrine, must prevent application of general regulations to individuals who would otherwise be unreasonably restrained in their exercise of religious freedom. This, it would seem, should have been done in the *Garber* case.

Unfortunately for the rest of us, the Amish, unlike such sects as the Jehovah's Witnesses, are religiously opposed to litigation. There may never be another chance to bring a case presenting the Amish position before the United States Supreme Court.[121] We may never have a really conclusive decision on their claim of religious liberty until with the passage of time we see that their argument has been vindicated, i.e., that their society has been destroyed.

---

on-the-job training in business or industry, or to accredited correspondence courses. A total of five hours of "learning activities" of one sort or another must be provided each day. The general requirement that all instruction must be given in the English language only, which formerly was applicable to all schools, was completely eliminated by the amendment.

[121] It may be noted, however, that a case comparable to the *Garber* case is now pending in a Wisconsin trial court.

BERNARD J. COUGHLIN, S.J.

Values and

the Constitution

Every society is based on values and depends on them for its continuity and development. It may even be said that a society is constituted by a group of people holding common values. To no nation should this be more evident than our own which was born in the pain of value conflict. The conflict was so acute that the small colonial societies tore away from the mother nation, and a new nation came to birth through a war over the nature of man and human rights, and the nature of political institutions and their responsibilities.

The ideas that inspired the revolution and the creation of a new nation flowed from two principal historical currents, the Judaeo-Christian tradition and the eighteenth-century Enlightenment, and the values from those currents thoroughly permeated the Declaration of Independence and the federal Constitution. Some question the relevance today of those values. Others feel adrift without any value-orientation on which to base personal decisions and group commitments. At no other time in our history have we so sensed the need to re-examine and explore more deeply the values of our culture and the assumptions on which rest our important social institutions — the family, church and state, education and welfare, labor, business, industry. As we and the other leading nations of the world achieve

Bernard J. Coughlin is Dean of the School of Social Service, Saint Louis University.

industrial and technological gains at an ever accelerating pace, our social institutions totter on the edge of spiritual and cultural impoverishment. Technological advance is good, but it is of parts. Man is one. We need to see the whole man. The times demand that our best talents explore the intellectual and moral values that shape our citizens, our institutions, and our national life.

This essay has as its theme two of the fundamental values of our society which are expressed in the Constitution and which are maintained today only with difficulty: religion and voluntarism. It is the responsibility of the Supreme Court to develop a constitutional construction of the First Amendment that will maintain them.

The Meaning of Value

Value pertains to and is part of the broader concept of culture. Definitions of culture vary from one discipline to another and within a given discipline; in general it refers to a design for living or to patterns of behavior that are distinctive for a group. It is defined by the anthropologists Kluckhohn and Kelly as "an historically derived system of explicit and implicit designs for living, which tends to be shared by all or specially designated members of a group."[1] In substantial agreement with this definition, the sociologist Parsons amplifies the meaning of culture by pointing out three of its characteristics: it includes the social traditions of a people that are transmitted as a heritage from generation to generation; it is not a product of man's genetic constitution but is learned; and it is shared by individuals and groups in the society.[2]

Now a group's design for living is the result of many interrelated conscious and unconscious ideas and beliefs that form a pattern and provide an orientation to guide the group in choosing social goals and means. Human beings through thought and experiment in living are forever interrelating, organizing, simplifying, and generalizing their

[1] Kluckhohn & Kelly, *The Concept of Culture,* in The Science of Man in the World Crisis 98 (R. Linton ed. 1945).
[2] T. Parsons, The Social System, 15 (1964).

views about life, man, and the world. Through these processes they develop a philosophy of life which gives a sense of coherence and unity to individual and social behavior.[3] The ideas, beliefs, and convictions that make up this more or less coherent pattern are called values, and they may be grouped into three types. First, the group has certain kinds of knowledge, beliefs, or assumptions about nature and man, society, time, and space. These are the cognitive values of the culture which are expressed in certain ways and through certain symbols. Second, the group has common ideas of beauty, of what is pleasing to the senses. These are the aesthetic values which are expressed in certain forms and styles and modes of being. Finally, the group shares a certain conception of good and bad behavior, of what is right and wrong in individual and group conduct. These are the moral values which are expressed in the mores and laws of a society and in the codes of ethics of business and professional groups.

In addition to developing these groups of ideas, beliefs, and feelings, a society also develops norms or value standards with regard to them. These ideas and beliefs, then, are more than mere existential propositions. They are normative propositions which the society elaborates and which function to achieve social unity and conformity. Every society holds some things to be false and others to be true; the latter it values and sets with regard to them a norm of belief. Every society has its ideas of what is ugly and what is beautiful; the latter it values and sets with regard to it a norm of style and expression. And every society has its idea of what is bad, what is wrong and "ought not to be done," and of what is good, what is right and "ought to be done"; the latter it values and sets with regard to it a norm of conduct. The culture of every society, therefore, includes not only values but value standards according to which it differentiates the true from the false, the beautiful from the ugly, and the good from the bad. In this way a society not only encourages certain cognitive, aesthetic, and moral values, but, as Tolman says, it tends "to impose its rules or *standards* about just what is 'so' or true, what is beautiful, and what

[3] Bateson, *Cultural Determinants of Personality,* in 2 PERSONALITY AND THE BEHAVIOR DISORDERS 723 (J. Hunt, ed. 1944).

is good."[4] Finally, a society achieves conformity to its value standards through a system of rewards and punishments.[5]

There are several corollaries to this. First, value is more than merely what one desires or prefers; it is that toward which one feels obligated. Preference merely assigns priority or at most indicates like and dislike. Value conveys obligation and responsibility with respect to a standard. Clyde Kluckhohn defines values as "a conception, explicit or implicit, distinctive of an individual or characteristic of a group, of the desirable which influences the selection from available modes, means, and ends of action."[6] The desirable in this definition influences action because it is true, or because it is beautiful, or because it is good. Again in Kluckhohn's words: "A value is not just a preference but is a preference which is felt and/or considered to be justified 'morally' or by reasoning or by aesthetic judgments, usually by two or all three of these."[7]

A second corollary is that value as such does not exist in reality. Since value is a conception it is not observable. Value is not a goal, policy, program, or organization; but it influences and directs individuals and groups in the selection and pursuit of goals, policies, programs, and organizations. Though it has conceptual existence, it influences choice because the ideas and beliefs that provide the value-content are not purely intellectual; they contain appreciative and affective content which give value its normative quality. The concept conveys what should be believed, admired, and done.

This is not to say that value is unrelated to reality. On the contrary, value is based on nature as understood by man. There is an ontological relationship between what is and what ought to be. "Do you want to find out what you ought to be?" asks Maslow; "Then find out what you are! ... The description of what one ought to be is almost

[4] Tolman, *Value Standards, Pattern Variables, Social Roles, Personality*, in TOWARD A GENERAL THEORY OF ACTION 344 (T. Parsons & E. Shils eds. 1959). (Emphasis in original.)

[5] Parsons & Shils, *Systems of Value-Orientation*, in TOWARD A GENERAL THEORY OF ACTION, *supra* n. 4, at 159.

[6] Kluckhohn, *Values and Value-Orientations*, in TOWARD A GENERAL THEORY OF ACTION, *supra* n. 4, at 395. (Original in italics.)

[7] *Id.* at 396.

the same as the description of what one deeply is."[8] What nature ought to be is nature's fulfillment and realization. Man contains within his being a thrust towards self-realization; this thrust is the ground of becoming; it impels him to be his full self. Again, in Maslow's words: "[t]he facts themselves carry, within their own nature, suggestions of what *ought* to be done with them."[9] Or again: "The more clearly something is seen or known, and the more true and unmistakable something becomes, the more ought-quality it acquires."[10] Nature is dynamic; it contains the seeds of the flower.

Therefore, while values are not found in nature, they presuppose it and are limited by it, and they develop out of man's experience with and understanding of nature. Because of this teleological relation between nature and values, value statements are existential as well as normative. "There can be no doubt," says Kluckhohn, "that an individual's or a group's conceptions of what is and of what ought to be are intimately connected."[11] A purely existential statement describes nature, and then the value statement in effect says: "This appears to be naturally possible. It does not exist or does not fully exist, but we want to move toward it, or, it already exists but we want to preserve and maintain it. Moreover, we aver that this is a proper or appropriate or justified want."[12] In this sense value statements are existential statements; "[j]udgments of value," Thorndike says, "are simply one sort of judgment of fact."[13] Judgments of value are judgments of the teleological or purposeful ordination of nature as understood by man. " 'This is a value for me' is an existential proposition about me."[14] "This is a value for me" means "this is my self-realization."

VALUES INFLUENCE ACTION

Much study and research are still needed to provide more comprehensive insight into the way that values influence action. Our concern

[8] Maslow, *Fusion of Facts and Values,* 23 AMERICAN JOURNAL OF PSYCHO-ANALYSIS 121 (1963).
[9] *Id.* at 130. (Emphasis in original.)   [10] *Id.* at 127
[11] Kluckhohn, *supra* n. 6, at 391.   [12] *Id.* at 393–94.
[13] Thorndike, *Science and Values,* 83 SCIENCE 2 (1936).
[14] Kluckhohn, *supra* n. 6, at 391.

here will be with one modest aspect only of a complex and elusive subject.

In recent writings on systems theory sociologists identify three interacting systems in the society. Two of these, the personality system and all social systems, are action systems. The third is the value system which greatly influences action, although it is not an action system. The society as a whole, and the social institutions in it, are made up of individual persons who fit into many roles which they must play — a man is son, brother, husband, father, lawyer, breadwinner, neighbor, civic leader. What the roles are and the demands they exact are determined largely by the way in which the society and its culture define them. Within limits, individuals modify these roles, the society allowing a degree of innovation and deviation from cultural expectations. The society is also made up of a great variety of social systems and subsystems — the family, the church, industry, the school, government, public and private associations and organizations. Like individual roles, the roles and functions of these social systems are structured with certain demands and expectations determined largely by the way that society and its culture define them. Social systems, likewise, within limits, may modify institutional roles.

Personality and social systems are empirical systems that act and directly determine the course of history. They interact and are interdependent. Individuals, each fulfilling particular roles, function as parts of various social systems. These roles, established over a period of time, are independent of the individuals who play them. Therefore, in a sense, social systems have an existence and effect apart from and independent of the individuals who function within them. It is obvious that social systems today, with their policies, laws, and structures, possess a power and wield an influence that did not exist in simpler societies.

The cultural system influences action through values and symbols. "Systems of action," says Parsons, "are functional systems; cultural systems are symbolic systems in which the components have logical or meaningful rather than functional relationships with one another." [15]

---

[15] Parsons & Shils, *supra* n. 5, at 173.

Values influence action by becoming internalized in the cognitive, appreciative, and moral powers of personality systems, and by becoming institutionalized in the goals, laws, policies, and principles of social systems. Both action systems become committed to a particular value system from which they derive normative standards.[16] The value system is expressed in formulas and symbols that serve a twofold purpose: they are visible guides to the society itself, and they are visible manifestations of the society's commitment to elected goals and means.[17] This does not mean that action systems are incapable of tolerating conflicting values and of accommodating them.[18] It does mean, and for our purposes this is the significant point, that a system of action can intelligently and consistently choose goals and means only if it has a recognized value-orientation on which to base choice. And it means, furthermore, that if a society is to transmit its value system from one generation to the next, that value system must be internalized in persons and institutionalized in the various social systems that make up the society—family and school, church and state, industry, business, labor.

Values and Law

The state, of all social systems, is perhaps the most influential, attaining its influence through the instruments of law. Through the law it reflects and projects a value orientation about man, nature, and society, and gives visibility to cognitive and moral values through the formulas and symbols over which it has control. That the law concerns values, Mr. Justice Holmes had no question. "The law," he wrote, "is the witness and external deposit of our moral life. Its history is the history of the moral development of the race."[19] Moreover, because of its concern with values, the law as a living instrument is forced to look into the future of a people as well as its past. This means that the court not only reflects but creates society's

[16] Tolman, *supra* n. 4, at 343.
[17] Parsons & Shils, *Categories of the Orientation and Organization of Action,* in TOWARD A GENERAL THEORY OF ACTION *supra* n. 4 at 54–56.
[18] Parsons & Shils, *supra* n. 5, at 179.
[19] O. W. HOLMES, COLLECTED LEGAL PAPERS 170 (M. Howe ed. 1920).

values. In the opinion of M. Smith, the primary concern of the judge is not with the values of yesterday, and "what the legislator willed a century ago, but what he would have willed if he had known what our present conditions would be."[20]

The law looks to the past, and so precedent is important, but because values are the yeast in law, the law considers what should be as well as what has been; it considers the purposes and ends behind the law and the reasons why those ends are desirable.[21] As Cardozo said, "Not the origin, but the goal, is the main thing. . . . The teleological conception of his function must be ever in the judge's mind."[22] Law is ever evolving, and the task today in American law especially is intelligently to guide the evolution "of 'the law that is' into the law we think it ought to become."[23] Thus Rostow stresses the existence of values in the law and the power of law over values.[24]

In sum, the link between values and law is this: the concern of law includes the end and purpose which it serves; end and purpose concern what "ought to be done"; and what "ought to be done" is the immediate concern of values and morality. This is the broadest power of the legislature and the court, that they shape social values and symbols which influence individuals and determine the course of social institutions.

Values and the First Amendment

Of the values that permeate constitutional law those of the First Amendment rise from the deepest roots in human nature, and cause the sharpest conflicts. The First Amendment states: "Congress shall make no law respecting an establishment of religion, or prohibiting

[20] M. Smith, Jurisprudence, 29–30, as quoted in B. Cardozo, The Nature of the Judicial Process 84 (1921).

[21] Cardozo, *supra* n. 20, at 66 (*see also id.* at 102).

[22] *Id.* at 102 (*see also id.* at 66 ff.).

[23] Rostow, *The Realist Tradition in American Law*, in Paths of American Thought 216 (A. Schlesinger, Jr., & M. White, eds. 1963).

[24] E. Rostow, The Sovereign Prerogative: The Supreme Court and the Quest for Law 79 (1962).

the free exercise thereof; or abridging the freedom of speech, or of the press; or the right of the people peaceably to assemble." The Amendment obviously contains a broad value-orientation well beyond the scope of this essay. This discussion will be limited to the values of religion and voluntarism; and I will assume that the First Amendment sought to guarantee, among other things, a social order that would allow religion and voluntarism ample opportunity to flourish.

For purposes of constitutional law it is extremely difficult to define religion. Recent efforts to define it, and the Supreme Court's seeming despair in doing so, illustrate how judicial interpretation is a reflection of the culture. The Founding Fathers were in agreement that religion embraced some form of man's relationship to God. This is clear from many writings and from the Declaration of Independence itself.[25] In 1890 the Supreme Court accepted a traditional definition in terms of the Creator-creature relationship: "The term 'religion' has reference to one's views of his relations to his Creator, and to the obligations they impose of reverence for his being and character, and of obedience to his will." [26] As recently as 1931 the Court's working definition had not changed much. In *United States v. Macintosh* the majority said: "We are a Christian people acknowledging with reverence the duty of obedience to the will of God." [27] Chief Justice Hughes in a dissenting opinion of the same case more pointedly stated that "The essence of religion is belief in a relation to God involving duties superior to those arising from any human relation." [28] More recently the Court has avoided defining religion. Sweeping cultural changes have rendered traditional definitions outmoded. Since many people consider that "religion" is a set of mere humanistic or naturalistic convictions exclusive of any divine reference, for them God is no

[25] R. M. HEALEY, JEFFERSON AND RELIGION IN PUBLIC EDUCATION 98 ff. (1962). Healey's book provides ample material on this subject. Concerning Jefferson's views he says: "In contemporary terms we might say that Jefferson believed there was a 'common core' of religious belief, a group of tenets on which all sects could be expected to agree. Obviously this common core did not include creed or dogma, but it did most certainly embrace the field of morality and also the rational or philosophic proofs of the existence of God." *Id.* at 98.

[26] Davis v. Beason, 133 U.S. 333, 342 (1890).

[27] United States v. Macintosh, 283 U.S. 605, 625 (1931).

[28] *Id.* at 633-34.

longer essential to religious belief. Thus, in 1961 the Court said: "Among religions in this country which do not teach what would generally be considered a belief in the existence of God are Buddhism, Taoism, Ethical Culture, Secular Humanism and others." [29]

Whatever its context, religion encompasses a set of personal beliefs that are expressed in social attitudes and conduct. Moreover, it is generally recognized that religion exacts of the individual a total commitment and claims a spiritual autonomy which eludes the reach of civil authority. Because it is an interior, free act, it demands liberty to fulfill its commitments. Therefore, the Founding Fathers ordained that the state would not prohibit the free exercise of religion.

Full religious freedom, however, requires a parallel guarantee that the police power of the state will not be used to establish a religion. The government of the society must be nonecclesiastical; the state has no direct authority over the spirit. It is a secular state. There is nothing irreligious about the "secular" in this sense, which merely means that government, its constitutional system, and laws have a legitimate and proper function independent of the church and of man's religious nature. [30]

Although government must be secular, nevertheless, "it is not the government's business to promote a secularistic philosophy." [31] The state may not "establish" secularism any more than it may "establish" any other religious belief, for within the meaning of constitutional law, secularism is a religious position. Indeed, the intent of the

---

[29] Torcaso v. Watkins, 367 U.S. 488, 495 n. 11 (1961). There are some who push this liberalism in defining religion to extreme conclusions and argue that communism is a religion since it believes in a definite ideology and meaning of life to which it is committed, namely the process of dialectical materialism which ultimately will bring man to the victory of the communistic society. The inclusion of communism in the definition of religion, of course, would bring it under the free exercise of the First Amendment where it would enjoy the same right and protection as any other religion. *See* Stahmer, *Defining Religion; Federal Aid and Academic Freedom,* 1963 RELIGION AND THE PUBLIC ORDER 116 (1964).

[30] P. KAUPER, RELIGION AND THE CONSTITUTION 86 (1964). The term secular has two meanings, political and philosophical. The former meaning refers to the state and public institutions as being nonreligious or neutral as far as religious ideologies are concerned. The latter refers to an antireligious ideology which considers God as irrelevant and is based on a deistic, agnostic, or atheistic position.

[31] *Ibid.*

First Amendment was not and has never been interpreted to be the establishment of state indifferentism to religion; rather the state has from the Constitution a commitment to religion as a cultural value. For the state is concerned with law, and law is concerned with values, and values are the concern of religion. No state can for long afford to ignore religion, or can so wall itself off from the churches as merely to tolerate them, without witnessing the crumbling of a culture. "Religion," says Dean Kolb, "is not only the anchorage and justification for the ultimate moral values of a social group, it is the source of such values." [32] When its value-springs dry up, the roots of a society shrivel, for its social institutions are cut off from meaning and purpose, moral clarity and spiritual hope.

Much of the present confusion about the role of the state in respect to religion is due to the rapid growth of religious pluralism. When there was greater unanimity about religious beliefs, the value of religion was unquestioned. Not until the 1930's, when the Jehovah's Witnesses initiated a series of church-state litigations, did the Supreme Court begin seriously to discriminate areas of religious freedom and government practices that constitute religious establishment.[33] Since that time the First Amendment has unleashed some thorny questions. What is religion? What is the state's responsibility to it? What constitutes religious freedom? What constitutes establishment of religion? When society held a single religious view, uniform answers were given to questions like these. But pluralism makes the questions doubly persistent, and the answers doubly difficult.

The freedoms of the First Amendment, considered singly and as a whole, foster another value, voluntarism, or citizen self-determination in societal affairs. Personal freedom implies the liberty of citizens to create and administer associations for private purposes, independent of governmental mandate; voluntarism refers to the free exercise of social institutions. It is not a rejection of authority; but it does reject paternalism and authoritarianism. Voluntarism is based on the demo-

[32] Kolb, *Images of Man and the Sociology of Religion,* in SOCIETY AND SELF 642 (B. Stoodley ed. 1962).

[33] Gilbert, *Religious Freedom and Social Change in a Pluralistic Society: A Historical Review,* 1964 RELIGION AND THE PUBLIC ORDER 97 (1965).

cratic ideal that man is free, responsible, and capable under normal conditions of conducting the affairs of his life. On the principle of voluntarism rests an extensive range of free institutions in our society: ours is a free government, of the people and by the people; business and industry are based on a free enterprise system that is by and large self-regulatory; commerce and the media of communications are free; and there are innumerable voluntary schools, hospitals and clinics, children's institutions and day-care centers, nursing homes and homes for the aged, citizen's councils, community funds, and social welfare programs.

Through these free associations citizens collaborate for purposes that are vital to the whole society. The private school, like the private hospital and the social welfare program, is the responsibility of a board of directors and administrators who establish policy, plan, execute, and finance programs. These organizations fulfill important societal needs; but equally important, they are schools in social responsibility where citizens learn to create and manage the institutions of a free society. They are schools in democratic government. By encouraging voluntarism, society renders remote the possibility of a monolithic press, radio, and television, monolithic business and industry, and monolithic systems of health, education, and welfare. Society needs both unity and diversity. A prudent system of laws based on common values guarantees unity; freedom, wisely fostered, guarantees diversity in sources of thought, creativity, and influence.

Although society has always been and is still deeply committed to voluntarism, the growth and complexity of modern times requires a different application of this value in today's world.

Early in our national life voluntary associations cut furrows of health, education, and welfare. Motivated by concern for human need and the desire to witness to faith, private groups, sectarian and nonsectarian, built hospitals, schools, and institutions, created and organized welfare programs of all kinds. These institutions and programs by their very origin and nature diffused the values of voluntarism and religion. Later, when voluntary effort was no longer adequate, government entered all of these fields. The need is so great that the power of government is necessary. Since the 1930's especially we have developed a philosophy of moderate state welfarism with the result that government today increasingly employs the tax power to provide for the general welfare; and year by year the scope of general welfare concerns widens.

Government's expanding activity has greatly affected voluntary effort. The accelerating demands for good education, good health, and welfare services, and the spiraling costs in every area make problematic the continuance of voluntary endeavors even at their present level of competence. To offer a recent example from one field of voluntary effort, higher education, the President of the Carnegie Foundation detailed the rising costs of education and then added: "We are forced, therefore, to a very simple conclusion. If this nation's needs for higher education are to be met in the years to come, the federal government will have to accept the principal part of the consequent financial burden." [34] Faced with realities like these and confronted with a state of virtual competition with government in many areas of service, voluntary effort is at the point of saying: "We will retire from the field. Let the government do it."

One consideration stops that decision: fundamental national values are at stake. Values like voluntarism and religion, which are intertwined and scarcely separated in practice, are to a considerable degree kept alive and relevant to the nation through institutions of service that express and transmit them. Through voluntary institutions the churches perform important public services; they also express and symbolize certain religious values. At some point society must come to grips with the role of the churches in modern times and give practical answers to questions like these: What positions should the churches occupy in the social life of the American community? What rights and responsibilities do they have as social institutions? Should government disregard the health, educational, and welfare institutions of the churches? Can government disregard them without fostering a religious secularism? Or should government effectively

[34] Pifer, *Toward a Coherent Set of National Policies for Higher Education*, THE CHRONICLE OF HIGHER EDUCATION, Jan. 26, 1968, p. 4.

and by policy encourage church-related health, education, and welfare programs? Can government encourage them without undermining the church-state separation principle?

All of these questions pertain to the role of the churches in the society. They require consistent answers. It is enigmatic to say that voluntarism is important to the national culture, and then by neglect or policy to squeeze into insignificance the role of voluntary health, education, and welfare programs. And it is enigmatic to say that religious values are important to the national culture, and then by neglect or legislation to prejudice the potential for church-related programs in these fields.

VALUES AND THE SUPREME COURT

It is the task and responsibility of the Supreme Court to unravel these enigmas. It is an especially perplexing task because they must be unraveled within the constitutional allowances of the First Amendment which conveys what almost seems to be an inherent contradiction: the state is told not to enter into matters of religion; and the state is told to protect religious freedom. How can the state protect a citizen's religious freedom without first defining religion and then inserting itself between that citizen and the individual or group that violates the citizen's religious right? Or how can the state guard and protect the religious liberty of a particular church without thereby in some degree "establishing" that church? Mr. Justice Douglas states the dilemma succinctly: "The First Amendment commands the government to have no interest in theology or ritual; it admonishes government to be interested in allowing religious freedom to flourish." [35]

In recent years especially the Supreme Court has directed its attention to this dilemma as it bears on the infringement of individual rights. But the Court's decisions have redounding cultural implications that deeply affect the entire society. The ultimate concern that the Court must face is this: how can the society, as it maintains a viable principle of church-state separation, sustain at the same time viable values of religion and voluntarism? Unfortunately its past

[35] McGowan v Maryland, 366 U.S. 420, 564 (1961) (dissenting opinion).

decisions have not clearly conveyed to what extent the Court will recognize the social and cultural dimensions of religion and voluntarism.

This ambivalence of the past, however, does not commit the Court to future decisions that will necessarily strengthen or weaken these values. A hurried review of recent church-state cases indicates that the Court's future decisions could lead down many paths. One course that could be followed, not inconsistent with the past, would reinforce these values.

Thus in *Cochran* the Court allowed tax-financed textbooks for parochial school children when they were challenged under the due process clause on the ground that public funds were being diverted to a private use. The Court rejected this challenge, finding that furnishing the textbooks served a public purpose since children and the state, not the parochial schools, were considered to be the beneficiaries.[36] Similarly in *Everson* the Court allowed New Jersey to provide bus transportation for children attending sectarian schools. Neither was this "establishment" because bus transportation was considered to be a public welfare benefit to which all citizens have equal right regardless of their religious affiliation or the school they attend.[37] However, in the same breath that the Court allowed this benefit it declared that the state may not aid any religion.[38] It spoke of separation in absolute terms: "The First Amendment has erected a wall between Church and State. That wall must be kept high and impregnable." [39] A year later, then, the Court stood on the wall metaphor and ruled in *McCollum* that use of public school classrooms for religious instruction on a released time basis was "establishment." [40]

Mr. Justice Reed was the sole dissenter in *McCollum*. He objected to the "wall of separation" metaphor on the ground that "A rule of law should not be drawn from a figure of speech." [41] While he agreed with *Everson* that government should not aid any or all religions, he insisted that what constitutes aid to religion is not at all clear. In his

---

[36] Cochran v. Board of Educ., 281 U.S. 370 (1930).

[37] Everson v. Board of Educ., 330 U.S. 1 (1947).

[38] *Id*. at 15.   [39] *Id*. at 18.

[40] Illinois *ex rel*. McCollum v. Board of Educ., 333 U.S. 203 (1948).

[41] *Id*. at 247.

opinion the kind of aid that violates the First Amendment is "purposeful assistance directly to the church itself or to some religious group or organization doing religious work of such a character that it may fairly be said to be performing ecclasiastical functions." [42] It seemed clear to Mr. Justice Reed that the First Amendment allows the state sufficient flexibility to accommodate the religious needs of the people. Neither religious liberty nor nonestablishment are absolutes. One citizen's right to religious freedom can be too readily violated by another's zeal to prevent the establishment of religion. In the case of *McCollum,* for example, one may ask: Whose right to the free exercise of religion is more infringed upon—those children who freely choose not to participate in religious instruction in the public schools on a released time basis, or those children who wish to participate but are prohibited by the *McCollum* decision?

Mr. Justice Reed's dissent was the spearhead of a strong popular reaction against strict state neutrality to religion. Members of the court itself testified to the reaction.[43] Many groups agreed with Mr. Justice Reed that the doctrine of *McCollum* consistently applied would make the state a hostile party to religion. This conclusion was based on premises such as these: neither a person nor a school or a society can be neutral in respect to ultimate meanings; so-called "neutrality" is merely the disinterestedness of those who are not concerned about religion in any form; neutrality is impossible because there is no middle ground between religious and nonreligious; a school that is not religious is simply irreligious in spirit and in principle. As Dean Kelley said: "A public school that excludes all religious content is not, therefore, 'non-sectarian'; instead it has established a new sectarianism of nontheism." [44] And as Tussman said:

"Religion is either in or out, and 'out' carries with it the overtones of rejection." [45]

---

[42] *Id.* at 248.

[43] See Mr. Justice Black's dissenting opinion in Zorach v. Clauson, 343 U.S. 306, 315 (1952).

[44] Kelley, *Beyond Separation of Church and State* 11 (address, 1962, published with some modifications in 5 A JOURNAL OF CHURCH AND STATE, 181 [1963]) as quoted in Stahmer, *supra* n. 29, at 120.

[45] J. TUSSMAN, THE SUPREME COURT ON CHURCH AND STATE xxiii (1962).

Four years later the Court swung from the strict neutrality and "non-establishment" emphasis of *McCollum* to the accommodation and "free exercise" emphasis of *Zorach*. The Court ruled that the public school system may cooperate with religious school authorities by arranging class schedules so that children may attend religion classes in the sectarian schools. The Court rested its decision on arguments like these: "We are a religious people whose institutions presuppose a Supreme Being";[46] our national life, policies and public practices clearly reflect an interdependence of government and religion; "the First Amendment . . . does not say that in every and all respects there shall be a separation of Church and State";[47] government fittingly cooperates with a wide variety of beliefs and creeds for the sake of the spiritual needs of man; "when the state encourages religious instruction or cooperates with religious authorities by adjusting the schedule of public events to sectarian needs, it follows the best of our traditions."[48] Thus principles of cooperation and accommodation were replacing the principle of strict neutrality.

Three members of the Court dissented strongly to *Zorach* and the Court's apparent retreat from *McCollum*. The stinging language of their dissents has become famous: "McCollum has passed like a storm in a tea cup"; cooperation is only a "soft euphemism" under which government will "steal into the sacred area of religious choice"; *Zorach* after *McCollum* "will be more interesting to students of psychology and of the judicial process than to students of constitutional law."[49]

The question persisted: "What constitutes aid to religion?" *McCollum* and *Zorach*—nonestablishment and free exercise—stood face to face, but solved nothing. They merely clarified the problem. In *Schempp* and *Sherbert* the Court first began to forge a test of establishment with the following reasoning: certain actions and forms of aid have as their purpose and primary effect the achieving of a religious objective; other actions and forms of aid have as their purpose and primary effect the achieving of a secular objective. The freedom

[46] Zorach v. Clauson, 343 U.S. 306, 313 (1952).
[47] *Id.* at 312.   [48] *Id.* at 313–14.
[49] *Id.* at 325 (Justice Jackson dissenting).

of religion clause forbids any action of the state the purpose and primary effect of which is to inhibit religion; the establishment clause
forbids any action of the state the purpose and primary effect of
which is to advance religion. The test as enunciated for the Court by
Mr. Justice Clark is this:

what are the purpose and primary effect of the enactment? If either is
the advancement or inhibition of religion then the enactment exceeds
the scope of legislative power as circumscribed by the Constitution. That
is to say that to withstand the strictures of the Establishment Clause
there must be a secular legislative purpose and primary effect that
neither advances nor inhibits religion.[50]

The Court first applied the test to two cases on one and the same
day and struck down one action as a violation of nonestablishment,
and the other as a violation of free exercise. In *Schempp* the Court
ruled that Bible reading in the public schools was a violation of nonestablishment because its purpose and primary effect is religious. In
Sherbert the Court ruled that for the state to deny unemployment
benefits to a citizen who for religious reasons refuses to accept Saturday employment is a violation of the free exercise right.

In *Sherbert,* then, the Court held that the state does not establish
religion by accommodating the citizen's religious needs; on the contrary, not to make this accommodation would prejudice the free
exercise of religion by exerting unlawful force on the worker to abandon her religious convictions.[51] In thus applying the test to *Sherbert*
the Court makes clear that it abandons strict neutrality and makes
religion, as Kauper said, "the ground of a preferred position" in the
application of the law.[52] Although the Court still uses the term
"neutrality," there is ample evidence that it is not presently committed
to a theory of strict neutrality.[53] It is a neutrality twice tempered by
considerations stemming from the two countervailing principles of the
religion clause: neutrality is first tempered by the state's responsibility

[50] School Dist. v. Schempp, 374 U.S. 203, 222 (1963).
[51] Sherbert v. Verner, 374 U.S. 398 (1963).
[52] Kauper, *Schempp and Sherbert: Studies in Neutrality and Accommodation,*
1963 RELIGION AND THE PUBLIC ORDER 3, 14 (1964).
[53] *See* Kauper, *supra* n. 52.

to respect religious freedom and to accommodate the religious needs and interests of citizens; this responsibility of the state to religion, however, is itself tempered by the state's obligation not to become involved with the primarily theological and evangelical aspects of religion. The test, of course, is no rigid rule of thumb. It is a pragmatic test that involves weighing the two principles of the First Amendment. As Mr. Justice Douglas said: "The constitutional standard is a separation of Church and State. The problem, like many problems in constitutional law, is one of degree." [54]

It is clear that in these efforts to draw the subtle line between free exercise and establishment, the focal point of the Court's attention has been individual rights. The very nature of the judicial contest places in the foreground individual grievances and leaves aside broader concerns about values and value-orientations. On a number of occasions, to be sure, members of the Court have obliquely referred to those broader areas. They have warned against a concept of neutrality that is tantamount to hostility toward religion,[55] and they have warned against "a brooding and pervasive devotion to the secular." [56]

On the other hand Mr. Justice Douglas has taken the position that "financing a church either in its strictly religious activities or in its other activities is equally unconstitutional." [57] Whether or not he still maintains this position is not clear. But should the Court follow this rule, religion, and to a considerable degree voluntarism likewise, would be in danger of losing much of their cultural significance. Such an absolute prohibition in a society where government plays a dominant role and has an all-pervasive influence would relegate religion and voluntarism to inconsequential roles. Mr. Justice Harlan perceived the cultural implications of such a prohibition. "There are," he wrote, "too many areas in which the pervasive activities of the State justify some special provision for religion to prevent it from being submerged by an all-embracing secularism." [58] A democratic

[54] Zorach v. Clauson, 343 U.S. 306, 314 (1952).
[55] School Dist. v. Schempp, 374 U.S. 203, 246 (1963) (Justice Brennan concurring).
[56] Id. at 306 (Justice Goldberg concurring).
[57] School Dist. v. Schempp, 374 U.S. 203, 229 (concurring opinion).
[58] Sherbert v. Verner, 374 U.S. 398, 422–23 (dissenting opinion).

and religious society that is committed to the principles of the social welfare state, as our society is, must build into itself instrumentalities that guarantee the continuance of voluntary institutions that from generation to generation transmit religious ideals. Without these instrumentalities society will be transformed into an absolute state. Then it will have lost both its democratic and its religious ideal.

If cultural values are important, it would behoove the Court, as it continues to develop a theory of church-state separation and a test for establishment, to keep a broader cultural perspective. Within that perspective should fall not only awareness of changing social needs but the following three propositions apropos of the First Amendment.

First, not indifference but partiality to religion inspired the First Amendment. There are those who hold that among the most important purposes of the First Amendment was the advancement of the interests of religion.[59] When the Bill of Rights was adopted, a number of states had established religions. As Professor Howe has shown, "at least in New England, a view of government prevailed which not merely permitted but required a state's public power to be exercised for the advancement of religion."[60] The fact of establishment, at least in New England, supports the view that the intention of the religion clause was to guarantee that the federal government would not interfere with the religious liberties of individuals and groups, and would not interfere with the states in their religious establishments.[61]

Second, the purpose of the religion clause of the First Amendment was not to place religion and nonreligion on an equal footing; rather it was, in part at least, "to allow all religions and all denominations to pursue, in freedom, the common enterprise of advancing what they conceived to be the spiritual welfare of the American people."[62] It is very unlikely that the religion clause was intended as a statement of rights protecting nonbelief and irreligion. The nonreligionist does not need a religious liberty guarantee. Other clauses of the Amendment protect the nonbeliever and his interests—freedom of speech, freedom of the press, freedom of assembly. Because of the special importance that the Founding Fathers assigned to religion, and be-

[59] M. Howe, The Garden and the Wilderness 1–15 (1965).
[60] Id. at 26.   [61] Id. at 22.   [62] Id. at 154.

cause of the oppression that some of the colonists had experienced in its name, religion is singled out and assigned a special right, and government is assigned a special responsibility with regard to it.[63]

Third, the First Amendment must be understood and interpreted in light of the momentous social and political changes that differentiate the mid-twentieth from the nineteenth century. The changes in the role of government since the previous century have affected considerably the social and cultural influence of religion and voluntarism. Both the police power of the state and its power to tax are broad powers. They are exercised quite differently today than in former times. During the nineteenth century when that government was thought best which governed least, the state assumed a laissez-faire posture not only toward religion, but toward all social and economic institutions. It was considered bad government, not to say bad morality, for the state to use its power to plan and direct the course of social and economic life. At the same time there existed what Howe has called a *de facto* establishment of religion.[64] The culture and the mores of all institutions, public and private, reflected the prevailing Protestantism. Many of our national customs, some of which are protected by law, are remnants of *de facto* establishment. Consequently an absence of government activity that cooperated with religion and accommodated the religious needs and desires of the people created no cultural void. The state was equally nonaccommodating to other social and economic needs for a time at least, but these needs were adequately met without government assistance. Likewise religious and other cultural needs were met independently of state aid. The state's interest in furthering religious values, as well as its interest in advancing economic growth and social development, was thought to be best manifested by policies of laissez-faire; and for a time it was.

Today, things are quite different. In a radically changing society the role of government has expanded and will continue to expand. As society has changed, government has developed policies based on a philosophy of cooperation with economic and social institutions.

---

[63] *Id.* at 150–57.   [64] *Id.* at 11.

These policies are designed to maintain vital economic and social institutions, and to preserve certain political and social values that nourish a democracy. It is no less important that government adopt policies based on a philosophy of cooperation with church-related health, education, and welfare institutions in order to maintain cultural values of religion and voluntarism that are equally vital to a democracy. It comes to this: in a welfare state where government must play such an all-pervasive role, can a secular state coexist only within a secular culture? Or, perhaps more simply, must the Great Society's commitment to the separation of church and state be likewise a commitment to a secular culture?

One can only hope that in its future decisions the Supreme Court so interprets church-state separation as to allow more fertile opportunities for the flowering of religious culture and the value of voluntarism. Happily past decisions of the Court are not so absolute as to predetermine future choices. Rather its opinions are sufficiently open-ended and express sufficient sensitivity to cultural values, as to make possible a test of constitutionality that would encourage these values.

There is sufficient precedent on which to build a constitutional construction that will be culturally enriching. The early *Bradfield* decision rests on the fact that there are church-sponsored and administered institutions that fulfill a recognized secular purpose.[65] The public funds that assist these institutions enable them to provide services comparable to those provided by nonsectarian institutions. While the motivation of these church-related institutions is frequently religious, the service they provide is not.

The Court could rely on *Zorach* and *Sherbert* as further developing the *Bradfield* position. Many citizens prefer church-related health, education, and welfare services. *Zorach* held that the state should accommodate the religious needs and wishes of the people. *Sherbert* held that if the primary purpose and effect of a service is secular, and government aid for it does not over-involve the state in religious affairs, it passes the test of nonestablishment. Not only church-related

---

[65] Bradfield v. Roberts, 175 U.S. 291 (1899).

hospitals, as recognized in *Bradfield*, but schools and welfare programs offer services comparable to public and private nonsectarian services. Voluntary and church-related programs, moreover, breathe into the society values that it needs—voluntarism and social reponsibility, a moral sense, social justice and a sense of human dignity, brotherhood and love, a religious ideal and dedication. Culturally, society is dessicated without these values. The Court, then, might well continue to develop this course as social and cultural conditions seem to advise.

Moreover, the Court could further develop the child-benefit theory in a way that would support the principle of accommodation and the primary purpose and effect test. The *Everson* case accommodated students who chose to attend parochial schools by providing them bus transportation out of tax funds. The Court could expand this concept to include other forms of aid to schoolchildren, applying in each case the primary purpose and effect test.

Both the decision and the opinion of the Supreme Court in *Board of Education v. Allen*[66] make clear that the Court has adopted the primary purpose and effect test as the ruling norm in all church-state cases. Applying this test, the Court upheld a New York law that requires local school boards to loan textbooks free of charge to children attending nonpublic schools, including parochial ones. The Court cited with approval[67] its earlier decision in the *Cochran* case, indicating that the child-benefit theory now meets not only general due process objections to public educational aids for parochial school students but also ones based on the establishment clause.

The Court's opinion in *Allen* is carefully limited to textbooks. The Court has left open the question of how far the secular purpose and effect test goes to accommodate the educational needs of parochial school students. In the future it may decide to limit aid on the basis of a somewhat circumscribed child-benefit theory. There is no language in the *Allen* opinion indicating such a development. The tone and approach of the opinion leaves open the possibility of substantial direct aid to parochial schools to support their secular educational

[66] 392 U.S. 236 (1968).   [67] *Id.* at 247.

programs. Writing for the majority, Mr. Justice White said that "private education is playing a significant and valuable role in raising national levels of knowledge, competence, and experience." [68]

There is considerable scholarly opinion supporting the constitutionality of substantial aid to church-related schools. Professor Choper submits that under the secular purpose and effect test, state financial aid may be extended directly to parochial schools so long as it does not exceed the value of the secular educational service rendered by the school.[69] Professor Howe, speaking before the Education Subcommittee of the Senate Committee on Labor and Public Welfare, could find no insurmountable legal obstacle to federal financing of sectarian schools for nonreligious purposes. "I am satisfied," he said, "that a valid line can be drawn between government support of activities that are predominantly of civil concern and those that are predominantly of religious significance." [70] Professor Katz urges direct tax support to the secular educational programs of church-related schools. "While the government," he said, "should not promote religion, it not only may, but should try to avoid restraining or burdening religious choices. And if groups wish to have parish schools there seems to me a presumption in favor of so moulding government fiscal policies as not to handicap that choice." [71]

Dean Drinan likewise argues that the value of religious freedom requires a greater accommodation by the state in favor of students who choose to attend church-related schools.[72] Basing his argument on *Sherbert* he says that, just as the state may not pressure a Sabbatarian to accept work on Saturday or be deprived of unemployment compensation, neither may it pressure a student to abandon education in a church-related school in favor of a strictly secular education. To deny state aid to sectarian colleges places, in effect, that kind of pressure on college students and their families. Finally, Giannella carries

[68] *Ibid.*

[69] Choper, *The Establishment Clause and Aid to Parochial Schools,* 56 CALIF. L. REV. 260 (1968).

[70] Quoted in W. KATZ, RELIGION AND AMERICAN CONSTITUTIONS at 73 (1964).

[71] *Id.* at 77.

[72] Drinan, *Does State Aid to Church-Related Colleges Constitute an Establishment of Religion?* 1967 UTAH L. REV. 491, 511.

the argument one step further: to deny state aid to sectarian colleges and universities not only indirectly pressures the student to favor a strictly secular education, but it also places sectarian colleges and universities at "a state created disadvantage vis-a-vis secular institutions."

In Giannella's words:

To argue that the establishment clause requires the creation of this disadvantage is to adopt a view of non-establishment which requires the state to throw its weight against religion when acting in areas that affect cultural development; in effect it calls for a secularistic culture as well as a secular state. The principles of free exercise and political neutrality converge to militate against this interpretation; both sanction the propriety of governmental support of religious institutions to the extent necessary to counter-balance the negative influences which the state's increased societal role has on religion.[73]

Thus, to use the tremendous tax power of the state for large government programs of health, education, and welfare, while denying similar assistance to voluntary programs, tends to pressure voluntary institutions out of business. And this has wide cultural reverberations; it not only infringes on individual rights to free exercise; it contributes to the corrosion of a culture.

SUMMARY AND CONCLUSION

Endless distinctions and qualifications are necessary to terminate properly a subject of such breadth and depth. Happily the purpose of this essay is not to terminate, but to contribute to a discussion that is momentous to the culture of this society. The many things that have gone unsaid, and the qualifications that should be made, may offer others a point of departure for further and more worthy discussion of a subject as yet too little explored.

By way of summary let me merely say that I have attempted to present the following views. First, values are the soul of a society be-

73 Giannella, *Religious Liberty, Nonestablishment and Doctrinal Development, Part II. The Nonestablishment Principle,* 81 HARV. L. REV. 513, 586–87 (1968).

cause they give it meaning and purpose; they inspire individual citizens and direct social institutions in the goals they elect and in the choice of means to achieve those goals. Second, the law incorporates the society's fundamental values; it molds the individual and group value-ideal, and is its crystallization. In today's world, government, in whose hands the law reposes, more definitively than other institutions determines society's value-orientation. Third, in an effort to maintain the constitutional principle of church-state separation two fundamental values have come under stress, religion and voluntarism. The constitutional obligation of maintaining a secular state poses the possibility of a culture that is secular because the expanding influence of the state threatens to remove the cultural significance and influence of religion and voluntarism. Finally, the Supreme Court has the unenviable task of upholding the principle of church-state separation on the one hand, and allowing policies that encourage the cultural contributions of religion and voluntarism on the other. In the past the Court has focused on the principle of separation as it affects individual rights, with little express attention directed to the long range cultural implications of its decisions. Nevertheless, there is a favorable climate of opinion and sufficient precedent on which to develop a view of separation that keeps the state and the church truly separate and at the same time encourages the social and cultural contribution of the churches. It would seem desirable to develop this precedent if religion and voluntarism are to endure as national values.

WILLIAM H. MARNELL

Civil Disobedience

and the Majority of One

"Any man more right than his neighbors constitutes a majority of one already."

—Henry David Thoreau

"Civil disobedience" is a phrase once more upon men's lips, as it tends to be in one form or another in any age beset by the seething of discontent and the lightning flash of violence. Like many another phrase rich in emotional overtones, it is at once a term of proud self-reliance, dogged opposition, moral recrimination, and total denunciation. It suggests the martyr and the patriot, but it also suggests the rebel and the revolutionary, and beyond them the anarchist.

Not infrequently the overtones and undertones of meanings that words and phrases can have operate with a greater impact than their literal, dictionary meanings. We are quite familiar with what are termed smear words, those words and phrases which contain within themselves derogatory implications that do not need to be spelled out, and sometimes could not be spelled out if put to that acid and specific test. Perhaps we need some term opposite to *smear word* to denote the words and phrases that contain within themselves laudatory implications that do not need to be spelled out, and sometimes could not be spelled out. The automatic praise word can be just as danger-

William H. Marnell is Professor of English at Boston State College.

ous as the automatic smear word. The latter damns without a trial, but the former vindicates without a test.

Civil disobedience is just such an automatic praise term. It conjures up a mental image of Socrates resolutely drinking the hemlock in obedience to the law of Athens which he has defied in the name of a higher law for the welfare of his city and its younger generation. It is the hallmark of the Christian martyr stepping into the arena with head erect. It is St. Thomas More mounting the block, with "the king's good servant but God's first" upon his lips. It is Henry David Thoreau, lover of human freedom, hater of human slavery, refusing to pay taxes to keep his fellow man in chains and going to jail for his refusal because he respects the law too much to be a fugitive from injustice. It is Mahatma Gandhi passively defying an empire in the name of justice and freedom for a conquered people, and restoring to its rightful place among the nations a subcontinent ancient in culture and creative in ways as impressive as they are foreign to western patterns.

Thus civil disobedience does what the automatic praise term always does. It casts its warm, protective coloration over men and their deeds profoundly and even totally different from such men as Socrates and More, and from the deeds which have shed glory on their names. The time is ripe for a long, hard look at precisely what the phrase implies, what motivation may lie behind its specific manifestations, what courses of action it may embrace, to what goals it may properly aspire, and what philosophy inspires it. The sad and solemn truth is that the United States is in a period when harassment and violence have largely taken the place of logic and reason as the necessary preludes to political action, and in the name of democracy are making a mockery of democracy and its processes. Civil disobedience is also the student demonstrator, yeasty with youth and untouched by maturity's wholesome frost, making an unholy nuisance of himself. It is the marchers abreast on a city street, disrupting the processes of society to present an image blurred in their own minds and totally different on the retina of society. Or it may indeed be the communist cadre, precisely aware of its objective. It is a phrase important enough today to warrant examination, and one rich enough in habitual emotionalism to make desirable a limitation of the flowers of rhetoric to the opening paragraphs of the examination. What follows will be, at least in intent, only logical herbs and simples.

Before proceeding to logical herbs and simples, however, one might be wise to cultivate the ground. Civil disobedience is currently associated in the public mind primarily but not exclusively with the Negro revolution. This is, of course, logical and reasonable enough; the difficulty is that to question the process of civil disobedience makes one appear to question the grounds, motivation, and objectives of the entire civil rights movement. This is illogical and, when carried to the extreme, unreasonable. One may feel the deepest sympathy with American blacks, recognize to the full the endless decades of repression and injustice to which they have been subjected, even dedicate oneself by specific action to the elimination of those evils in American racial life to which the Kerner report gave eloquent testimony, and still question gravely the process of civil disobedience, just as one may be bitterly opposed to American participation in the Vietnam war and yet view with repugnance the burning of a draft card as a gesture of flamboyant protest and defiance. One may plausibly argue that an ounce of constructive deeds is worth a pound of sympathetic emotion, and maintain that the real hope for racial justice in America lies less in protest than in affirmative action, in promoting black ownership of business in black communities, in the financing by private agencies of Negro enterprises with the full opportunity for economic development that the American system affords, in the systematic and vigorous reconstruction under black control of the areas in which blacks live until the homes there befit human dignity, and in similar constructive manifestations of what in reality is simply the American system at work. Let us now proceed to logical herbs and simples.

In examining the various categories of resistance to constituted authority which at times lay claim to the moral legitimacy surrounding the concept of civil disobedience, it will be helpful at the outset to state what most people would consider to be the paradigm of civil disobedience so that we can see why it is enveloped with a somewhat benign and salutary aura. The model case of civil disobedience involves the violation, in obedience to a higher law, of some duly enacted and applied governmental regulation, by one who accepts in general the legal order of the society of which he is a loyal member, who limits his resistance to nonviolent means, and who is willing to accept the prescribed penalty for his act in the hope that his example will lead to an amendment of what he deems offensive in the law, its interpretation, or application. The essential purpose of civil disobedience—to alter a particular unjust law or institution—leads most to regard it as a fundamentally different kind of resistance to civil authority than that which is designed to serve either the end of anarchy or that of rebellion.

In order to distinguish civil disobedience from anarchy it is necessary for the dissenter to appeal to some higher law. If he arrogates to himself the moral right to decide in all cases what is in the common good, he is in effect espousing anarchy. Civil disobedience is not commonly regarded as coincidental with such radical individualism; if it were, it would lose many of its benign connotations. Similarly, civil disobedience is not commonly equated with rebellion and the total social upheaval that it indicates; consequently, the dissenter who limits himself to civil disobedience is willing to accept the constituted legal and civic order except for the particular, unjust laws against which his protest is directed.

Since he is committed to the prevailing public order generally, such a dissenter is constrained to register his protest in a nonviolent manner and to accept the legally ordained punishment. These necessary conditions of an act of civil disobedience—that it be an open, peaceful, albeit illegal act accompanied by nonviolent submission to the legally constituted authorities—are sometimes observed by persons who act in accordance with anarchic or rebellious ends. Nonetheless, because their style conforms to that of civil disobedience, their acts are frequently labeled as such.

The phrase civil disobedience historically is associated with two men, Henry David Thoreau and Mahatma Gandhi. The very juxtaposition of their names reveals how elusive the phrase is, how difficult to define, how vastly more difficult to limit in its valid application. Thoreau defined himself as "a mystic, a transcendentalist, and a natural philosopher to boot." It is not without significance that

Thoreau really lives in the last capacity, the natural philosopher whose *Walden* is an enduring delight of American letters. Thoreau was the sort of mystic whose mysticism turns inward and not upward to the eternal, the transcendentalist who did not transcend himself but rather the rest of his fellow mortals. He lived "to observe what transpires, not in the street, but in the mind and heart of me." Thoreau was something of a foreigner in his natal Concord and he was wise enough not to join those more formally known as Transcendentalists at Brook Farm. The simple truth is that Thoreau was an utter individualist, and therefore an anarchist. "That government is best which governs not at all," said Thoreau. And again, "There will never be a really free and enlightened State until the State comes to recognize the individual as a higher and independent power, from which all its own power and authority are derived." This last doctrine can be confused with democracy, and indeed was so confused by Thoreau himself.

Thoreau enters the annals of civil disobedience by an act and an essay. He came to the conclusion that the government of the United States, which conducted a war with Mexico, abused the Indians, and condoned slavery, was unworthy of his tax payments. He refused to pay his poll tax and went quietly to jail for one day. The rationale of his act was spelled out in a lecture first printed under the title "Resistance to Civil Government" in Elizabeth Peabody's *Aesthetic Papers* (1849), but now known as "Civil Disobedience."

Thoreau denounces what he deems the iniquitous conduct of the federal government, but does so on the thesis that government is at best an expedient and that the best government is the one that governs not at all. He makes the criterion of justifiable civil disobedience his personal and unsupported moral sense: "The only obligation which I have a right to assume is to do at any time what I think is right." Thus he does more than make his personal moral sense his criterion of right and wrong; he denies that for him any other criterion is morally admissible. Thoreau was a philosophic anarchist, and it is not unfair to point out that philosophic anarchy was possible for him because he lived in the unusually orderly, tolerant, and law abiding town of Concord, Massachusetts.

On the other hand, Thoreau was willing to accept the legal consequences of his philosophic anarchy. When a quite disturbed Emerson
went to the jail and asked Thoreau what he was doing in there,
Thoreau asked Emerson what he was doing out there. The clever
riposte revealed what is so often true of philosophic anarchists, that
they are far more willing to indulge themselves in their own moral
sense than to extend the same indulgence to others.

Mahatma Gandhi included in the phrase civil disobedience the refusal to obey bad laws, and also the refusal to obey any laws, provided that the refusal "does not involve moral turpitude and is undertaken as a symbol of revolt against the State." The first question to
be answered is, what did Gandhi understand by a bad law? A law
may be bad because it is unwise or because it is unjust, and of course
it may properly be contended that any unjust law is unwise. There are
two distinct criteria of judgment involved in the words *unwise* and
unjust. An action is unwise if it runs counter to human experience of
what is effective and judicious, or if it runs counter to reasonable
anticipation of what may be effective and judicious. That is to say,
the judgment of an action as wise or unwise is a pragmatic judgment.
On the other hand, an action is unjust if it runs counter to an accepted code of right and wrong. This may mean a legally accepted
code, such as the Constitution of the United States. It may mean a
code that is believed to exist apart from man's contrivance, what is
variously termed a higher law, a moral law, a natural law, a divine
law. Ordinarily, when an action is branded as unjust, it is so branded
in terms of what may for convenience's sake be termed natural law.
An action deemed to run counter to a legally accepted code is usually termed illegal.

To Thoreau his personal moral sense and natural law were identical. Believers in natural law believe in the existence of a code of
conduct either divinely instituted or inherent in the natural order,
which is basically the same for all men and independent in its ordainments of the dictates of their individual consciences. If civil disobedience is taken to mean a violation of statute law in obedience to
natural law, one must believe in natural law in this objective sense.
Thoreau was capable of breaking the statute law, but he was not

capable of doing so in obedience to natural law since he recognized no natural law except his own moral standards.

To Gandhi, however, civil disobedience was possible since he recognized the existence of natural law. When he passively resisted what he considered unjust laws, he did so in obedience to what he considered natural law. Furthermore, he did so with a demonstrated willingness to accept the legal consequences. In the case of Thoreau there is present only one presumptive axiom of civil disobedience, the willingness to accept its legal consequences. In the case of Gandhi there are two, disobedience of unjust statute law in obedience to natural law and willingness to accept the legal consequences.

There is, however, a very different aspect to Gandhi's civil disobedience which sets his case entirely apart from that of Thoreau. Gandhi was disobedient to what was certainly a foreign government and one that he deemed unjust. Gandhi believed that one is morally justified in disobeying any law of an unjust government, even if the law itself is just, provided that the breaking of the law does not involve moral turpitude. He carefully limited the morality of this kind of civil disobedience to symbolic opposition to unjust and tyrannical governments. Thus Gandhi had a twofold criterion for justifiable civil disobedience, the injustice of the law and the injustice of the government. Gandhi employed the tactics of passive resistance to what he considered a despotic government and the government of a foreign conqueror. He did not owe true allegiance to the British government in India. Hence it may properly be contended that his acts against that government, however passive in nature and however accompanied by a willingness to accept the consequences, were not acts of civil disobedience at all but acts of rebellion. Gandhi was a revolutionist just as truly as George Washington, and with just about the same justification. Each used the tactics which circumstances dictated as the ones best adapted to gain the revolutionary end. Each man's actions are to be justified on the principle of inalienable rights, with the right of self-government among them and the connotation of the right of revolution against despotic government or indeed against any government imposed by a conqueror. Gandhi's passive resistance was civil disobedience only in the sense of technique. In rationale it was revolution, and was to be justified by the arguments which have long been accepted by believers in democratic processes as justifying revolution.

Thus a problem of one sort faces us when we analyze what is termed civil disobedience on the part of Thoreau, and a problem of another sort when the case of Gandhi is considered. Thoreau was entangled in a logical inconsistency. In effect, he either believed that he should accept democratically attained conclusions except when he found himself in conscientious conflict with them or he believed that the American government had departed so far from its principles as to be despotic and unworthy of obedience. In the first case he would be elevating his private conscience above the corporate conscience of the society of which he claimed in general to be a faithful member, and so be an anarchist, or he would be rejecting the society of which he claimed inconsistently to be a faithful member, and so be a revolutionist. In neither case would his act be one of civil disobedience. Gandhi, on the other hand, did base his passive resistance upon belief in natural law and was willing to accept the legal consequences of his act. In these respects his actions did conform to the concept of civil disobedience, but his attitude was not that of civil disobedience because he did not accept as legitimate the government against which he was protesting. He was a revolutionist, with the presumptive justification for his acts which revolution may have. Although civil disobedience has been associated with Thoreau and Gandhi, the thought pattern behind the actions of both is not consistent with what is usually considered the thought pattern of civil disobedience. Put another way, the man whose thought pattern is anarchistic cannot cloak it in the rationale of civil disobedience, and neither can the man whose thought pattern is revolutionary.

We may now turn to three other men whose thought patterns were neither anarchistic nor revolutionary. One is Socrates, a second is a hypothetical Christian martyr, and the third is St. Thomas More. Between the first two is a certain parallelism. Socrates was accused of corrupting the youth of Athens and of not worshiping the gods whom the city worshiped. The latter charge was obviously leveled against the martyrs, who actually were branded as atheists, and the former charge might be leveled as well. To a certain extent the attitude of Socrates was the precise opposite of civil disobedience, since part of the defense of Socrates was that he had not broken the laws of the city in either his teaching or his religious attitude. There are aspects of the case of Socrates, however, suggestive of civil disobedience.

Socrates maintanied that his actions were done in accordance with the moral instruction of his *daimon,* his voice of conscience. Like the ancients in general he believed in a higher moral law which was the same for all men and was revealed to individual man by his conscience. His attitude was also suggestive of civil disobedience in that he made no effort to escape the consequences of his acts. As the *Crito* makes clear, he could have escaped from prison but chose not to do so, since escape is illegal. His actions, then, were typical of civil disobedience in that he maintained that they were in accordance with natural law as revealed to him by his conscience and that he was willing to accept the legal consequences of his act, thereby showing his basic allegiance to the society of which he was a member and to its laws. But Socrates always maintained that he had not broken the law. Obviously one cannot do a deliberate act of civil disobedience unless one both intends to break the law and does so. Unintentional breaking of the law, or deliberate breaking of the law for some motive other than passive resistance to a specific statute of a government the statutes of which in general one accepts, is not what is commonly considered civil disobedience. Thus the technical breaking of a law in order to provide a test case of constitutionality is hardly civil disobedience.

The element of motive naturally introduces the case of the Christian martyr. Martyrdom typically was the consequence of refusing to perform an act of religious homage to a pagan deity. Since the Church and the State were one in ancient Rome, there was no distinction between a civil law and a religious ordainment. If one did not offer the required homage to the deity, one broke the law. A Christian martyr might be quite unwilling to perform the act of worship, yet equally unwilling in other respects to disobey the laws of Rome or to renounce either the rights or duties of Roman citizenship. Hence the person who broke the specific law which required the worship of a pagan deity, who did so without renouncing his general allegiance to Rome and his general obedience to its laws, and who accepted willingly the martyrdom which was the quasi-legal consequence of his act would seem to offer a more clear-cut example of what civil disobedience really means than do Thoreau, Gandhi, and Socrates.

This is precisely the point at which the brakes must be applied most firmly to speculation. An act cannot qualify as civil disobedience unless it has the requisite motivation. If the motivation of the martyr was disobedience to the statute law in obedience to a higher law, possibly with the additional hope that such disobedience might prompt society to amend the statute law, then his act was one of civil disobedience. But if the martyr was seeking the martyr's crown, then his motivation was very different indeed and so was the nature of his act. If his motive was to purchase an eternity of bliss by some minutes of hideous torture, then his case belongs to some discipline other than the law—perhaps theology, perhaps psychiatry. The point is not hypothetical, since the voice of rational faith and prudence was steadily raised in the age of the martyrs against the emotion-packed, apocalyptic Christianity of the millenarians in whom faith drifted into the hinterland of fanaticism, and even to the darkness beyond which was madness. To pass to what may from one viewpoint be considered self-inflicted martyrdom, one might question if those Buddhists in Vietnam who doused themselves in gasoline and then applied the match may not have had a motivation similar to that of the fanatics and madmen who, along with the steadfast Christians, sought the martyr's crown. The element of motive is all-important.

The case of St. Thomas More may also be instructive. King Henry VIII had called upon him to furnish the legal justification the king sought for his divorce of Catherine of Aragon and his marriage to Anne Boleyn. Let us pass over the thorny question of the validity of the king's marriage to Catherine and his belated scruples on the point. It suffices for the present purpose that Thomas More thought the marriage valid, and the break between the king and his minister was occasioned by a conflict of judgment concerning a marital case.

The execution of Thomas More was occasioned in the immediate sense by his refusal to accept the Supremacy Act of 1534 whereby Henry was declared head of the English Church. We may pass over another thorny question concerning that curious and spineless Parliament which was packed by the king and moved only when he beckoned. One may concede that the law of England is the king acting through Parliament and still question, as More is said to have, the omnicompetence of the sovereign. Could Parliament make Henry the head of the English church? In More's mind it was not within the power of Parliament or of the king acting through Parliament to do so, and hence to him the Supremacy Act simply had no validity. In other respects More acted as a loyal subject of the king and accepted without any attempt to evade it the penalty of his act. Thus the case of More conforms to the definition of civil disobedience except for a point of some subtlety. Does a man break the law for the purpose of making a moral protest against its alleged inequity if he does not believe that the law really exists? The point would be quite academic were it not for one very pertinent and contemporary fact: this has been precisely the point at issue when blacks have broken Jim Crow "laws." How can you in intent break a law if you have reason to believe that it does not exist?

The only common denominator in the five cases we have considered appears to be the voluntary acceptance of the penalty for the acts in question. The case which can come closest to the model of civil disobedience is that of the Christian martyr who refuses to comply with the law of the land because of his allegiance to a higher law. In his case, however, motivation is all-important. If his motivation fits the definition of civil disobedience, then his is the clearest case of all; if he sought the martyr's crown to the exclusion of any other motivation, then his act was not one of civil disobedience at all. The other cases are simpler. Thoreau's act was rather an affirmation of anarchy than an act of civil disobedience. Gandhi's act was one of rebellion. Socrates believed that he had not broken the law, and the crux in More's case was one of resisting the acts of civil authorities on the ground that they were not in accordance with the proper application of the law of the land.

This is a long preamble to a tale, and its justification must be that a great many of the acts which in the twentieth century are labeled as civil disobedience have prototypes in the acts of the men we have considered. Let us consider the act of a man who challenges the validity of the remnants of Jim Crowism. His is not an act of civil disobedience since he has not only morality on his side but the law as well. The disobedience is on the part of those who try to perpetuate what has been declared unconstitutional. Since there is no particular evidence that proponents of Jim Crow are actuated by reverence for higher law or stand ready to accept the legal consequences of their acts, they can hardly enjoy the protective coloration of civil disobedience. Of our five cases, the man who defies Jim Crow comes closest to Socrates, although there is present in his reasoning something close to the reasoning of Thomas More. He acts in accordance with a higher law, he is willing to accept the consequences of his act, he is motivated by the hope of stimulating the general conscience, but he does not perform an act of civil disobedience for the simple reason that he has not broken a law. His deeds may be thoroughly admirable, but they cannot be used as a precedent and justification for civil disobedience.

Then we may consider the hippie, with his doctrine of love and his disregard for all the conventions and ordainments of the society whose police and fire departments protect him, whose civil services make possible his lilies-of-the-field existence, whose absolute independence paradoxically is absolutely dependent upon the discipline of the society within which he is a maverick and outside which he could not endure. When he comes into the toils of the law, it is not because he has performed an act of civil disobedience since (if one grasps with some exactness his mental processes) he recognizes no moral order higher than the one he has fashioned for himself. Like Thoreau, he makes his personal moral sense his criterion of right and wrong and denies that for him any other criterion is morally admissible. The lover of *Walden* may bridle at the suggestion, but the hippie is the ideological son of Henry David Thoreau. He follows Thoreau and all other extreme individualists who confuse anarchy with democracy when he makes his individual will the one valid criterion of his actions. To the hippie, as to Thoreau, and as to the great intellectual prototype in English thought of all individualistic skepticism, David Hume, reason is inert and cannot be a source of moral judgments since morality is a matter of feeling and not of fact. Such men are incapable of true acts of civil disobedience, since civil disobedience to a statute law implies obedience to a higher law and they recognize no law higher than their personal ideologies. Anarchy and disobedience are mutually inconsistent terms, since one can be disobedient only to some order external to oneself and anarchy denies that such exists.

A characteristic form of civil disobedience during the Vietnam war has been the burning of the draft card. It conforms in its externals at least to civil disobedience as we have defined it: a statute law is broken, presumably in obedience to a higher law, for the moral impact the act may have on the general conscience, and the typical draft card burner is ready to face the legal consequences of his act. There are certain aspects to the business of draft card burning, however, that tend to give one pause. The steps of a State House make a suitable locale, a crowd of on-lookers is a prerequisite, the presence of newspapermen a necessity, and a television squad at least a desideratum. Morality and publicity stand shoulder to shoulder, as the match is applied to a bit of paper—this part one takes on trust—said to be a draft card. One recalls that in the early Christian centuries emotion-packed, apocalyptic Christianity had a way of drifting into the hinterland of fanaticism accompanied by publicity. It may well be true that some young men have burned draft cards in the true spirit of civil disobedience, and the history of the Vietnam conflict being what it has been, they may well have felt an entire sense of obedience to a higher law in thus violating a statute law. It may be equally true that others were sensationalists, rhapsodic in their emotional displays, given to the grandiloquent gesture which will be imprinted on the retina of television and reproduced from coast to coast via Huntley-Brinkley or its equivalent. There were the pseudomartyrs in the early Christian centuries as well as the true martyrs, and martyrdom for the sake of the martyr's crown was pseudomartyrdom. The same is undoubtedly true of the draft card burners today. It would be cynical to say that none is actuated by the principles that underlie true civil disobedience, and it would be naive to say that all are, and possibly naive to say that many are. Only the young men themselves know, if their thinking is clear enough to let them know. One might also add that the martyr's crown the draft card burner may be forced to wear is not a crown of glory, but neither is it a crown of thorns.

Thus Socrates, Thoreau, the Christian martyr, and the pseudo-martyr have their modern parallels, if one allows for the bit of stretching always necessary to create historic parallels. What of St. Thomas More and Gandhi? This is the point at which distinctions need to be drawn with the greatest care. St. Thomas More performed an act of civil disobedience, not to the basic law either of his own country or his Church, but to what may be termed an administrative interpretation of the royal power. It was the belief of the king concerning his powers when acting through Parliament and his will to enforce his belief which More opposed, not what he considered the law of the land. More was the king's true servant, not a revolutionary. Gandhi, on the other hand, performed acts of passive resistance to a government imposed upon his people by an alien power. He was in rebellion against both the injustice of the law and the injustice of the government. Thus the acts of Gandhi were not acts of civil disobedience but acts of revolution, although Gandhi buttressed his moral position by limiting himself to acts involving no moral turpitude.

By and large disobedience in the civil rights movement—and this is the chief justification for writing on this topic at the present time —has tended to seek justification on grounds most closely approximating those employed by St. Thomas More. Martin Luther King defined civil disobedience as the violation of laws "out of harmony with the moral law of the universe," maintaining that one has a "moral responsibility to obey just laws." He consistently joined to his constitutional argument, as his criterion for justified civil disobedience, the incompatibility with natural law either of a specific statute law or the judicial interpretation of some law. The person who uses this criterion in the hope of bettering the general moral climate and couples with it the willingness to accept the legal consequences of his act, performs an act of civil disobedience. King's actions resembled those of More since he claimed that the basic law of the United States, the Constitution, requires that governmental action conform to basic canons of racial and social justice. However, the moment that Gandhi's criterion, the alleged injustice of the government itself, becomes the motivating force, the act is not one of civil disobedience but an act of revolution. There are definite circumstances under which revolution can be morally justified; we are not ready yet to renounce the Founding Fathers. But revolution is not entitled to the protective moral cover accorded civil disobedience, and everyone knows that the civil rights movement is at the very least in imminent peril of crossing the shadowy borderline which separates civil disobedience from outright rebellion. The extremists have said so, and we have no reason to believe that they do not mean what they say. One might add that people have been known to mean what they say without understanding what they say.

Since our concern is civil disobedience, our subject is not the extremists, however disturbed the nation may rightfully be about them. Those who have performed acts of civil disobedience after the fashion of Dr. King accept the premises of American society and American democracy. The most fundamental premise of all is that in a democracy decisions are reached, after mature and open debate, by the legislative processes set up for that purpose, and then such decisions are accepted by all until such time as the same processes may modify or reverse them. The corollary is that the legislative process reflects accurately, in either a direct fashion or by representation, the majority will. It follows that one cannot believe in the democratic process and not accept its conclusions unless the process itself is so corrupted and distorted that it no longer fulfills its appointed purpose. In the very nature of things no one can believe in the democratic process and protest against its theory by an act of civil disobedience. The believer in democracy logically can protest only against its corruption and distortion.

There is a question that everyone must ask himself who makes his own conscience the criterion for his acts. To what extent can one reconcile belief in the democratic process with belief in a subjective judgment about the validity of its procedures? To obey the utterly unsupported voice of conscience when it is in opposition to the law is to deny the validity of law itself. It is, in the root meaning of the word, anarchy. On the other hand, democratic absolutism or the total denial of the moral right to disobey any law passed by the democratic process is at least the handmaid of tyranny. Furthermore, it is fundamentally contrary to the Constitution of the United States. The whole purpose of the Bill of Rights is to establish the fact that there are human rights antecedent to statute law and that any law which violates one of them is *ipso facto* invalid.

How, then, are we to avoid the Scylla of anarchy and the Charybdis of democratic absolutism? The logical answer, and to one who believes in the fundamental justice of American governmental processes the true answer, is by appeal to the courts. It is precisely for this purpose that the higher courts exist, and it might even be plausibly argued that the Supreme Court of the United States exists for no other purpose than to insure that the acts of the majority are subject to the norms of justice found in the Constitution, and most particularly in the Bill of Rights. Such is the established mode of appeal against what one might deem a substantive violation of the basic law or a procedural disregard of it. The statement is trite and, like most trite statements, true. Since an act of civil disobedience connotes either a disrespect for the established procedures of democratic government or a distrust in their just and effective operation, it follows that a loyal American citizen will test the issue fully in the courts before accepting as inevitable either disrespect or distrust.

If our reasoning is correct, it provides us with an explanation of the Supreme Court's holding in *Walker v. City of Birmingham*,[1] which places restrictions on legitimate resistance to laws that may be later found to have been invalid under the Constitution at the time of the actor's disobedience. In April 1963, officials of Birmingham obtained from the judge of a state circuit court an injunction enjoining certain organizations and individuals from mass parading in the streets of Birmingham without a permit. The next afternoon, which

---

[1] 388 U.S. 307 (1967).

was Good Friday, a group did parade without a permit, defying the injunction as "raw tyranny under the guise of maintaining law and order." They paraded again on Easter Sunday. When the city officials applied to the circuit court for an order holding the petitioners in contempt of court, the petitioners attacked the injunction as unconstitutional, maintaining that it was vague, too broad, and in restraint of free speech. The court refused to consider these contentions on the grounds that the petitioners had not sought either to have the injunction dissolved or to obtain a permit for the parade. It considered the only issues to be whether it had the power to issue the injunction and whether the petitioners had knowingly violated it. On these issues the court found against the petitioners, fining each $50 and sentencing each to five days in jail. The most distinguished of those fined and sentenced to jail was Martin Luther King.

The Supreme Court of Alabama upheld the finding of the lower court on the grounds that the petitioners did not file a motion to dissolve the injunction but rather ignored it and held the parade anyway, thus disregarding the orders of the circuit court in contempt of its lawful authority. Since they ignored the authority of the circuit court to determine the validity of the ordinance and likewise disregarded the procedure of orderly review by a higher court of the findings of the lower court, they were guilty of contempt of lawful authority and properly subject to punishment. This finding of the Supreme Court of Alabama was affirmed by the Supreme Court of the United States, which relied on and quoted from its decision in *Howat v. Kansas*.[2] "It is for the court of first instance to determine the question of the validity of the law, and until its decision is reversed for error by orderly review, either by itself or by a higher court, its orders based on its decision are to be respected, and disobedience of them is contempt of its lawful authority, to be punished."[3] The *Howat* case was decided nearly a half century ago, and its abiding validity was affirmed by the Supreme Court in this case as it had been in eight other cases in the intervening years.

The point at issue was not the constitutionality of the Birmingham

2 258 U.S. 181 (1922).   3 *Id.* at 190.

ordinance. The Court recognized that it had a breadth and vague-
ness that rendered it open to substantial constitutional question.
Neither was it the arbitrary fashion in which the ordinance was applied by city authorities accused of being insensitive to the mandates
of justice. The point at issue was that the petitioners had made themselves judges of the constitutionality of the ordinance and the legality
of its administration. They had made up their minds that justice was
not to be obtained from the city government of Birmingham or the
courts of Alabama without endeavoring to prove the truth of the
contention by applying to the Alabama courts. Alabama had been
found guilty by them without a trial. They had done to Alabama
what they suspected Alabama would do to them. They had tarred
themselves with a brush with which Alabama might or might not
have tarred itself. The fact is that Alabama justice did not tar itself
with that brush in 1960, when in the "white supremacy" case of
Fields v. City of Fairfield [4] it made precisely the same finding against
white supremacy advocates that it made in 1963 against civil rights
advocates.

The central point, however, is not justice to the civil rights advocates or to Alabama, but justice as the objective and impersonal
foundation of the free American society. As Mr. Justice Potter Stewart
well put it in the final paragraph of the Supreme Court opinion, "The
rule of law that Alabama followed in this case reflects a belief that in
the fair administration of justice no man can be judge in his own
case, however exalted his station, however righteous his motives, and
irrespective of his race, color, politics, or religion. This Court cannot
hold that the petitioners were constitutionally free to ignore all the
procedures of the law and carry their battle to the streets. One may
sympathize with the petitioners' impatient commitment to their
cause. But respect for judicial process is a small price to pay for the
civilizing hand of law, which alone can give abiding meaning to constitutional freedom." [5] The various dissents written by Chief Justice
Warren,[6] Justice Douglas,[7] and Justice Brennan[8] do little more than
skirt this central issue, since all beg the question of the constitutionality

[4] 273 Ala. 588, 143 So.2d 177 (1960).   [5] 388 U.S. at 320–21.
[6] *Id.* at 324.   [7] *Id.* at 334.   [8] *Id.* at 338.

of the Birmingham ordinance. Perhaps the ordinance was unconstitutional. The Court admitted the possibility. The fact remains unchanged that decisions on points of constitutionality are not made by aggrieved parties. They are made by the duly constituted courts. Nor would the point, raised by Chief Justice Warren, that it was "important for the significance of the demonstrations" that they be held on Good Friday and Easter Sunday and hence that the issuing of the injunction may have been a delaying action designed to harass,[9] recommend itself, one suspects, to the more careful sort of theologian. There is no obvious connection of the spirit between a demonstration in favor of civil rights and what in Christian belief was Christ's vicarious atonement for the sins of men. The theology is not nearly so obvious as the theatricality.

Beyond all this is another consideration to which thoughtful and concerned Americans give increased and disturbed attention. When all is said and done, Thoreau, Gandhi, Socrates, the martyr, and Thomas More were individuals. Civil disobedience in the 1960's has been the work of groups, and frequently of large, disorderly, and at least potentially dangerous groups. To what extent may an act of civil disobedience disrupt the orderly processes of society and still be covered by the moral justification traditionally offered for civil disobedience? The issue does not tend to arise when the act of civil disobedience is that of an individual, since under ordinary circumstances an individual is not in a position to disrupt the orderly processes of society. A little ingenuity might enable one to conjure up a situation in which an individual could do precisely that. Let us assume that a man in a position to govern the flow of electric power to a community decides to shut it off as an act of civil disobedience designed as a protest against American involvement in a foreign war. Few would argue that either his belief that such involvement was contrary to moral law or his willingness to suffer the legal penalty for his act would provide moral justification for his imperiling the safety of the community. But one must contrive a situation to illustrate the principle where an individual is concerned, and the contriving is bound

9 *Id.* at 325.

to be far-fetched. The real problem is presented by the group of people who jointly disrupt the orderly processes of society by what they consider an act of civil disobedience.

Certain rights guaranteed to Americans by the Constitution are in potential conflict with certain other rights. Americans enjoy the rights of free speech, free assembly, and free petition by the First and Fourteenth Amendments to the Constitution. But Americans also enjoy the right to peaceable and orderly living by the very nature and purpose of society itself. Those who wish to march, demonstrate, and picket are not the only ones with the right to appeal to natural law. As the Court said in *Walker v. City of Birmingham,* "When protest takes the form of mass demonstrations, parades, or picketing on public streets and sidewalks, the free passage of traffic and the prevention of public disorder and violence become important objects of legitimate state concern." [10] The Court had already spelled out the principle in *Cox v. Louisiana:* [11] We emphatically reject the notion . . . that the First and Fourteenth Amendments afford the same kind of freedom to those who would communicate ideas by conduct such as patrolling, marching, and picketing on streets and highways, as these amendments afford to those who communicate ideas by pure speech." [12] Americans indeed have the rights of free speech, free assembly, and free petition. They are guaranteed by the Constitution. But American society also has the right and the duty to maintain the public order as the framework within which rights are exercised. As the Court stated in *Cox v. New Hampshire,*[13] "Civil liberties, as guaranteed by the Constitution, imply the existence of an organized society maintaining public order without which liberty itself would be lost in the excesses of unrestrained abuses." [14]

A very real difficulty confronts the attempt to apply to group action the principles which may justify civil disobedience. An orderly march or demonstration conducted in accordance with local ordinances by some group intent on bringing to public attention what it considers a violation of human rights or of statute law is not an act of civil disobedience. One cannot disobey the law when the law is on

[10] 388 U.S. at 316.   [11] 379 U.S. 536 (1965).   [12] 379 U.S. at 555.
[13] 312 U.S. 569 (1941).   [14] 312 at 574.

one's side. On the other hand, when the march or demonstration does disregard or disrupt the orderly processes of society the question of culpability does not hinge on the issue of civil disobedience unless the objective of the demonstration is to focus attention on the social processes themselves. Once more we see that the area of true civil disobedience is extremely circumscribed. Group acts of protest are not acts of civil disobedience if they are orderly and do not violate the orderly processes of society since they are performed in accordance with rights guaranteed to Americans by their Constitution. On the other hand, no group can accept the principles on which its government rests and consider itself in general a law-abiding element in the society of which it is physically a part, and yet ignore or disrupt the orderly processes of that society in the name of civil disobedience. The end no more justifies the means for demonstrators than it does for other people.

The fact remains, however, that four justices of the Supreme Court dissented in *Walker v. City of Birmingham*; their viewpoint is necessarily worthy of consideration. There have been acts of state legislatures and local courts that, in the general judgment of dispassionate and informed men, are unconstitutional. It is true that such acts or injunctions may do a substantial damage, and possibly an irremediable damage, during the time that it takes to test their constitutionality. The technique of the delaying action is not confined to the military. Finally, it is true that the individual or group which disobeys what it considers clearly an unconstitutional law or an illegal injunction is not, in its own judgment, disobeying the law itself but rather its limited perversion. It is not in rebellion against the government under which it lives or the society of which it is a part, but rather against the presumably illicit action of a unit of that government. The dissenting justices in *Walker v. City of Birmingham* found the petitioners in that position. But were they? In the opinion of the majority the fact is that they were not, since they had not begun to exhaust their legal recourse. In the opinion of the minority, they were. Once more, we see illustrated the fact that cases of civil disobedience tend to be judged, not on a basis of principle, but on a basis of fact. But courts exist to determine points of fact and to adjudicate them by the principles of law. In *Walker v. City of Birmingham* both legal theory and American tradition support, not the dissenting opinions, but the Court opinion.

A more difficult situation is presented when an act is found constitutional by the appropriate court but the decision is contested on moral grounds by an individual or group. Can failure to obey such an act be covered by the principle of civil disobedience? One may surmise that it can, provided the purpose of those disobedient is to promote the moral education of society, to bring home to it the error of its legal ways, and to facilitate a change, be it in the law or in the Constitution. Naturally there must be no interference with the orderly processes of society, and the disobedient must be willing to accept the legal consequences. However, to disobey an act of established constitutionality demands a higher degree of moral certitude than to disobey an act of unestablished and dubious constitutionality. In the latter case the disobedient party may buttress his position by such arguments as legal precedent and clear intent of the law afford. In the former case the Court has already spoken. The appeal is now simply and solely moral, and the higher degree of certitude is a clear necessity. Having said that by way of theory, one might add that civil disobedience as a device designed to bring home the necessity for constitutional amendment is uniquely unpromising, unless it really be open rebellion, after the fashion of John Brown.

This brings up the final issue. Any act of intended civil disobedience rests on the placing of one's conscience, or that of the group, ahead of the law of the land, its legal administrators, and its duly appointed interpreters. Part of the law of the land in democratic countries is the legal process. One certainly has the right in the United States to spur on the legal process by exercising the rights of free speech, free assembly, and free petition. So long as the exercise of such rights is in each appropriate sense orderly, there is no element of disobedience involved. When such exercises cease to observe the orderly processes of society, their culpability rests in the disorganization they cause, not in the motivation that inspires them. But a true act of civil disobedience in a democracy is a confession of distrust in the legal process. It may be a distrust of those legally responsible for the exercise of the legal process, such as a legislature or court. It may be a distrust of the intellectual or moral competence of the people themselves and hence a distrust of their competence to create the atmosphere in which just legislation is enacted. True civil disobedience must rest on the conviction that one has a more acute moral sensibility than his fellows and a moral duty to instil in the society of which he is in general a loyal member an acceptance of the moral principle which inspires his act of civil disobedience. There are few acts in life that impose a more rigorous test upon the moral convictions of a person than the act of civil disobedience, few acts that require more intensive searching of the soul, more painstaking and dispassionate weighing of the possible consequences.

The peril forever present in the concept of civil disobedience is well illustrated by what has actually happened in the course of the civil rights movement. The early stages were entirely within the framework of American tradition and the pattern of American law. Such acts as the freedom rides and the march on Washington in 1963 were entirely legal manifestations of American rights as spelled out in the Bill of Rights and protected by the spirit and the letter alike of the Constitution. But, for that very reason they were not acts of civil disobedience. What Jim Crow connoted had been declared unconstitutional years before the freedom rides took place. Those who challenged the validity of the remnants of Jim Crowism were not only in the moral right but in the legal right as well.

That was the first stage. The next stage was the sit-in. In theory a sit-in may be effected as a passive protest either against what the protesting parties consider an unjust law or against what they consider a failure to enforce a just law. The appeal in the former case is to the conscience of society, in the latter case to the consciences of the responsible officials and, of course, obliquely to society. A sit-in by its nature at least renders inconvenient the orderly processes of society, but it may not obstruct them to an intolerable degree. On the other hand a sit-in ordinarily comes into some sort of collision with the law, if only with a statute that prohibits loitering. It would seem that a passive sit-in, organized to prod the official and public conscience, may be a valid example of civil disobedience if the other elements of civil disobedience are present.

The record of recent years shows in tragic fashion how transitory and unreliable is the passive nature of the sit-in. The next stage is the sit-in that does obstruct to an intolerable degree the orderly processes of society and hence is an act of harassment with a nuisance value designed to force compliance with the will of those indulging in the sit-in. With a slightly Pickwickian employment of the term *sit-in,* the act of demonstrators in blocking with their bodies the Triborough Bridge in New York is an example of the sit-in which crosses the shadowy borderline that divides civil disobediences from unprincipled defiance of the law. The truth is that acts of civil disobedience are simpler for individuals to perform than for groups, since it is physical-ly easier for the group to slip across that borderline than for the indi-vidual. There is no difference in theory where the individual and the group are concerned, but a very substantial difference in practice.

From this point on the record becomes increasingly tragic and foreboding. Ahead lie Watts, Newark, and Detroit. Ahead lie the mobs and the riots, the fires and the looting. By now the final vestige of legality has disappeared and nothing remains but lawlessness rampant. In that tragic hour the policemen, the firemen, and the National Guardsmen are there. They may face the rocks, the bottles, and the sniper's bullets. But the college students who took the freedom rides and joined the sit-ins have returned to their classrooms, the sympathizers have returned to their suburbs, and the clergymen to their studies.

The perils implicit in the pattern of thinking of which civil dis-obedience is a part are to be found in the streets of Newark and De-troit, Milwaukee and New Haven and Rochester. The melancholy truth of life is that we must take into account not only the planned consequences of our actions but the unplanned, not only the intend-ed but the unintended, not only the rational but the irrational, when we undertake to stir the passions of our fellow men. And we must be very certain indeed of what we are doing when we urge on others a philosophy of disobedience which implies that the law is bankrupt and every man is a law unto himself. There was nothing in the plan, the logic, or the reason for the freedom rides, the orderly marches, the peaceful demonstrations, the passive sit-ins that was designed to bring wild lawlessness and rampant destruction to the cities of America. There is nothing in the concept of civil disobedience that calls in plan, logic, or reason for violent and outrageous violation of the law. But history has a way of being unplanned, illogical, and irrational because the acts of men reveal an instinct for such violent ways.

For this reason we have law, and really for no other. The rule of law is slow, it can be uncertain, without constant watch it has a tendency to be unjust. This is true because it is an instrument of men, who have a slow and wavering dedication to justice. On the other hand, the entire theory of democracy rests on the belief that rational men, free to expound their personal beliefs, to bring to the fore their deeply held convictions, but binding themselves to the rule of a majority operating through legal channels and voluntarily limiting itself by observance of individual and minority rights, can order their affairs in a planned, logical, rational, and legal fashion. By and large the history of the United States justifies this belief.

One must accept the thesis that civil disobedience is on occasion licit, or accept the grim alternative to that thesis, legal absolutism. There is a place in a free society for civil disobedience and the world needs an occasional martyr. That it needs them in the mass is far less clear, but it is conceivable that it does; the Christian martyrs on occasion marched in companies to horror and to glory. But civil disobedience is by its very nature a second last resort. Beyond it lies only rebellion. Therefore civil disobedience must be carefully examined and accurately understood, so that it may never be confused with acts that superficially resemble it. Civil disobedience is an extremely limited concept, and even more limited in fact than in theory. There is nothing in the history of the United States to make one wish it more common than it has been. There is everything in American history to make one trust that good will, honest intentions, sincere conscience, and hard work within the legal framework will produce more beneficial results, more surely and even more quickly, than acts rooted in unchecked individualism and the rejection of social controls. The law may be slow, cumbersome, uncertain, and at times even cynical and unjust, but it is still the best principle we have and are likely to have this side of the Celestial City. There is nothing more salutary than the rule of the majority honestly arrived at. Few things are more perilous than Thoreau's majority of one.

DEXTER L. HANLEY, S.J.

The Military

Chaplaincy

The military chaplaincy stands as a venerable governmental institution which recognizes the important role that religion plays in American life. A highly conceptualistic approach to separation of church and state—one is tempted to say a highly doctrinaire one—might find this institution unconstitutional. An interpretation of the establishment clause which regards that provision as barring any and all governmental aid to religion implies that the chaplaincy is vulnerable to constitutional challenge.[1] First, there is the material and moral support extended to religion by the chaplaincy; the government pays the chaplains for their services, provides them with facilities for religious exercises and instruction, and accords them the rank of officers. Second, the state becomes involved with religion through its supervision of the functions and duties of the chaplains. Even when the chaplain's duties are not strictly religious, as when he acts as an instructor in morality, the question of undue governmental involvement with religion is apt to be raised because the religious interests

Dexter L. Hanley, S.J. is Professor of Law at Georgetown University Law Center.

[1] Some of the language in Everson v. Board of Educ., 330 U.S. 1, 15 (1947) implies that all aids to religion are unconstitutional. See pp. 10–11 infra. Mr. Justice Douglas seems to conclude that all financial aids from the state are unconstitutional and on this ground questions the legitimacy of use of tax funds to support the chaplaincy. Engel v. Vitale 370 U.S. 421, 437 n. 1 (1962) (concurring opinion).

and commitments of the chaplain as clergyman usually bear on these activities, a fact that explains in large part why he is assigned such duties.

The courts have never ruled on the constitutionality of the chaplaincy, mainly because no one had standing to bring suit until very recently, and perhaps not even now.[2] The Supreme Court in *Frothingham v. Mellon*[3] held that a taxpayer does not have the requisite standing to litigate the constitutionality of federal tax expenditures and programs. That case required the litigant to show not only the invalidity of the statute challenged, but also a direct injury to himself or an immediate threat of harm. It was not enough to show that he suffered in "some indefinite way with people generally," for example with millions of other taxpayers who object to allegedly unconstitutional expenditures. However, this doctrine has come in for substantial criticism by legal scholars.[4] Some urge that an exception be made in sensitive areas where the constitutional issues involved are amenable to effective investigation and resolution by the judicial process, as in cases involving the establishment clause of the First Amendment.[5] This argument was raised in a recent taxpayer suit [6] challenging the constitutionality of the Elementary and Secondary Education Act of 1965 [7] because of the benefits extended there-

[2] Lower courts have dismissed for want of standing those cases thus far initiated against the chaplaincy. Hughes v. Priest, Civil No. 4681–55, D.D.C., Jan. 12, 1956, *appeal dismissed,* Appeal No. 13293, D.C. Cir. May 16, 1956; Elliott v. White, 23 F.2d 997 (D.C. Cir. 1928). The Supreme Court, however, has *sub silentio* acknowledged the legality of the chaplaincy by upholding a judgment of the Court of Claims awarding a deceased chaplain's longevity pay to his executrix. United States v. LaTourette, 151 U.S. 572 (1894). Even though the parties did not raise the question of constitutionality the Court would have done so if it had serious doubts on the matter since the award would have been without jurisdiction if the chaplaincy is illegal.

[3] 262 U.S. 447 (1923).

[4] *E.g.,* Davis, *Standing to Challenge Governmental Action,* 39 MINN. L. REV. 353, 386–91 (1955); Jaffe, *Standing to Secure Judicial Review: Public Actions,* 74 HARV. L. REV. 1265 (1961).

[5] *See, e.g.,* Jaffe, *supra* n. 4.

[6] Flast v. Gardner, 271 F.Supp. 1 (S.D.N.Y. 1967).

[7] 20 U.S.C. §§ 236–44, 331–36, 821–27, 841–48, 861–70, 881–85 (Supp. 1965). Title I of the Act provides for multi-purpose grants to local boards of education to improve the quality of education in school districts having a substantial number of low-income families. 20 U.S.C. § 241a (Supp. 1965). The theory is that grants

under to children attending church-related schools. A three-judge court convened in the Second Circuit dismissed the case, relying on the *Frothingham* decision. There was a vigorous dissent which argued that a federal taxpayer who claimed that tax funds were being applied in violation of the establishment clause alleged a sufficiently personal interest to justify standing. The dissent took the position that a taxpayer who claimed that he was being compelled to provide financial support to a religion, particularly when not of his choosing, alleged a "vital, intimate and grave hurt against which the establishment clause was meant to guard." [8]

The Supreme Court reversed the decision, but did so on grounds that leave some doubt whether a taxpayer has standing to challenge the chaplaincy.[9] Chief Justice Warren, who wrote the Court's opinion, did not repudiate the *Frothingham* rule entirely, nor make an unqualified exception for all cases arising under the establishment clause. He held instead that a taxpayer has standing to sue when two conditions are met: first, that the challenge be to an expenditure of funds made pursuant to a "spending" program rather than one made incidentally to a "regulatory" program; and second, that the challenge rest on a specific constitutional limitation. The second requirement is met by a taxpayer's suit claiming the chaplaincy to be in violation of the establishment clause. There may be some question whether the first requirement is met. Expenditures necessary to support the chaplaincy can be characterized as incidental to the "regulatory" program

---

to such districts will benefit "educationally deprived children." The Act provides that some provision be made to benefit students in private elementary and secondary schools "to the extent consistent with the number of educationally deprived children" of the district who are enrolled in private schools. 20 U.S.C. § 241e (2) (Supp. 1965). The Act specifies that such benefits may include "special educational services and arrangements (such as dual enrollment, educational radio and television, and mobile educational services)." *Id.* Pursuant to this section of the Act the New York City school board undertook to send public school teachers into the local parochial schools to offer remedial instruction in mathematics and reading as well as guidance services. The petitioners in the *Flast* case challenged these arrangements as contrary to the "special services" standard of the Act and as unconstitutional aids to religion in any event. They also challenged the constitutionality of Title II of the Act, which provides for the loan of publicly owned textbooks for use by children attending private schools. 20 U.S.C. §§ 821–827 (Supp. 1965).

[8] 271 F.Supp. at 6.   [9] 392 U.S. 83 (1968).

of integrating clergymen into the military services to satisfy the spiritual needs of the men and therefore may not clearly fall within the category of a "spending" program.

Despite these doubts there is good reason to expect that a taxpayer will be able to challenge any governmental expenditure under the establishment clause. The Supreme Court has shown a growing disposition to make available a forum in which the individual citizen can challenge governmental action under that clause. At one point the Court refused to take an appeal from a state court suit unsuccessfully challenging local Bible-reading ordinances and practices because the petitioners had failed to allege any expenditures of public funds that would give them an interest as taxpayers.[10] However, in *Engel v. Vitale* [11] and *School District of Abington Township v. Schempp* [12] the Court heard appeals from cases challenging similar devotional exercises in the public schools by schoolchildren and their parents. The Court did not even advert to the standing problem in *Engel,* while in *Schempp* it did point out in a footnote that schoolchildren and their parents surely had standing to complain about being subjected to practices violative of the First Amendment.[13]

In any event, the staunchest supporters of the chaplaincy probably would not want to rely on the doctrine of standing to sue to remove that institution from scrutiny under constitutional standards. The doctrine is a technical and constitutionally important device for maintaining the proper balance between the judiciary and the other branches of government, and it ensures "that the plaintiffs have 'such a personal stake in the outcome of the controversy as to assure that concrete adverseness which sharpens the presentation of issues upon which the court so largely depends for illumination of difficult constitutional questions.' " [14] When a suit is dismissed for want of standing, no decision is rendered on the practices which are being challenged. Since chaplains as theologians and as government of-

---

[10] Doremus v. Board of Educ., 342 U.S. 429 (1952).
[11] 370 U.S. 421 (1962).   [12] 374 U.S. 203 (1963).   [13] *Id.* at 224 n. 9.
[14] School Dist. v. Schempp, 374 U.S. 203, 266 n. 30 (Justice Brennan concurring) (citing and quoting Baker v. Carr, 369 U.S. 186, 204 [1962]).

ficials have the duty to act within the confines of the Constitution, their concern should not be with standing but rather with the substantive question: Does the existence of the chaplaincy contravene the Constitution?

A TRADITION OF CONSTITUTIONALITY

The chaplaincy shares the heritage of the United States Armed Forces.[15] The institution antedates the Constitution, and its uninterrupted history through the prerevolutionary period up to the present bears witness that it is generally accepted as legitimate. With few exceptions early American statesmen did not think that the chaplaincy's legitimacy was put into question by the establishment clause. As early as 1758, Virginia established a chaplain program which was subsequently embraced by Colonel George Washington. The first federal or national chaplaincy was created by a Continental Congress resolution of July 29, 1775; and in the following year, General Washington specifically authorized and encouraged the use of chaplains.[16] In 1791, two years after the organization of the American Army, the same Congress which studied the "wall of separation" and formulated the First Amendment increased the salaries of chaplains to fifty dollars per month and established the policy which exists today—the chaplain serves with rank but without command function.[17]

James Madison, perhaps the most articulate spokesman of separation, opposed these congressional appropriations to the chaplains. Although he was successful in urging two-thirds of the House of Representatives to propose the First Amendment to the Constitution, he was

---

[15] For historical discussions of the chaplaincy see 1 A. P. STOKES, CHURCH AND STATE IN THE UNITED STATES 267–73 (1950) [hereinafter cited as STOKES]; 3 STOKES & PFEFFER, CHURCH AND STATE IN THE UNITED STATES 35–36 (1967) [hereinafter cited as STOKES & PFEFFER] Hermann, *Some Considerations on the Constitutionality of the U.S. Military Chaplaincy,* 22 THE CHAPLAIN 32, 33–38, 42–43 (1965); Klug, *The Chaplaincy in American Life,* 23 THE CHAPLAIN 15, 17–30 (1966); U.S. DEPT. OF THE ARMY, AMERICAN ARMY CHAPLAINCY—A BRIEF HISTORY, PAM 165–1 (1955).

[16] 1 STOKES 271.

[17] Act of Mar. 3, 1791, tit XXVIII, ch. 28 §§ 5, 6, 1 Stat. 222–23.

unsuccessful in convincing the House that expenditures for the chaplaincy contravened the amendment upon which they had acted. Of this defeat he later wrote:

It would have been a much better proof to their constituents of their pious feeling if the members contributed for the purpose a pittance from their own pockets. As the precedent is not likely to be rescinded, the best that can now be done may be to apply to the Constitution the maxim of the law, *de minimis non curat*.[18]

From 1852 through 1854 various congressional studies of the constitutionality of the chaplaincy were made, and all challenges to the chaplaincy were roundly defeated. The Committee on the Judiciary of the House of Representatives reported:

While your committee believes that neither Congress nor the army or navy should be deprived of the service of chaplains, they freely concede that the ecclesiastical and civil powers have been, and should continue to be entirely divorced from each other. But we beg leave to rescue ourselves from the imputation of asserting that religion is not needed to the safety of civil society. It must be considered as the foundation on which the whole structure rests. Laws will not have permanence or power without the sanction of religious sentiment—without a firm belief that there is a power above us that will reward our virtues and punish our vices.[19]

[18] Letter from James Madison to Edward Livingston, July 10, 1822, 3 LETTERS AND WRITINGS OF JAMES MADISON 274 (1884). See also 1 STOKES 347. The timing of the First Amendment and of the appropriations for the chaplaincy is not entirely clear but this disagreement does not disprove that the framers of the First Amendment rejected the argument that the chaplaincy was unconstitutional. Professor Sutherland contends that: "[I]n Spring 1792, with the First Amendment just two months old, the House of Representatives undertook to expand the Armed Forces. They set up a Table of Organization in the statute which took effect March 5, 1792. It provided for one Major General . . . and a chaplain. His pay was the very considerable sum of $50 per month. . . . One of the congressmen who voted to establish the chaplain and give him pay was James Madison, who had provided the First Amendment, which had been a part of the Constitution for two months."
Sutherland, *The U.S. Constitution and the Military Chaplaincy*, THE MILITARY CHAPLAIN, May–June 1965, pp. 21, 28.
[19] H.R. REP. No. 124, 33d Cong., 1st Sess., March 27, 1854. *See also* STOKES & PFEFFER 480.

Briefly assessed, the impact of the chaplaincy upon the country has been a healthy one. Before the Revolutionary War an American colonial's ties were primarily to his own colony and to the dominant sect in that area, as A. P. Stokes and Leo Pfeffer have pointed out, but the war changed this.

> Massachusetts Congregationalists, Rhode Island Baptists, New York Episcopalians and Dutch Reformed, New Jersey Presbyterians, Pennsylvania members of many small Protestant sects with a continental background, Maryland Roman Catholics, and a scattering of Jews from seaboard cities . . . met in the same camps and acquired a new idea of the need and possibility of religious tolerance. . . .
> The contribution of the chaplains to these results was important. Detached from their own local church, they developed a sense of responsibility for all the men in their regiment and rendered a large service.[20]

Professor Pfeffer, a scholar who usually reads the establishment clause restrictively, suggests that the "overwhelming majority of the American people are satisfied with the chaplaincy system in the military forces and do not seriously doubt its constitutionality or its wisdom." [21] He further suggests that the chaplaincy is not an old-world relic doomed to extinction; rather, it characterizes "the government's attitude toward religion. It is sympathetic with the cause of religion, appreciates its significance in individual and national life, and encourages provisions for worship in all branches of military service, while at the same time retaining an impartial attitude toward the various denominations." [22] The institution is "a tradition that commends itself to the great majority of Americans." [23]

Thus the origin and continued existence of the Chaplains Corps manifest "a rationally conceived and deep-seated policy, and not an accidental or vestigal survival of outmoded practices." [24] In fact, the historical data on the interplay in 1791 between the appropriation of chaplaincy funds and the proposal of the First Amendment compels the inference that the First Amendment was not intended to disrupt the tradition of the chaplaincy.

---

[20] *Id.* at 35.   [21] *Id.* at 472.   [22] *Id.* at 471.   [23] *Id.* at 482.
[24] Kauper, *The Constitutionality of Tax Exemptions for Religious Activities*, THE WALL BETWEEN CHURCH AND STATE 95, 110 (Oaks ed. 1963).

Nevertheless, the Supreme Court has warned that arguments relying on history, logic, or efficacy to reject the distinctions which have
been made about the First Amendment are "entirely untenable and
of value only as academic exercises." [25] And again it is said that "a
too literal quest for the advice of the Founding Fathers upon the
issues of these cases seems . . . futile and misdirected." [26] While this
advice is sound, it does not, and should not, require the Court to shun
entirely the wisdom of the past. The words of Mr. Justice Holmes
bear repeating: "[I]f a thing has been practiced for two hundred
years, it will need a strong case . . . to affect it." [27] What is clear
from the cases later to be discussed is that the Supreme Court has
held beyond cavil that the First Amendment is applicable to the
states through the Fourteenth Amendment and that the government
may not support or prefer either individual religious beliefs or religion in general. We shall consider how these distinctions apply to
the Chaplains Corps in the following section.

THE GOVERNING LEGAL PRINCIPLES

Starting with *Everson v. Board of Education*,[28] one can find language in Supreme Court decisions indicating that aid to religion violates the establishment clause. Although the Court in that case upheld
a New Jersey statute that authorized the state to reimburse parents
whose children used regular bus transportation to and from school, including parochial institutions, today it is obvious that the greatest constitutional impact of the Court's opinion came from the following
statement:

The "establishment of religion" clause of the First Amendment means
at least this: Neither a state nor the Federal Government can set up a
church. Neither can pass laws which aid one religion, aid all religions,
or prefer one religion over another . . . No tax in any amount, large

[25] School Dist. v. Schempp, 374 U.S. 203, 217 (1963). The Supreme Court has
often uprooted long-standing practices. *E.g.,* Torcaso v. Watkins, 367 U.S. 488
(1961) (requirement of oath-taking in Maryland for public office).

[26] School Dist. v. Schempp, 374 U.S. 203, 237 (Justice Brennan concurring).

[27] Jackman v. Rosenbaum Co., 260 U.S. 22, 31 (1922).

[28] 330 U.S. 1 (1947).

or small, can be levied to support any religious activities or institutions, whatever they may be called, or whatever form they may adopt to teach or practice religion.[29]

The Court reinforced this statement with its holding in *McCollum v. Board of Education* [30] which declared unconstitutional religious instruction given by private religious agencies in regular public school classrooms during school time to students whose parents consented. The Court, relying on a no-aid theory of establishment, summarily rejected the argument that "historically the First Amendment was intended to forbid only government preference of one religion over another, not an impartial governmental assistance of all religions." [31]

The theme that the state cannot aid religion in general even when all sects are treated equally was repeated in *Engel v. Vitale*,[32] which declared unconstitutional the daily recitation in New York schools of a nonsectarian prayer officially formulated by the Board of Regents. Even though the recitation by the students was voluntary, the Court found a clear violation of the establishment clause because its prohibition "does not depend upon any showing of direct governmental compulsion and is violated by the enactment of laws which establish an official religion whether those laws operated directly to coerce non-observing individuals or not." [33]

Meanwhile, in cases decided after the *McCollum* decision, the Court developed two different themes that have provided counterpoint to the no-aid strain. In *Zorach v. Clauson* [34] the Court, speaking through Mr. Justice Douglas, referred to the concept of accommodation. Pursuant to this concept the state may provide religion with aid to relieve it of disadvantages resulting from governmental action. Thus in *Zorach* the Court held that the strictures of the *McCollum* decision did not apply to "released time" programs allowing public school students to leave the school grounds during classroom time to attend privately conducted classes in religious instruction. Mr. Justice Douglas said: "When the state encourages religious instruction or cooperates with religious authorities by adjusting the schedule of public events to sectarian needs, it follows the best of our traditions. For

---

[29] *Id.* at 15.   [30] 333 U.S. 203 (1948).   [31] *Id.* at 211.
[32] 370 U.S. 421 (1962).   [33] *Id.* at 430.   [34] 343 U.S. 306 (1948).

it then respects the religious nature of our people and accommodates the public service to their spiritual needs." [35] This limitation of the no-aid principle arises from the interplay of the free exercise and establishment clauses, which was noted by Mr. Justice Brennan in his concurring opinion in the *Schempp* case:

This case [*Quick Bear v. Leupp,* 210 U.S. 50 (1908)] forecast, however, an increasingly troublesome First Amendment paradox: that the logical interrelationship between the Establishment and Free Exercise Clauses may produce situations where an injunction against an apparent establishment must be withheld in order to avoid infringement of free exercise.[36]

In the *Zorach* case the public's interest in religious education permitted the accommodation of religion represented by released time programs; there was no constitutional compulsion requiring that the aid be given. However, as the language of Mr. Justice Brennan quoted above suggests, there are times when the free exercise clause requires that religion be accommodated. The case of *Sherbert v. Verner* [37] is an instance of required accommodation. In that case the Court compelled South Carolina to excuse a claimant for unemployment compensation from the condition that she stand ready to accept available employment when to do so would require her to violate observance of her Sabbath.

The second theme running counter to the no-aid motif is the secular purpose and primary effect test of nonestablishment. This test does not depend on the free exercise clause. It proceeds, instead, from the premise that the establishment clause was not meant to deny religion all the incidental benefits arising from governmental programs directed to a secular structuring of the public order. The test was first applied in *McGowan v. Maryland,*[38] a case challenging state Sunday-closing laws. The Court upheld the laws involved because their present purpose and effect is to serve the general welfare of society, wholly apart from any religious considerations. Nonetheless,

---

[35] *Id.* at 313–14.
[36] School Dist. v. Schempp, 374 U.S. 203, 247 (Justice Brennan concurring).
[37] 374 U.S. 398 (1963).   [38] 366 U.S. 420 (1961).

the Court recognized that the preference for Sunday as a day of recreation and rest was based on religious associations and that recognition of such a preference, even though for secular reasons, would
coincide with the religious interests of those who observe Sunday as
the Sabbath. This was conceived to be a legitimate, incidental aid to
religion not violative of the establishment clause.

The most recent pronouncement of the Court on the establishment
clause in the *Schempp* Bible-reading case [39] explicitly adopted this
test as the basic standard to determine constitutionality pursuant to
the establishment clause. Speaking for the court, Mr. Justice Clark
said:

[W]hat are the *purpose and primary effect* of the enactment? If either is
the advancement or inhibition of religion then the enactment exceeds
the scope of legislative power as circumscribed by the Constitution. That
is to say that to withstand the strictures of the Establishment Clause
there must be a *secular legislative purpose and a primary effect that
neither advances nor inhibits religion.*[40]

When the no-aid aspects of the establishment clause are harmonized
and integrated with the accommodation and secular purpose-effect
themes, the benefits accruing to religion from the chaplaincy are
readily justified. First, the general restraints of military life deprive
the individual of his freedom to such a degree that special provision
must be made to insure that he is able to exercise his religious right.
Some members of the Supreme Court, notably Justices Goldberg,[41]
Harlan,[42] and Stewart[43] have implied that the failure of the government to provide military chaplains could in itself be a violation of the
First Amendment. Mr. Justice Brennan, while not saying that the government *must* provide chaplains, points out why the government *may*
do so. He says:

[The chaplaincy may] be sustained on constitutional grounds as necessary
to secure to the members of the Armed Forces . . . those rights of worship guaranteed under the Free Exercise Clause. Since government has

[39] School Dist. v. Schempp, 374 U.S. 203 (1963).
[40] 374 U.S. at 222 (emphasis added).
[41] School Dist. v. Schempp, 374 U.S. 203, 306 (1963) (concurring opinion).
[42] *Ibid.*   [43] *Id.* at 309 (dissenting opinion).

[152] DEXTER L. HANLEY, S.J.

deprived such persons of the opportunity to practice their faith at places of their choice, the argument runs, government may, in order to avoid infringing the free exercise guarantees, provide substitutes where it requires such persons to be. . . .

[H]ostility, not neutrality, would characterize the refusal to provide chaplains and places of worship for prisoners and soldiers cut off by the State from all civilian opportunities for public communion.[44]

In short, to constrict the right of free exercise and yet to press the establishment clause to its limits would be unnecessary, or perhaps even hostile to religion. It would be ironic indeed to deny the soldier the opportunity of celebrating his marriage, baptizing his children, or receiving last rites when those who do not believe in a Supreme Being and yet conscientiously object to war may be exempted from military service in order that they may practice their convictions.[45]

Thus, the applicability of the establishment clause of the First Amendment can be determined only if the amendment is read and applied in its entirety. To evaluate the chaplaincy upon the establishment clause alone is to deny the right of free exercise which the framers of the Bill of Rights sought to protect.

Second, the chaplaincy can be justified under the secular purpose and primary effect test of the *Schempp* case. In structuring the total environment of the serviceman's life the Government is interested in providing appropriate facilities and opportunities to fulfill his various needs, including that for religious services and guidance. The ordinary citizen integrates, if he wishes, his religious and secular life. He lives near a church or he establishes patterns of private conduct which bear upon his religious practices. He has a *stability* by reason of his environment. People in government hospitals, in prisons, in the military service, Indians, those associated with the military academies, congressmen assembled in deliberation—for these there is not the same opportunity. A soldier subject to military orders does

---

[44] *Id.* at 297–99
[45] United States v. Seeger, 380 U.S. 163 (1965). *See* Conklin, *Conscientious Objector Provisions: A View in the Light of Torcaso v. Watkins*, 51 GEO. L. J. 252 (1963).

not have the same opportunity as a civilian to seek religious counsel on his own time and in his own way. Thus the government has compensated for certain hindrances to be found in these situations, as for instance, the lack of stability.

Another aspect of the government's secular interest in providing opportunities for religious activities should be distinguished. This is the interest in satisfying the basic psychological and spiritual needs of the men in order to maintain their morale. The effectiveness of the chaplaincy in such matters cannot be overestimated. It is a fundamental principle of our government that access to religious services raises the morale and increases the effectiveness of our fighting force.[46] The executive branch of the government has declared that it is the "policy of the government to encourage and promote the religious, moral, and recreational welfare and character guidance of persons in the Armed Forces" and thereby to enhance the military preparedness and security of the nation.[47]

Men in uniform need more than military discipline to weld them into an effective fighting force. An army may fight on its stomach but it lives on its morale. High morale is essential in producing victories. Men, deprived of the opportunity to practice their religion, will, undoubtedly, lack that positive spirit that brings victory. Likewise, spiritual support given to their wives and families will increase the morale of the soldiers. There is no strictly "secular" alternative that can satisfy these needs of the fighting man.

If chaplains are considered essential to the successful conduct of war in Vietnam or anywhere else, then to support the unconstitutionality of the Chaplains Corps is to deny the use of what could be fairly called a bulwark of the "national defense."[48] For in addition to the power to conscript men and to requisition the properties necessary and proper to enable it to raise and support the armed forces, Congress not only has the power but the primary obligation to

---

[46] Governmental concern in bolstering the morale of our fighting forces by providing them with chaplains goes back to action taken by the First Congress. *See* n. 17 *supra*.

[47] Exec. Order No. 10013, Oct. 27, 1948.

[48] *Cf*. Ashwander v. TVA, 297 U.S. 288 (1936).

provide all the equipment and resources that may be necessary to win a war.[49]

The proper exercise of the war power is clearly not limited to time of war. It may be used also in time of peace,[50] during preparation for war,[51] and during the denouement after war.[52] Certainly, the power is not restricted to the winning of victories in the field, but it extends to every matter and activity related to war which substantially affect its conduct and outcome.[53] Thus regulations pertaining to the military service and its branches, such as the chaplaincy, if valid during actual wartime, may also be valid during peacetime, so long as they are reasonably related to military preparedness. The impossibility of creating and maintaining a Chaplains Corps only during war is a strong reason for its secular justification during peacetime.[54]

There is still another important secular reason why the state should take steps to satisfy the religious needs of enlisted men; it is to ensure that men subjected to a military regime are given appropriate and undiminished opportunities to exercise their *civil rights*. Surely one of the most basic *secular* interests of a democracy is the securing and promot-

[49] Alexander Wool Combing Co. v. United States, 334 U.S. 742 (1948); Lichter v. United States, 334 U.S. 742 (1948).

[50] Ashwander v. TVA, 297 U.S. 288 (1936).

[51] Silesian American Corp. v. Clark, 332 U.S. 469 (1947), *see* 3 STORY, COMMENTARIES ON THE CONSTITUTION §§ 1184–86 (1833).

[52] Woods v. Miller Co. 333 U.S. 138 (1948); Hamilton v. Kentucky Distilleries Co., 251 U.S. 146 (1919).

[53] Atherton v. United States, 176 F.2d 835, *cert. denied*, 338 U.S. 378 (1949).

[54] The advantages to the military are well summarized, though presented as an objection on constitutional grounds, by Herrmann, *supra* n. 15. These arguments, which go to the establishment clause, seem in fact to add weight to any argument founded on the war power: "Undeniably, a chaplaincy operating outside the realm of governmental employment is bound to create serious administrative problems. Thus military posts and stations might be expected to be besieged by a host of religious societies, each one of them vying for the support of Armed Services' personnel. Attendant disorder, and possible breaches of military security might well be occasioned. Further, the peculiar nature of the military establishment, maneuver exercises, and preparation for actual combat do represent serious obstacles to a wholly voluntary religious ministration. Granted also, that the present, orderly and systematized chaplaincy establishment has much to commend itself from pragmatic aspects: a method of apportioning chaplain's vacancies on the basis of nominal troop adherence to the particular religious grouping, a well functioning procurement and training schedule, satisfactory tenure, promotion and retirement incentives." *Id.* at 40.

ing of the freedom of its citizens in all areas. Freedom of religion appropriately falls within the scope of this secular interest, a relationship that is clearly evidenced by the inclusion of the religious liberty guarantee in the First Amendment along with such basic civil rights as freedom of speech and the press.

Although this argument depends to a significant extent on the free exercise clause, it differs from the accommodation argument previously made which attempts to reconcile the tension between the free exercise and establishment clauses. We are not talking here about a *conflict* of constitutional rights, a situation which would arise where a governmental action made it impossible for a person to practice his religion unless some special provision were made contrary to the strictures of an absolute no-aid view of the establishment clause. Such a case would arise where the government dispatched enlisted men to the battlefield or to an isolated outpost. Rather, what we are considering is the role that religion can play in governmental structuring of military life so that servicemen will have appropriate opportunities to practice their religion as they would have in civilian life. The chaplaincy, then, is one of those areas where pervasive governmental regulation affects religion in such a way that freely determined and developed religious interests can be properly taken into account in order to ensure that the government gives *civil rights* their proper scope. Mr. Justice Frankfurter, a staunch supporter of the doctrine of separation of church and state, recognized that the legitimate interaction between religion and government necessarily increased as the scope of the state's activities increased. He observed: "As the state interest in the individual becomes more comprehensive, its concerns and the concerns of religion perforce overlap. . . . No constitutional command which leaves religion free can avoid this quality of interplay." [55]

Constitutionality of Specific Aspects of the Chaplaincy

The reasons for upholding the constitutionality of the chaplaincy are so convincing that there are few dissenters from the proposition

[55] McGowan v. Maryland, 366 U.S. 420, 461–62 (1961) (Justice Frankfurter concurring).

that the Government should make some provision for clergymen in military life. A number of Supreme Court justices have through the years spoken with approval of the chaplaincy.[56] The one justice who has suggested that the chaplaincy runs afoul of the Constitution, Mr. Justice Douglas, appears to single out for criticism only the use of tax funds to support the religious ministry of chaplains.[57] Elsewhere he speaks of the chaplaincy with approval.[58] Similarly, Stokes and Pfeffer, although questioning the use of tax funds to support the chaplaincy,[59] nonetheless acknowledge the value of this institution to our nation.[60] Some people have been concerned about the intimate involvement of government with religion that the institution seems to necessitate. Since chaplains are integrated into the military forces, the state seemingly is directly regulating the activities of the churches. Thus fears are raised that the church will be subjugated to the state and the latter will be able to favor certain sects and dogmas. A related fear is that the relationship of the chaplain to the enlisted men will contain overtones of coercion, since his office appears to have the full weight of the military establishment behind it.

It is appropriate, therefore, to examine in some detail various aspects of the chaplaincy that might be questioned under either or both of the religion clauses. Problems arising because of (1) governmental regulation of the chaplaincy, (2) material support made available thereunder to religion and (3) the danger of coercion will be discussed separately. Finally, I will consider some special problems.

---

[56] Mr. Justice Reed spoke approvingly of the chaplaincy in McCollum v. Board of Educ., 333 U.S. 203, 253–55 (1948). Mr. Justice Goldberg, joined by Mr. Justice Harlan, states in his concurring opinion in School Dist. v. Schempp, 374 U.S. 203, 306 (1963) that "it seems clear . . . that the Court would recognize the propriety of military chaplains." Mr. Justice Stewart, in his dissenting opinion, refers to the chaplaincy as a necessary accommodation of religion required by the free exercise clause. Id. at 309. Mr. Justice Brennan, concurring in Schempp, cites the chaplaincy as a practice that is constitutional despite the aid it extends religion. Id. at 296.

[57] Engel v. Vitale, 370 U.S. 421, 437 n. 1 (1962) (concurring opinion).

[58] In Girouard v. United States, 328 U.S. 61, 64 (1946) Mr. Justice Douglas talks about the "essential contributions" made to the war effort by chaplains, along with others.

[59] See STOKES & PFEFFER 482.   [60] Id. at 35.

Integration of the Chaplaincy into the Military

The duties and functions of a chaplain encompass a broad spectrum. He conducts religious services for military personnel and their dependents, providing them with opportunities for public and private worship consistent with their religious belief, and administering the rites and sacraments they desire. He undertakes pastoral duties, providing counseling, spiritual guidance, visitation of the sick and the incarcerated. These functions often involve him with activities of religious groups and welfare agencies in civilian communities. The provision of religious instruction consonant with the persuasion of the individual is another one of the chaplain's duties. Because of his special competence he also acts as adviser and consultant to the commander and his staff on matters which pertain to religion, morals, and morale. This aspect of his duties calls for him to provide instruction directed to character guidance. It also involves him in the planning of cultural and social activities consistent with the religious needs of the command. In all these activities the chaplain acts pursuant to regulations established by the military authorities.

One can argue that the chaplain is thus subjected to military discipline in his religious ministry in an apparent violation of the separation of church and state. Although the argument makes some abstract logical sense, it is not at all weighty when one examines the realities of the chaplaincy, or even its formal legal structure, for that matter. As one commentator puts it: "[T]he churches alone, through their chaplains, provide the spiritual content and activation of the government's regulations." [61] Under the relevant regulations the chaplain is regarded as a "representative of his denomination in the Army." [62] Army regulations make a distinction between the chaplain's functions that directly concern religion or the spiritual needs of the enlisted men and those that concern the morale and general well-being of the command. With regard to the former the chaplain is regarded as a "religious leader," with duties "which normally pertain

[61] Klug, *The Chaplaincy in American Public Life,* 23 THE CHAPLAIN 15, 32–33 (1966).
[62] AR 165–15, para. 2e.

to his profession as a clergyman"; with regard to the latter he is a "staff officer," with duties "prescribed by law, modified by the mission, and distinctive condition and circumstances of the Department of the Army." [63]

Perhaps the clearest indication of the autonomy of the chaplaincy in matters spiritual, as well as an effective means of maintaining it, is the requirement in Army regulations that a chaplain obtain ecclesiastical endorsement prior to his appointment and that he maintain it in order to continue in the service.[64] Although such endorsement raises some problems concerning governmental coercion which will be discussed later, it does serve to maintain ecclesiastical control over the religious ministry of the chaplaincy. Thus, one of the official duties of the chaplain is to satisfy the religious obligations established by ecclesiastical authorities to ensure maintenance of denominational endorsement.[65]

Although the legal and administrative structure of the chaplaincy is designed to eliminate intrusions by military authorities, implementation of the regulations governing the ministry may create occasions for practices contrary to constitutional standards. Aside from isolated abuses resulting from a disregard of regulations, the operations of the chaplaincy have not for the most part raised issues of improper military interference in religious matters. A notable exception has been the chaplain corps' unified curriculum for religious instruction, which has provoked criticism in some quarters. The following objection touches upon the chaplain's role of religious instructor to dependents of the enlisted men:

For some years a situation has existed in the Protestant Sunday schools in the Armed Forces that gives cause for concern regarding violation of the First Amendment of the Constitution. Affected is the religious freedom of hundreds of Protestant chaplains and about 150,000 pupils in military Sunday schools. At issue is the official promotion of the "United Protestant Sunday School Curriculum for Armed Forces" (UPSSC) and, in the case of the Air Force, the mandatory use of this curriculum in all Sunday schools on Air Force bases. Also in question is the use of Unified Course materials. While these materials are not tech-

[63] *Id.* at para. 2a.   [64] FM 16–5, para. 15.   [65] *Id.* at para. 4.

nically required in the Armed Forces, they are so firmly backed by senior officers of the respective chaplaincies as to tip the scales heavily in favor of their use by chaplains. In the Air Force, only by special permission may substitute materials be used.[66]

This matter has also been raised in correspondence between the Department of Defense and a member of Congress.[67]

The chaplain has a responsibility for providing religious education to military personnel and their families.[68] To this end, "an Army-wide program of religious education has been approved by the Chief of Chaplains. Programs have been developed for the three faiths by representatives of those faiths to provide a progressive curriculum for religious instruction throughout the Army."[69] These programs are known as the "Unified Curriculum for Protestants," the "Our Way to God" series for the Catholics, and the "Religious School Curriculum for Jews."[70] Although the objection made to the programs is that their requirement or approval violates the right of religious freedom, it would seem to violate the establishment clause rather than the free exercise one. An absolute requirement to use the unified curriculum, whether by Army Regulations or by a directive of the Chief of Chaplains exercising military command within the Chaplains Corps, would be giving a preference to one viewpoint and denying equal expression to any other.[71]

But, as a matter of fact, such is not the case;[72] the use of the unified curriculum is not required by any army regulation or by any directive of the Chief of Chaplains. This writer can testify from his

[66] Christianity Today, July 17, 1964 p. 21.

[67] Letters from Congressman Anderson to the Secretary of Defense, July 27, 1964 and to Chaplain Rhea, Sept. 29, 1964; replies from the Armed Forces Chaplain Board, Chaplain John I. Rhea, July 31, 1964, and Oct. 5, 1964.

[68] FM 16-5, paras. 33-34 (1964).

[69] Id. para. 34a.

[70] Ibid.

[71] Cf. School Dist. v. Schempp, 374 U.S. 203 (1963); Engel v. Vitale, 370 U.S. 421 (1962). It is less clear that there would be any violation of freedom of exercise. So long as there is no compulsion to attend classes, such a procedure lacks even the appearance of coercion which has elicited some comment in the School Prayer Cases—though even here, the Court has never relied on coercion.

[72] The author has here relied on materials supplied by the Chaplain Board containing excerpts from the Chief of Chaplains policy.

own experience [73] that the proffered freedom of choice is indeed exercised by individual chaplains. The Office of the Chief of Chaplains supports efforts to implement the curriculum and positively encourages denominational Sunday schools separate and apart from the general-type Sunday school. This approach, allowing full freedom to the chaplain and to the church, should be immune from constitutional attack.

Nevertheless, it has been urged that the Armed Services Chaplains Board "should do nothing more than make available information about materials." [74] Yet the frequent shifting of Army personnel makes it highly desirable that a uniform course of study be followed by the dependents as they transfer from post to post. The advantages of co-ordinated buying are obvious, both in terms of cost and of availability. The training of teachers by chaplains is important, and the skills gained in one course of study should not be lost because a different plan of study is used in a later station. For the military man, the armed forces constitute a "single parish," for it is only within the service as a *whole* that he can find stability. Thus, the Armed Forces Chaplains Board performs a necessary service when it makes available a single course on a world-wide basis, co-ordinated with audio-visual aids [75] and specialized libraries.[76]

A brief comment may be in place here on another aspect of military control of religious material and facilities. Nonappropriated funds are administered under military regulations and controls.[77] This form of administration is necessitated by the nature of the military, the

[73] During the summers of 1961–1964, he was engaged in helping chaplains in Europe to set up religious instruction programs and in the training of teachers for these programs. Visiting posts and bases in Germany, France, and Italy, he had extensive contact with the chaplains and with the programs. The programs differed widely and were under the direct control of the local chaplains. The availability of approved texts and the opportunity for simplified ordering commended the approved programs to many of the chaplains, while many others used texts of their own choices.

[74] CHRISTIANITY TODAY, July 17, 1964, p. 22.

[75] *See, e.g.,* Guide to Films and Filmstrips, Hq., Second U.S. Army, August 1964.

[76] Basic Religious Education Libraries have been set up for the major faiths and distributed throughout the Army commands.

[77] AR 230–36.

possibility of frequent transfer, and the need to account for the use of the funds. The regulations may be interpreted as saying: "A chaplain will not accept voluntary offerings unless they are given with the understanding that they are subject to accounting and disbursement proceedings as outlined in regulations." This is not an exercise of control by the government over church property and is not an undue interference in church administration.

Material Aid Extended to Religion

Once it is conceded that some governmental action can appropriately be taken to meet the religious needs of the men, the practicalities of the situation prevent separate arrangements for each of the many denominations ministering to the enlisted men. Some degree of coordination and standardization is necessary and is most efficiently achieved by having the Government undertake the responsibility for furnishing the necessary facilities and material. More than efficient use of resources is involved. Government coordination is probably the only way in which to see that the greatest provision is made for numerous different denominations so that the diverse religious interests of the men will be satisfied as far as is practical. The coordination and standardization accompanying governmental action tend to secure equal treatment of the various denominations as required by the establishment clause. As long as conformity is not imposed on dissenting denominations contrary to their religious principles, no serious constitutional harm is threatened.

Army regulations provide for a chapel, activity room, and educational facilities. It should be noted that all religious facilities and ecclesiastical materials purchased from appropriated funds are nondenominational in character.[78] This standardization of equipment and supplies "has meant a substantial economy in dollars as well as the actual betterment of individual items of religious equipment and supplies."[79] This over-all planning enables the services to provide for

[78] See AR 210–115, paras. 5–8, 10–11, 13–15. Some few items, supplied by the military, are denominational in character. *See, e.g., id.* para 13 (chaplain's kits). *But see id.* para 14 (sacred items).

[79] Address by Chaplain C. E. Zielinski, Office Chief of Air Force Chaplains (undated).

religious needs either "in a well-appointed standard chapel or under the severest conditions of improvision in combat zones." [80] The military supply system provides only those materials which can be used by all chaplains. Thus, both by reason of economy and of military need, standardization and regulations serve the good of the serviceman and of the services. If, then, the chaplaincy itself is justified, there seems to be no special constitutional question which arises from implementing the function of the chaplain by providing chapels and equipment.

Of a somewhat different nature is the problem of adequate facilities for religious education. The following may help to put the problem into focus:

We have planned chapel annexes to serve the purpose of a religious community center, available for such allied activities as religious education, character guidance lectures, youth activities, scouting activities and the like. It might be of interest at this point to stress the fact that there exists a very cogent reason on the part of the Government to provide (these facilities). . . . Personnel serving in the Armed Forces have given up all personal freedom of movement for the common good and must live out their lives where directed by the military. Thus, in many instances, a military reservation must become a self-contained community. An integral part of its life is the fostering of all factors which develop personnel not only physically but spiritually too.

In addition, please bear in mind that the Military Establishment today does not consist of men who have left their families behind them and have gone "off to war." Their families, in great part, are with them. Many of these dependents of service personnel live in government-sponsored housing areas adjacent to or located on military installations. It is not uncommon for chaplains to number their Sunday School children in the hundreds. This important fact demands continued vigilance on the part of the chaplain to insure that these young lives are developed fully in spiritual matters in accordance with the will of their parents.[81]

Basic materials for religious instruction, whether chosen from items in the unified curriculum or individually selected by the chaplain, may be purchased from appropriated funds.[82] All other literature of

[80] *Ibid.*   [81] *Ibid.*   [82] AR 210–15, para. 13.

a denominational nature must be purchased through the nonappropriated funds.[83] This limited use of appropriated funds for the approved purchases is based on the same reasoning which permits the erection of chapels. The military personnel, moving at government command, cannot take their own facilities with them. A properly set up and administered religious education program, effectively operating on large and small posts, requires over-all planning and some government expenditures.

A slightly different question may arise where the dependent schools are utilized for religious instruction. If this instruction is carried on as part of the school day, it may well run afoul of the constitutional limitations spelled out in *McCollum*. As a result of school-attendance requirements, school administrators would be lending their authority to a program of religious instruction. This is what *McCollum* considered an unconstitutional vice. But there should be no reason to prohibit the use of the school building during nonschool time. The general administration and care of buildings is committed to the commanding officer, who has a command responsibility both for the schooling and the religious education of his personnel.[84] He may lawfully permit the use of the school buildings by the chaplains, either for weekly instruction or for vacation schools. There would be no logic in requiring the government to build at its expense parallel facilities, although, of course, as we have seen, it is authorized to do so wherever these are thought to be feasible.

Finally, there is the question of salaries and pensions. Considered in the abstract, they can be viewed as a form of state subsidy to religion. Thus there are those who feel that the military personnel should contribute to their own religious care.[85] However, when the appropriations made to support clergymen enlisted in the military

---

[83] *See* AR 210–115, para. 16. These funds are established to support and promote the moral, spiritual, and social activities related to the religious program of the command. Dep't. of the Army, Army Regulation AR 230–36, para. 3 (1963). These funds consist of voluntary offerings, grants from other non-appropriated funds, interest on bank deposits or investments, and proceeds from sale of fund-owned property. *Id.* para. 15.

[84] AR 165–15, para. 8 (responsibility for religious life, morals, and morale of the command).

[85] See comments of James Madison set out in text at n. 18 *supra.*

service are placed in the context of a chaplaincy that not only is integrated into the military command but that also has welfare functions extending beyond a strictly "religious" ministry—and, as we have seen, such an office is such a highly desirable, perhaps necessary, means to achieving both secular and religious liberty ends as to be readily justified under the establishment clause—then such appropriations are not properly classified as grants-in-aid to religion. They are payments to chaplains for the special services they perform for the benefit of the military. To deny chaplains pay for their services, which are highly valued and encouraged by the government itself, would be an anomalous result that would convert the concept of non-establishment from one indicating neutrality to one indicating hostility toward religion.

The appointment of auxiliary chaplains and the use of these chaplains and of civilian clergymen paid by appropriated funds are also authorized.[86] Because of the chaplain's responsibility to all members of the command, he is instructed:

So far as practicable, opportunity will be provided for members of the command to receive the ministrations of their own religious faith in such ways and on such occasions as are appropriate to their respective denominational requirements. The responsible chaplain may accomplish this objective through his own services and through the cooperative efforts of other chaplains, civilian clergymen, or authorized lay leaders.[87]

Thus, while guaranteeing the freedom of the chaplain, regulations also provide for the opportunity of denominational worship. This seems consonant with the reasoning offered for the establishment of the chaplaincy itself, and the utilization where helpful or necessary of civilian personnel does not become unconstitutional.[88]

[86] Provisions for the employment and payment of civilian clergymen for religious services are contained in Army Regulations AR 1-11-FY, AR 165-35, AR 230-10, and AR 230-36. *See* FM 16-5, para. 26a.

[87] AR 165-16, para. 3b.

[88] Anyone familiar with the difficulty of getting adequate civilian coverage at major installations and in the outposts will realize the impracticality of trying to afford an opportunity to worship if the military chaplaincy were not in existence to supervise and to minister.

Coercion and Religious Freedom

It might be argued that any co-operation of the Armed Services with religious exercises is enough to create an atmosphere of coercion.[89] Even though personnel are under no obligation to attend divine services, it might be argued further that this does not alter the unconstitutional vice. In this regard, one can recall the concurring opinion of Mr. Justice Brennan in *School Dist. v. Schempp*: "[T]he excusal procedure itself necessarily operates in such a way as to infringe the rights of free exercise of those children who wish to be excused." [90] Yet, even Mr. Justice Brennan recognized in the same opinion that the case of the military is distinguishable from that of the schools.

For one thing, there is no element of coercion present in the appointment of military . . . chaplains; the soldier . . . who declines the opportunities for worship would not ordinarily subject himself to the suspicion or obloquy of his peers. Of special significance to this distinction is the fact that we are here usually dealing with adults, not with impressionable children as in the public schools. Moreover, the school exercises are not designed to provide the pupils with general opportunities for worship denied them by the legal obligation to attend school.[91]

Further, although Mr. Justice Brennan in *Schempp* [92] and Mr. Justice Frankfurter in *McCollum* [93] found the excusal provisions to be coercive when coupled with religious exercise, this was not the ground for the Court's decision in the *School Prayer Cases*. Nor, for adults at least, should the right to dissent "involve the right to be spared the occasions for dissenting," nor should the privilege of dissent be equated with coercion of belief.[94]

In addition, it should be noted that an argument based on coercion can be met by establishing procedures which will guarantee the freedom of religious exercise. In *West Virginia Bd. of Educ. v. Barnette* [95]

---

[89] The general problems of coercion are aptly dissected by Brown, *Quis Custodiet Ipsos Custodes?—The School Prayer Cases,* 1963 THE SUPREME COURT REVIEW 1, 26–31 (Kurland, ed.).

[90] 374 U.S. 203, 288 (1963) (Justice Brennan concurring).

[91] *Id.* at 298–99.   [92] *Id.* at 288–90.   [93] 333 U.S. at 227.

[94] Brown, *supra* n. 89, at 28–29.   [95] 319 U.S. 624 (1943).

the Court held that public school children can not be required to salute the American flag, if this is contrary to their religious conviction. And, again, in *Torcaso v. Watkins* [96] the Court held that a candidate for public office could not be required to take an oath affirming a belief in God. Yet, in neither of these cases was there the slightest hint that the petitioner could enjoin the practice of either the flag salute or of the oath taking by others.

Thus, there does not seem to be any direct threat to the chaplaincy based on the free-exercise clause. Yet, surely, this is an area of constitutional protection where the chaplaincy should be most sensitive and concerned. It befits neither the officer nor the clergyman to overlook elements of subtle coercion which can be present if care is not taken. For this reason, this writer concurs in the suggestion of the U.S. Army Chaplain Board [97] that the field manual be changed from "the mission of the chaplain is to promote religion and morality" [98] to read "the mission of the chaplain is to assure the opportunity for religious worship and continued spiritual development for soldiers, their dependents and authorized personnel." This spirit of concern for the welfare of military personnel bespeaks the highest tradition of the chaplaincy and better expresses the fundamental reason for the Corps —service.

Attendance at services. In the Army, attendance at religious services *is not and may not* be compulsory.[99] Nevertheless, chaplains, under the direction of the commander, arrange and participate in military and public ceremonies.[100] The regulations provide that "although these ceremonies may include an invocation, prayer, or benediction, they will not be conducted as religious services but as military exercises." [101] There are many patriotic and public occasions in which the military are expected to participate, even though an invocation be offered. As an example, one might cite an inaugural parade. An honor guard, too, may be ordered as a military courtesy at a funeral.

---

[96] 367 U.S. 488 (1961).

[97] See Special Study in Connection with Project 65–13, wth accompanying Memorandum From Chaplain Wallace M. Hale, President (undated).

[98] FM 16–5, para. 3.   [99] AR 165–15, para. 11d(2).   [100] *Id.* at para. 3f.

[101] *Ibid.* It is also provided that, for patriotic affairs, tri-faith participation should occur when appropriate and possible. FM 16–5, para. 32.

The examples need not be multiplied to show that, so long as the affair is a *bona fide* military event, there is no constitutional need to eliminate the prayer.

Occasionally troops have been assembled to participate in maneuvers on some patronal feast day.[102] Although a particular sect may, during denominational services, call attention to some religious facet of a military occasion, it would seem to be unconstitutional to turn the military operation into a religious ceremony. Hence, it is suggested that such formations should not be denominated by the commander as religiously oriented. Nevertheless, should a particular chaplain desire to call attention to the coincidence of a formation and a feast day, he should be permitted to do so. Indeed, if a formation would otherwise be held or is thought militarily necessary, there seems to be no constitutional prohibition forbidding the commander from scheduling it so as to reflect a religious desire of some of the troops.[103] However, the wisdom of such a practice is subject to question, both from the military and the religious points of view.

The chaplain himself is not required to participate in any service contrary to the requirements of his denomination,[104] although, as pointed out, he has an obligation to see that the personnel are cared for so far as possible.[105]

In making announcements of church services and religious programs, the chaplain has various media at his disposal.[106] These include official bulletins, posted announcements, the sounding of "Church Call," display of the chaplain's flag, and the rotation among units for specific duties which contribute to the service. But "such participation must not be allowed to assume the appearance of compulsory attendance." [107]

A special problem is posed by the mandatory chapel programs of the military academies.[108] Although there may be a difference between requirements which can be imposed on a volunteer as opposed to the

102 *See* Herrmann, *Some Considerations on the Constitutionality of the U.S. Military Chaplaincy,* 22 THE CHAPLAIN 32, 44 (1965), citing CHURCH AND STATE, Sept. 1963, pp. 13, 15.

103 *Cf.* McGowan v. Maryland, 366 U.S. 420 (1961).

104 FM 16–5, para. 21b.   105 *Id.* at para. 25.   106 *Id.* at para. 31.

107 Id. at para. 31e.   108 *See* Herrmann, *supra* n. 102, at 45 n. 39.

soldier who is drafted, nevertheless there seems to be legitimate constitutional objection to any compulsory attendance at religious services.
Not only does the procedure seem to offend the guarantees involved
in *Barnette* and *Torcaso,* but analogically seems contrary to *Speiser
v. Randall.*[109] That case protected the freedom to engage in constitutionally protected activities by holding that a tax exemption could
not be conditioned upon a willingness to take a loyalty oath. So here,
the right to enter military service and to seek education as a professional officer cannot be conditioned upon attendance at religious
services. The regulations, it is true, are promulgated by the academies
and are not part of ordinary army procedure. Nevertheless, the chaplaincy should disassociate itself from all such mandatory programs.

Character guidance. The importance of the Army character-
guidance program is emphasized in Army training.[110] The objective
of the program is to instill into all the members of the Army a sense
of individual moral responsibility.[111] It is concerned with the moral
fiber of the soldier: the kind of man he is, the principles and standards of his conduct and service.[112] The key words emphasized in the
program are "Duty-Honor-Country," which are held to be an integral
part of the military tradition.[113] The program is mandatory for all
enlisted personnel below the grade of E-6, who must participate one
hour per month.[114] Other personnel receive a monthly briefing.[115] The
instruction is confined to basic ethical and philosophical ideals, and,
as such, is not part of any particular religious belief.[116]

While the chaplain is the normal instructor for all character-
guidance training, the commander himself has over-all responsibility [117]
and is instructed to periodically assume the position of instructor.[118]

To avoid giving the program a superficially religious appearance,
instruction is forbidden in chapels or chapel facilities, except in case

---

[109] 357 U.S. 513 (1958).

[110] Dep't. of the Army, Training Circular 16–1 (1965) (hereinafter cited as TC
16–1).

[111] *Id.* para. 2a.   [112] *Id.* para. 3.   [113] *Ibid.*

[114] *Id.* para. 3a.   [115] *Id.* para. 3b.

[116] *Id.* para. 4a. The ideals of prudence, justice, fortitude, and temperance are
outlined. *Id.* para. 4b.

[117] AR 165–15, para. 8.   [118] TC 16–1, para. 4d.

of military necessity.[119] Special materials are made available for the program, along with teaching manuals, aids, and specific instructions. Nevertheless, it is common experience that chaplains are free to develop the materials as they think best. It might also be noted in passing that the task of conducting the character-guidance programs is not one which is sought after by the chaplain, but is a duty imposed on him, as one who is specially suited to develop basic philosophical tenets.

As so conceived and generally executed, this program runs afoul neither of the free exercise nor of the establishment clauses. It is oriented to developing in the soldier the character and the characteristics needed to defend our nation.[120] It seems to accord with the dicta of the Supreme Court in the *School Prayer Cases* where it was made clear that a school can offer courses in the history of religion, the literary study of the Bible, comparative religion, and so forth.[121]

The only feature of the program which could conceivably be attacked is the use of the chaplain, rather than other military personnel. However, his special qualifications are justification enough for assigning him to the task. Still, both the chaplaincy and commanders should remain vigilant to see that none of the programs in fact becomes a vehicle for proselytizing; they should remain basic ethical and philosophical courses. At the same time, one must recognize that religion and religious codes of conduct have much in common with philosophy and ethical codes.[122] This coincidence, however, should not lead to timidity in discussions.[123]

Forms and interviews. Upon entering a reception center, recruits are addressed by a chaplain and are informed of the religious programs offered. In addition to any general talk, each recruit has an

---

119 *Id.* para. 4e.   120 *See id.,* Appendix II, para. 3.

121 *See e.g.,* School Dist. v. Schempp, 374 U.S. 203, 225 (1963).

122 *See* McGowan v. Maryland, 366 U.S. 420, 442 (1961): "In many instances, the Congress or state legislatures concluded that the general welfare of society, wholly apart from any religious considerations, demands such regulation. Thus, for temporal purposes, murder is illegal. And the fact that this agrees with the dictates of the Judaeo-Christian religions while it may disagree with others does not invalidate the regulation."

123 *Cf.* Brown, *supra* n. 89, at 32–33 (speaking of the "establishment" of political, economic, and social ideals).

interview with a chaplain of his choice.[124] It is recognized that the new recruit is impressionable at this time and that the chaplain can influence his attitude toward religious activity.[125] The chaplain is instructed that he can indicate his own position as a volunteer in the army and speak of the services he is prepared to offer and of the opportunities in the service for worship, education, and personal growth.[126] The recruit is asked to fill out a card, setting forth his name, next of kin, home address, date and place of birth, and religious preference, along with other items.[127]

In the reception center, the chaplain is as much a counselor as a clergyman. Considering the problems attendant upon a shift to military service from civilian life and the desire of the recruit to be informed of the opportunities available to him, a compulsory interview with the chaplain seems justified. The general requirement that a form be completed and that a place be given to show a religious preference is likewise unassailable, especially since the chaplain is normally charged with conveying a notice of death when necessary.[128]

However, two points may give rise to legitimate objections. First, as regards the forms to be filled out, any requirement that a religious preference must be given should be eliminated. The form should clearly state that the marking of a religious preference is voluntary. Second, concerning the relationship between the recruit and the chaplain, any intimation by the recruit that he does not wish spiritual guidance should be respected. It is recognized that the time of induction is a critical one and that many a problem can best be settled before the soldier leaves for training. Nevertheless, if the over-all program of the chaplaincy is not to suffer and if all appearance of compulsion is to be avoided, the delicate balance which respects freedom of conscience must be achieved. This approach should be reflected in the Field Manual and in army regulations.

Other reports which the chaplain is asked to fill out and to forward

[124] "[An interview is] an integral part of the overall program of orientation given to the new men as soon as possible." FM 16–5, para. 74a.
[125] *Ibid.*   [126] *Ibid.*
[127] *See, e.g.,* Officer Qualification Record, DA Form 66, and Enlisted Qualification Record, DA Form 20.
[128] FM 16–5, para. 51. See also *id.* para. 27 (providing for a religious census).

through channels during the course of a soldier's military service seem immune from constitutional objection.[129] These reports are done either with the obvious approval of the subject (as in the case of a baptismal record), or in necessary accounting for military personnel (as in the case of marriage and funeral reports).

Endorsement. A principal requirement for appointment as a chaplain in any component of the Army is an ecclesiastical endorsement. The withdrawal of a chaplain's ecclesiastical endorsement by the denomination which he represents is a basis for terminating his commission and separating him from the service.[130] The requirement of an ecclesiastical endorsement is a matter of army regulations, not of statutory origin.[131]

Several questions may be posed regarding this requirement. First, may a man be deprived of his commission and separated from the military service on the ground that he does not have the endorsement of a religious body? The answer to this is "yes," so long as it is accepted that the very reason which justifies the existence of the chaplaincy is that it is a governmental effort to preserve and protect freedom of worship. It could hardly be said that the military service had properly cared for its personnel if the assigned chaplain did not have good standing in his denomination. Endorsement is necessary to serve the men adequately because quotas for assignments to the Chaplains Corps are based on the estimated needs of the military personnel.[132] Even though a chaplain not in good standing could see to the needs of his personnel through auxiliary chaplains and civilian aid, he would

[129] *See* Dep't. of the Army, Army Regulation AR 165–20 (1964) (religious and character-guidance activities reports).

[130] FM 16–5, para. 15.

[131] The National Defense Act, 41 Stat. 774 (1920), did provide that appointments as chaplains should be made from among persons duly accredited by some religious denomination and of good standing. Prior to World War II, it was discovered that many reserve chaplains had changed their ecclesiastical status and were no longer engaging in the ministry. Thus Dep't of the Army, Army Regulation AR 140–25, para, 2b–d (1941) required that there be an annual re-accreditation. In 1947, Sec. 506(g)(1) of the Officer Personnel Act of 1947, 61 Stat. 892, repealed the applicable section of the National Defense Act of 1920. See Dep't of the Army, Office of the Chief of Chaplains, Memorandum, Denominational Indorsing Agencies, para. 9, June 27, 1956.

[132] *See* AR 165–15, para. 2e.

not be performing the primary duties assigned, at least in the field
and for troops for whom he could not provide other coverage. The
added problem of costs for regular coverage also militates against
holding a man in service after he has lost denominational approval.

It can be admitted that the answer given above does not necessarily require severance; a situation can be imagined where a "nondenominational" chaplain could encourage religion and morality and
see to the spiritual and moral needs of the command.[133] But, on the
balance, the procedure to relieve him from duty is justified.[134]

The second and related question is, should a change of denomination on the part of the chaplain necessarily result in his dismissal from
the Chaplains Corps? The answer may depend on several factors.
What is the change and does this affect the quota? What are the
anticipated reactions of military personnel? Has he gotten ecclesiastical
endorsement from the new denomination? No hard and fast rule can
be given, and it is suggested that it is a matter for military determination by command officers and by the Office of the Chief of Chaplains.

Lastly, attention may be given for a moment to the objection that
a requirement of ecclesiastical endorsement is a violation of article six
of the Constitution, which provides that "no religious Test shall ever
be required as a Qualification to any Office or public Trust under the
United States." The objection, raised in the 1850's, was rejected by
the Congress, which in the Committee on the Judiciary stated:
"Everyone must perceive that this refers to a class of persons entirely distinct from chaplains." [135] Yet, in another sense, no religious
test *is* in fact imposed upon the chaplain. The purpose of the chaplaincy is to serve the needs of military personnel. Selection of chaplains is by quota as a matter of administrative necessity. If there were
a sufficient demand by humanists for religious guidance, even by those
who do not profess a belief in God, there would be no real barrier to
the appointment of a secular humanist to the chaplaincy. Thus, the

[133] *See* FM 16–5, para. 3 (status and mission).

[134] It has been stated that the withdrawal of indorsement is occasioned by immoral conduct or by an unacceptable change in theology. See Memorandum, Status
of the U.S. Army Chaplaincy, CHTCB, Dec. 14, 1965.

[135] *See* Herrmann, *supra* n. 102, at 37.

Corps is "open" to any belief; the appointment depends upon needs.

Rank. There is a conflict of views about the advisability and the constitutionality of giving military rank to the chaplain.[136] The fear that rank can add a sense of coercion to otherwise unobjectionable remarks is not without some justification. A parallel may be found in the field of labor law. "Slight suggestions," it has been said, "as to the employer's choice between unions may have telling effect among men who know the consequences of incurring that employer's strong displeasure." [137] But the fallacy in the argument when applied to the chaplain is that he is without command function over the soldier.[138] Further removing any appearance of command authority is the regulation that chaplains are addressed as "chaplain" in all official communications and in the performance of duty as staff officers; in writing, his grade is given in parentheses.[139]

The chaplain is assigned to the staff of the commander.[140] In this capacity and in order to co-ordinate the chaplain's work in large units, a description of his staff position by rank is helpful. Further, the use of rank is helpful, if not necessary, in determining pay scales commensurate with office and function.[141] It may be also pointed out that, with rank, the chaplain is better fitted to carry out his assigned duties of counseling and of helping the enlisted personnel.[142] For these reasons, it is submitted that the practice of giving rank to the chaplains should be continued and that a successful constitutional attack, based on coercion, is unlikely.

Special Questions

In concluding, three other topics will be touched upon—the performance of the duty to visit personnel, the privileged status of com-

---

[136] *Compare* Klug, *The Chaplaincy in American Public Life,* 23 THE CHAPLAIN, 15, 33–34 (1966) *with* Herrmann, *supra* n. 102, at 39–40. Klug, *supra* at 38, cites THE CHRISTIAN CENTURY as being opposed.

[137] International Ass'n of Machinists v. NLRB, 311 U.S. 72, 78 (1940).

[138] 10 U.S.C. 3581 (1964); FM 16–5, para. 12c.

[139] AR 165–15, para. 2f; FM 16–5, para. 9b. This prescription, while apparently more directed to the prohibition of ecclesiastical titles, serves the purpose of indicating the function of the chaplain as being without command.

[140] AR 165–15, para. 2b.   [141] *See* Klug, *supra* n. 136, at 34.

[142] *See* Herrmann, *supra* n. 102, at 40.

munication to a chaplain, and the function of the chaplaincy in matters of national interest.

Visitations. The chaplain is obliged to visit and spend time with the personnel, especially with the troops.[143] He may have special assignments in ministering to prisoners,[144] and to hospitalized personnel.[145] He has an unusual opportunity to visit because of the openness of military life and because of his own staff function and duties, but he must correspondingly beware of any invasion of privacy or of pressure upon the personnel to accept his spiritual counseling and ministrations.[146] While he should energetically carry out his mission to visit the sick and the incarcerated and to make pastoral visits to barracks, quarters, training, and recreation areas,[147] he should do so in the spirit of helping all the personnel and he should distinguish this mission from that of religious ministrations. Where, for instance, a soldier clearly objects to being visited by the chaplain, the chaplain should accord to him the same courtesy of privacy as he would to a civilian family in an outside parish or congregation. This is in accord with official regulations.[148]

Privileged communications. Communications between a chaplain and an individual are privileged when the chaplain acts in his capacity as a clergyman or spiritual adviser, or when the individual performs a religious act.[149] While the emphasis of the privilege is on the fact that the chaplain is not required to divulge the information to investigators or at trial, the dimensions of the privilege should be marked out and safeguarded. In his relations to the commanding officer [150] and in conversation with other chaplains and military personnel, he must take great care to protect personal secrets. It would be

---

[143] FM 16–5, paras. 4f, 10b–c.

[144] Dep't. of the Army, Army Regulation AR 210–181, paras. 10, 21 (1957).

[145] *See* Dep't of the Army, The Chaplain's Ministry to Hospital Patients, Pamphlet 16–61 (1962).

[146] *See id.* paras. 4n, 28. The chaplain is cautioned against beginning prayer without the expressed desire of the patient and against baptizing without the consent of the parents.

[147] *See* FM 16–5, para. 4f.

[148] *See* AR 165–15, para. 4c(1).

[149] MCMUS 151(b)(2)(1951); AR 165–15, para. 3a; FM 16–5, para. 42.

[150] *See* AR 165–15, para. 5.

an improper, if not an unconstitutional, procedure to reveal confidential information, even to the commander. A failure to observe professional secrecy would seem, in part, to make the ministry serve purely secular aims and would deprive the soldier of a truly free exercise of religion.

Declarations on matters of public interest. A troublesome question which illustrates how delicate is the relationship of the church to the military has been broached by an editorial in *Ave Maria*.[151] The editorial questions a resolution passed by the Military Chaplains' Association at its convention at Atlanta, Georgia, strongly endorsing American policies in Vietnam. The major criticism of the editorial is that there is no presentation of *religious evidence* for the judgment which was given. Pointing out the dangers inherent in having the state further its political aims by appeals to religious conviction, it states: "One can muse about the fate of the chaplain who would go about the country discussing the morality of war in negative terms."

Three postures are theoretically possible. The chaplain may be free to disagree with military and political objectives; he may be required to maintain a neutrality and be limited to more directly spiritual discussions; he may be forbidden to express a view contrary to accepted military and political aims. Although from the church's vantage point the first choice is almost mandatory, it does not follow that the churchman is free to disagree with such policies while wearing the uniform. The premise of the American form of government is that it is a pursuit of justice and equality, that our domestic and foreign policies concord with our spiritual ideals. Lacking a touchstone of infallibility, political and military procedures must support decisions made by legitimate authority. The churchman who disagrees with these decisions can, it seems to this writer, either resign from the chaplaincy and speak out, or remain in the service to minister and remain silent. No other solution is politically feasible. For the government to require outspoken conformity to its judgments would be to infringe upon the constitutional freedom to follow one's conscience. On the other hand, to utilize the post of chaplain (set up by the government to safeguard

---

[151] May 21, 1966, pp. 4–5.

religious freedom while furthering legitimate secular and political aims) in order to undermine the secular aims of government is politically self-contradictory. While conscience must be a guide, one does not have the right to insist that his dissent can be expressed contrary to his military appointment or privileges.

RECENT DEVELOPMENTS

THOMAS J. O'TOOLE

Books on Religion, Law, and Society, September 1966–September 1967

In the relevant literature of the period surveyed nothing of striking novelty or force appeared. Several works of sound scholarship can be reported, and a few books of uncommon interest. The topics covered are so disparate that any scheme of organization seems somewhat arbitrary. Nevertheless, two major areas of interest can be readily discerned. Apparently as an aftermath of the Vatican Council, considerable attention continues to be paid to the concept of religious liberty, especially its logic and its limits. The relationship between law and morals continues to interest a number of authors, perhaps stimulated by legislative proposals and enactments in England and some of the states on such topics as homosexuality and abortion. Book-length treatment of the relationship between religion and our domestic and international problems is not found in the publishers' lists. This itself is perhaps the most significant feature of the year's literature.

RELIGIOUS FREEDOM

The late John Courtney Murray is the editor of a book of essays exploring the Declaration on Religious Freedom entitled *Religious Liberty: An End and a Beginning*.[1] His own contribution is an

Thomas J. O'Toole is Dean of Northeastern University School of Law.
[1] New York: The Macmillan Company, 1966. Pp. 192. $4.95.

especially revealing analysis of the manner in which the Declaration underwent fundamental change as it passed through revisions in the Vatican Council. The original draft or schema was based on concepts of freedom of conscience understood within an ecumenical context. Religious liberty was not proclaimed as intrinsically a human right, but as something which must be recognized if we are to practice moral virtue in interpersonal relations among religiously divided people. This moral virtue could not be realized unless civil society also respected freedom of conscience.

Such a formulation was not acceptable to the Council because there was no clear-cut relevant Catholic tradition on rights of conscience. The second draft, while essentially similar to the first, added the notion of human dignity as the source of religious freedom. This idea became central in the final draft, which approached the topic apart from the context of ecumenism and as a formally juridical concept. Religious freedom became an immunity from coercion by society. This idea was well rooted in historical experience, including our First Amendment. The immunity extends to both belief and action pursuant to belief. Hence dignity requires the grant of this immunity.

In the same volume, Frank J. Canavan expresses significant reservations concerning the Declaration. He views it as so wedded to the natural law tradition as to be unlikely to appeal to those outside this philosophical heritage. More seriously, he raises queries concerning the limits of religious freedom. The document itself recognizes the legitimacy of state restrictions on actions (even when religiously motivated) which endanger the "public order." This concept is vaguely defined in terms of the essentials for public peace, public morality, and the rights of citizens. The public morality notion is especially troublesome. Who is to define it? Is it subject to definition in terms of the predominant religious group in a society? Or is it a covert reference to the morality espoused by Catholics? Canavan would have preferred that the document argue for constitutional government rather than assume it to be normative. With such a provision there would be less concern over how public morality would be defined.

Other essays in this volume criticize the absence of Old Testament sources and the poor selection of New Testament texts in the Declaration. But throughout the book there are repeated expressions of concern over the verbal formula employed to sanction limitations on religious liberty. A wise and deeply tolerant concluding chapter by the Belgian Jesuit, George van Massenhose, focuses on the inadequacy of verbal formulations concerning the limits of religious freedom. He urges a personalist approach, directed towards the common good defined in nonsectarian terms. This would permit—indeed require— the state to curb aggressive intolerance even though it results from religious zeal. The state's role would be to protect persons, not to favor particular doctrines. Hopefully, mutual tolerance would lead to a social togetherness which would gradually dissolve the need for state intervention against religiously-motivated acts. Taken as a whole, this book provides a stimulating enquiry into the meaning of the Vatican Council's Declaration on Religious Freedom, with particular emphasis on the problems left unanswered by the Declaration.

Moved in part by concern over the vague limits on religious freedom experienced in the Vatican Council's Declaration, Philip Wogaman attempts to explicate a Protestant theological basis for religious freedom in *Protestant Faith and Religious Liberty*.[2] He suggests indeed that the doctrine of religious liberty may be a distinctively Protestant contribution to ecumenical dialogue. After analyzing several of the grounds which have been used as a foundation for theories of religious freedom, he declares each of them inadequate. The core of the inadequacy is that they are not efficacious against absolutist notions of truth and salvation.

For himself Wogaman finds the most dependable basis for religious liberty in two affirmations of traditional Protestant faith: a) God is always more than any human symbol or institution and b) man has direct access to God; therefore it is blasphemous for the state to intervene between God and man. Whatever value these principles may have in convincing Protestants of the validity of claims to religious freedom, they suffer from the fatal defect of being nonpersuasive to persons of some other faiths and to persons of no faith. If they are inherent aspects of traditional Protestantism, one must take note of

[2] Nashville: Abingdon Press, 1967. Pp. 254. $4.75.

the historical fact they have not sufficed to deter Protestants from denying religious freedom to others. They also do nothing towards defining the juridical limits of state authority to curb actions which are religiously motivated. Even if the central threat to religious liberty lies in absolutist doctrines of religious truth, an ecumenically acceptable theory of religious liberty still cannot be based on a begging of this question. Rather, ground must be sought which is common to all participants in the dialogue. At the moment it seems unlikely that a better basis than human dignity can be found.

Indeed, Lukas Vischer, contributing to a volume of essays entitled *Religious Freedom,*[3] issues a persuasive call for all the churches to join in accepting a common formula of convictions about religious freedom. He suggests that this would be the most effective way to give witness against any power which might seek to interfere with liberty. Other essays in the volume indicate some of the difficulties which now obstruct the path to this goal, especially in Israel, in Islamic or Hindu countries, and in Africa. This book, Volume 18 in the encyclopedic Concilium series, is extremely disappointing. Designed to reflect the contemporary renewal of theology, it fails to reflect the exciting developments in this vital area of religious freedom.

The age of apologetics has not entirely ended. The traditional Roman Catholic view that doctrine may develop but must never change underlies Dom Pius Augustin's book, *Religious Freedom in Church and State.*[4] This is essentially a reexamination of the Roman Catholic tradition on church and state in the light of the Second Vatican Council. It is an attempt, not fully successful, to demonstrate that Catholic doctrine has developed in a "unidirectual" fashion. The power cemented by Pope Innocent III to depose kings is viewed as a consequence of the accidental role of the papacy as Europe's only unifying force. The author emphasizes that the medieval popes refrained from *unequivocal* claims of a "direct" power in civil matters despite their frequent assertions of an "indirect" power. This thesis is very hard to maintain concerning Boniface VIII, and the claim

---

[3] Edelby & Jimenez–Urresti (eds.), New York: Paulist Press, 1966. Pp. 183. $4.50.

[4] Baltimore: Helicon Press, 1966. Pp. 328. $6.95.

of power over two swords he made in the bull *Unam Sanctum* is treated by the author as the product of polemics rather than of theology. In this fashion some of the inconvenient facts of history are fitted into the thesis that the Declaration on Religious Freedom is the most recent product of a strictly consistent line of development which began with the New Testament. If one cannot always share his theory of lineal development of doctrine, one must nevertheless admire the author's ability to set forth clearly and candidly the major episodes in the long history of the encounter between the Catholic Church and the states of the Western world. Not profound, but highly readable, this book provides a useful summary.

LAW AND MORALITY

Prominent among contemporary writers who have the happy faculty of presenting unpredictable propositions is Sidney Hook. He has an added and highly useful talent for defending his conclusions with a skill which serves to illuminate brightly the key issues. This is what he does in *Religion in a Free Society*.[5] Proceeding from secularist premises, he reaches some conclusions about the role of religion in democracy which may not be widely shared by persons of similar philosophical persuasion. For example, he deplores the heavy reliance which secularists have placed on the Supreme Court to maintain the neutrality of the state in matters religious. He sees the Court's judgments as shifting and uncertain, a poor safeguard for the maintenance of principles central to a pluralist society. The Court's false use of history leaves him scornful.

Rather than relying on litigation, Hook urges that confidence be placed in education to insure neutrality in religion. Only thus can we be secure against shifting majorities on the Court. Meanwhile, he would allow vestigial practices violating strict separation of church and state to continue. Bible reading in public schools presents to him no issue of religious liberty, because he does not believe that students who seek exemption from these exercises are viewed hostilely. These

[5] Lincoln, Neb.: University of Nebraska Press. 1967. Pp. 120. $4.00.

ceremonies are to him inconsequential pieties. Their uprooting causes great distress and, still worse, adds impetus to sectarian education. It follows that he would not exclude such programs as shared time, which is preferable to totally separate church schools.

Despite his willingness to make these practical accommodations, Hook remains rigorously secularist in his outlook. Religion is viewed as superfluous in public affairs, and can be no more than a private matter. Our political institutions, he insists, do not presuppose a Supreme Being. Indeed, if Justice Douglas' famous dictum were true, the state should support religious education. Hook's democratic state stands apart from all religious views but gives morality primacy over all social phenomena, including religion. This is a pragmatic morality, independent of religion both in theory and in practice. Religion and nonreligion are equally entitled to enjoy freedom in his democracy, but only if they play by the rules. As a caustic commentary on the history of church politics, Hook labels political liberty the residuary legatee of ecclesiastical animosities.

Hook's vigorous insistence that social morality is absolutely independent of religion is not fully explored in his slim volume. Obviously, it is central to his entire approach to church-state issues. He asserts that those moral views which we ascribe to our religion are actually established independently and are then transferred to God in order to make them more authoritative. Although recognizing that the efficacy of the religious sanction is a complicated empirical question, Hook declares that the role of religion in morality is at least superfluous and probably insignificant. Early moral training occurs without religion and is more nearly determinative of conduct than is any other factor.

This same problem of the relationship between law and morality is gently but incisively explored by Basil Mitchell in a volume based upon his Edward Cadbury Lectures at the University of Birmingham.[6] He begins with an examination of the debate between Lord Devlin and Professor Hart and concludes with his own views concerning the propriety of a Christian asserting on legislative issues his own moral

---

[6] London: Oxford University Press, 1967. Pp. 141. 25s.

position derived from his religious traditions. Scrupulously fair in his treatment of the views of others, tentative in his criticism, he nevertheless concludes that there are public issues which involve moral issues to which a religious morality has relevance. Rejected by him are views such as those of Professor Hook that a strictly utilitarian morality has greater legitimacy in the public forum than has Christian morality. This is not to suggest anything concerning the proper use of the institutional power of a church, an issue not explored by the author.

When Lord Devlin explored these issues,[7] he used the Wolfenden Report[8] as his sounding board. Rejecting a utilitarian ethic, he declared that Western civilization was shaped by values derived from Christianity. To preserve the civilization, one must preserve the values. Hence, the suppression of vice (as defined by Christian standards) is as vital as suppressing subversive activities. Private morality becomes of public relevance, and we rely upon the judgment of "right-minded" persons to set the standards, with the jury being a device for ascertaining that judgment.

Hart[9] took the position that punishment by law of immoral conduct is prima facie unjustifiable—indeed, immoral. It can properly be done only for persuasive reasons. Some of Devlin's examples are distinguished by Hart as being paternalism rather than enforcement of Christian morality. While *a* morality is essential to a society, it need not be the morality of the moment. He claims Devlin comes close to saying that enforcement of morality is an end in itself, but he concedes Devlin probably treats it merely as a social cement. Hart admits that every society needs some fundamental values, but he would limit these to basic, universal ones. Any values not necessary to preserve society would be denied penal enforcement.

After analyzing these positions, Mitchell proceeds to suggest some conclusions of his own. In addition to universal social values, every society has special values without which it could not continue to be

---

[7] P. Devlin, The Enforcement of Morals (1965).

[8] Report of the Committee on Homosexual Offences and Prostitution. Cmd. 247 (1957).

[9] H. L. A. Hart, Law, Liberty and Morality (1962).

the same kind of society. In the Western world these do in fact reflect Christianity. The author rejects the notion that religious values are irrational and that the values of secular humanism are rational. He views as a legitimate function of law the protection of the essential institutions of society, and this may entail the reinforcement of the moral principles underlying these institutions. In this reinforcement the onus should be heavily upon those who would interfere in private behavior, but a clear line cannot be drawn between public and private morality. A free society does not shun moral judgments; it makes them openly and after full discussion. All relevant human experience should be consulted in making these judgments. The author's conclusion is that religious experience is a relevant datum which can properly be urged in the communal forum.

It is perhaps unfortunate that discussions of law and morality have focused almost exclusively on criminal law. Modern law impinges upon individuals much more significantly through its civil and administrative branches, yet the terms of the debate remain as they were cast by John Stuart Mill. In today's world, if religion is to have a significant impact on the public order, it will have to be principally through the noncriminal chapters of the law. For example, criminal penalties for adultery have less impact on our institution of marriage than do some of the rules for receiving welfare payments, such as the "man in the house" rule in the District of Columbia. On this and a host of other contemporary issues, value judgments must be formed to fix the course of our public policy. Are values derived from religious commitment to be excluded from consideration?

A book edited by Elwyn Smith, *Church-State Relations in Ecumenical Perspective*,[10] is of some relevance to this question. It presents papers delivered at a graduate seminar in ecumenism which was conducted jointly by Duquesne University and Pittsburgh Theological Seminary. A realistic tone is set by Daniel Callahan who, while examining the impact of ecumenism, suggests that the churches should reflect on the characteristics of our secular society and the positive values which secularism itself entails. In a kindred spirit, Dean Kelley

---

[10] Louvain: Duquesne University Press, 1966. Pp. 280. $4.95.

persuasively argues that respect for the principle of subsidiarity does not justify a liaison between church and state and, consequently, the churches cannot expect to continue those functions which require funds from the public treasury. Several of the essays explore various concepts of "natural law" without succeeding in establishing any relevance to contemporary social thought.

CONSTITUTIONAL LAW

Constitutional law in the United States has long benefited from the contributions of scholars who are not lawyers. Prominent among them today is Professor Henry J. Abraham, of the University of Pennsylvania. His tolerant wisdom is evident throughout the pages of *Freedom and the Court*,[11] a study of civil liberties. Of present interest is his extensive chapter on religion. He admirably accomplishes his basic task of presenting a concise and accurate picture of the Supreme Court decisions in this area. Through a combination of text and tables, the author depicts the chronological development of doctrine. It would be difficult to find a better brief exposition of the religious freedom and nonestablishment case law.

Abraham is quite content with the work of the Supreme Court under the free exercise clause. He characterizes the line of development as one of increasing liberality in the protection of personal liberty. The Sunday Closing Law cases are viewed by him as out of line in refusing to give immunity to Sabbatarians.[12] This appears strikingly so when these cases are contrasted with *Sherbert v. Verner*.[13] It is characteristic of Abraham's gentle scholarship to shrug off this apparent inconsistency by remarking that subjective factors enter into the judgment process. This gives him an opportunity to emphasize one of his central themes: the work of the Supreme Court is not simply legal but also governmental and political.

On the more complex questions raised by the nonestablishment clause the author is unable to describe the Court's decisions in terms

[11] New York: Oxford University Press, 1967. Pp. 335. $7.50.
[12] Braunfeld v. Brown, 366 U.S. 599 (1961).
[13] 374 U.S. 398 (1963).

of a coherent line of development. He finds himself in sympathy with Mr. Justice Reed's complaint that the "wall of separation" is only a figure of speech.[14] Following Kauper's [15] analysis, he sees three competing theories: strict separation, neutrality and accommodation. He suggests that pragmatic accommodation between church and state would be supported by a majority of our people and would bridge the gap between the two religion clauses of the First Amendment. Federal aid to education is to him, a test-ground on which the Court can work out a general theory on establishment. Conscious of the politics of the situation, Abraham seems to expect some degree of "accommodation" between church and state. This would permit, as a minimum, the provision of free textbooks for children in church-related schools. He refrains from predicting what will happen to shared time and tax-supported special teaching services in parochial schools. His discussion of these problems reveals the basic difficulty of an "accommodation" theory: one man's accommodation is another man's establishment.

It would be captious to criticize Abraham for not proceeding to make a more detailed examination of First Amendment values and their relation to specific current issues. His inquiry into the religion clause is only one chapter in what deserves to be recognized as a superb panorama of the Supreme Court's work on the gamut of personal liberties protected by the Constitution. He achieves a degree of incisiveness that is rare in writings whose sweep is so broad.

A posthumous volume of Edward Cahn's essays, *Confronting Injustice*,[16] edited by his widow, includes a chapter on church and state and religious liberty. Despite the consistent charm of his literary style, Cahn's contributions on these topics remain insignificant. On nonestablishment he presents an essentially unexamined position of absolute separation. Viewing separation of church and state as the principal device for securing religious liberty, he fails to recognize any tension between the two religion clauses of the First Amendment.

---

[14] Illinois *ex rel.* McCollum v. Board of Educ., 333 U.S. 203, 238–256 (1948) (dissenting opinion).

[15] P. KAUPER, CIVIL LIBERTIES AND THE CONSTITUTION (1962).

[16] Boston: Little, Brown. 1966. Pp. 428. $8.95.

This is particularly disappointing because Cahn was fully conscious that the working premises of Supreme Court Justices were more volatile in establishment of religion cases than in any other area of constitutional law.[17] This same volume of essays includes much that is valuable and stimulating but on topics outside the range of our present concern.

HISTORY

William Penn's contributions to freedom of religion in America are too real to be treated lightly. Nevertheless, it is fair to say that a comprehensive picture of his uneasy and uncertain relationships with the chartered territory bearing his name must give only a minor place to his libertarian views. Thus it is not surprising to find that Mary M. Dunn's study, *William Penn: Politics and Conscience*,[18] is more politics than conscience. She tells the story with impeccable scholarship wedded to a lively style. On the whole, Penn's efforts to mediate religious liberty in England are more instructive than his American experience. He took the view that it was not religious dissent which endangered the peace of the realm, but the refusal to grant religious toleration. Events forced him to modify his views when the efforts of James II to dispense Catholics from The Test Acts gave rise to a serious public reaction. It is fair to say he never abandoned his basic devotion to the principle of toleration, but his efforts to translate it into political reality in England were doomed to failure. In his colony he was able to give expression to this ideal, but his failure to give timely modification to his views on the privileges of a proprietor insured an unhappy and unprofitable relationship with his colonists.

In Louisiana during the same period the French were applying the double sovereignty of church and state. The operation of this firm but jealous alliance is told with entrancing detail by Charles E. O'Neill in *Church and State in French Colonial Louisiana*.[19] The scheme laid down the ideal of perfect harmony and complete co-

---

[17] P. 177.

[18] Princeton: Princeton University Press, 1967. Pp. 206. $6.00.

[19] New Haven: Yale University Press, 1966. Pp. 315. $10.00.

operation between the two realms. What developed was confrontation and conflict, policed by a remarkably pervasive set of rules which maintained outward forms without successfully coordinating realities. The church knew the place of honor which must be accorded the king's civil officers at divine services—whether within or outside the sanctuary, whether with or without *prie-dieu*. Similarly, the priest had his protected civil status, entitling him to an honored role even in such minor events as igniting holiday bonfires. Behind this facade of mutual respect, the rivalry for power continued. The author writes history and in doing so he cannot escape presenting a persuasive argument for separation of church and state. This is not his purpose, and he warns his readers against anachronistic judgments, but the record speaks for itself. It is interesting to note that the burdens of this liaison did not impinge solely upon the dissenters. Though few in number, and barred from free land grants, they enjoyed toleration despite an official ban on their entry into the colony. It was the Church itself which paid a price for its official protection. Indeed, it was in servitude to the Crown, which went so far as to deny Louisiana a bishopric while Baltimore (in Protestant territory) acquired one.

For nearly a century our country pursued a partnership of church and state in a limited aspect of the national scene. Liquidated before the turn of the century, this partnership operated the Indian missions. R. Pierce Beaver reviews this national experience in *Church, State, and The American Indian*.[20] The original aim was to promote the civilization of the Indians, with mission boards assigned the responsibility and given the finances for conducting educational programs. Despite some early involvement in programs of Indian removal, the record of the churches was on the whole one of beneficent concern for Indian welfare. The mission boards played a major role in reforming the Indian service in the post-Civil War period. The system of public subsidies to the missions was doomed by the increase in Protestant-Catholic hostility and the evolution of the public understanding of the establishment clause. It does the churches little credit to report that

[20] St. Louis: Concordia Press, 1966. Pp. 230. $6.75.

their interest in the welfare of the tribes declined sharply when public subventions ended. For this the entire nation has been poorer, and we have only recently begun a re-examination of conscience in this matter.

The acquisition of former Spanish territories as a result of our military and naval adventures in 1898 is a closed chapter in American history. Puerto Rico remains, together with the opportunities and difficulties posed by special links with Cuba and the Philippines, but our relations with Spain seem to carry no shadows from San Juan or Manila Bay. It was not always like that, and Frank T. Reuter has written an illuminating study of a difficult aspect of our adjustment to the spoils of war. Under the title *Catholic Influence On American Colonial Policies 1898–1904*,[21] he traces the efforts of our government to adjust Spanish church claims in the Philippines and the repercussions these efforts had on Catholic opinion in America. The thorniest issue was that of compensation to the religious orders for their properties in the Islands. President Theodore Roosevelt had a keen sense of the significance of the Catholic segment of the voting population. He was anxious not to offend this group, but wanted to move in a manner consistent with our separationist traditions. Moreover, the unpopularity of the Spanish clergy with the Philippine natives made it imperative that their role in the Islands be liquidated. The close alliance between church and state which the Spanish pattern imposed was so much taken for granted that formal records of property titles were not decisive in resolving the claims of the religious orders. Both Roosevelt and Taft (who served as governor in the Islands) seemed anxious to resolve the issues promptly and fairly. The author's survey of the Catholic press indicates the extent of concern in church circles, but leaves him in great doubt concerning the extent to which Catholic voters were genuinely interested. Nevertheless, it is clear that the manner in which our government proceeded to reach agreement with the Vatican was molded by a determination to avoid undue excitement of either the Protestant or the Catholic domestic camps. There may have been an excess of caution. Catholic public opinion

[21] Austin, Tex.: University of Texas Press, 1966. Pp. 185. $6.50.

was not a bloc. Even the hierarchy was split on the issues. Editorial opinion in the Catholic press was directed at the apathy of the rank-and-file Catholic as much as at the government. One is left with the feeling that politics at the turn of the century was happily free of the full force of group pressures that have developed in our time.

It is doubtful whether any other state can match New York in the field of church-state relations for her full array of experiences and encounters from the time of the Dutch settlement to the present. This history is recounted by John Webb Pratt in a highly readable work of scholarship, *Religion, Politics, and Diversity.*[22] Two themes emerge from this historical survey. One is the Protestant hostility towards Catholicism, originating in antipapal sentiment, which colored and controlled church-state controversies in New York for more than a century. This was evident in the debates leading to the Constitution of 1777 and in the Constitutional Convention of 1894. In the twentieth century, Catholic pressures for aid to parochial schools or the students attending them has been the major theme. The author's tolerant judgments can best be summarized by reciting his adoption of the view that a society must have both guiding principles and a capacity for practical compromise.

MISCELLANEOUS

The late Cardinal Spellman's declaration of patriotism serves as an apt point of departure for a serious but very limited study entitled *Nationalism and American Catholicism,*[23] by Dorothy Dohen. She uses six members of the hierarchy to illustrate what she calls a "peculiar admixture of religion and nationalism in America." (One of these, Bishop John Spalding, serves as an example of a churchman who succeeded in keeping his religion independent of his citizenship.) In some measure, this was part of the Irish-Catholic heritage which saw nation and faith intertwined. The nativist movement reinforced this attitude, challenging the Catholic to demonstrate his Americanism. Inevitably, the effect was to limit religious motivation as a source of

[22] Ithaca: Cornell University Press, 1967. Pp. 327. $7.50.
[23] New York: Sheed and Ward, 1967. Pp. 210. $6.00.

social criticism. Ultimately there comes a watering down of the distinctive parts of a religious tradition in favor of a unified national community. Professor Dohen has given us a case study in Will Herberg's schematic of the American way of religion.

There has been a reissue of Lea's classic study *The Censorship of the Church of Rome.*[24] This two-volume work, whose title suggests a monument to anti-Catholicism, is the product of high scholarship. By detailed examples, it shows the operation of censorship in the period 1540–1900. The author is balanced in his judgment and recognizes the equal zeal with which Protestants censored books in the century following the Reformation.

[24] New York: Benjamin Blom, 1967 (1906). 2 vols, pp. 375 and 510. $25.00.

The Year in Review,

July 1966–September 1967

JUDICIAL DEVELOPMENTS

Religious Liberty

Despite the broad language of the Supreme Court in *Sherbert v. Verner* [1] requiring justification of governmental action that "substantially infringes" an individual's freedom of religion on the ground that it protects a "paramount interest," persons claiming exemptions from various legal duties because of conflict with their religious beliefs were unsuccessful in several cases.

The Kansas Supreme Court refused to grant an exemption from its compulsory education laws on religious grounds. [2] The case involved an Amish farmer who enrolled his daughter in a high school correspondence course after she had graduated from public elementary school; he did this to comply with the state's requirement that she attend either a public or a private school full time until she was sixteen years of age. When local authorities informed him that enrollment in a correspondence school did not satisfy attendance requirements, he enrolled his daughter in an Amish school called Harmony. The Harmony school meets one morning a week and emphasizes training in

[1] 374 U.S. 398 (1963).
[2] State v. Garber, 197 Kan. 567, 419 P.2d 896 (1966), *cert denied,* 389 U.S. 51 (1967).

farming projects for boys and home management subjects for girls. During the remainder of the week students receive vocational training at their homes. The defendant was found guilty of violating the compulsory education laws because the Harmony program was not considered full-time attendance at a private school.

The Kansas Supreme Court upheld the conviction over the defendant's contention that his right to religious freedom required him to be exempt from the compulsory attendance laws. The basis of defendant's objection was the biblical injunction: "Be not conformed to this world." He claimed that exposure to the influences of a secondary school education would lead to the violation of the biblical rule. The court rejected this claim, relying mainly on the argument that religious freedom encompasses essentially the freedom to believe, and not the freedom to engage in religious practices contrary to reasonable requirements of law. It referred to language of the Supreme Court in *Prince v. Massachusetts* [3] which said that the state, as *parens patriae,* could require school attendance despite contrary parental wishes, including religious ones. The Kansas court pointed out that defendant's objection to the secular education did not allege an infringement of the right to worship, nor did it interfere with his freedom to believe. In its view the question of how long a child should attend school was not a religious one. Since the defendant did not object to all secular education, but only to such education beyond the elementary grades, this view of the court undercut the defendant's claim to religious liberty.

The court also dealt with the question of parental rights in education. It noted that the defendant did not claim an absolute parental right to control the education of his children. Since the Kansas statute permitted attendance at a private or parochial school, the court concluded that the state had recognized the parental right in education to the extent required by the Constitution. (See Casad, *Compulsory Education and Individual Rights, infra,* for a critical discussion of this case.)

A California Appellate Court rejected the defense of religious lib-

---

[3] 321 U.S. 158, 166 (1944).

erty in a prosecution for the possession of marijuana.[4] The defendant did not claim to take marijuana as part of a ritual prescribed by a religious body. He justified his use on rather general notions concerning the relation of religion to a free life style. He relied heavily on the *Woody* case,[5] in which the California Supreme Court held that members of the American Native Church had the constitutional right to smoke peyote at their religious ceremonies, state criminal laws notwithstanding. The court in the instant case distinguished *Woody* on the grounds that the central religious event in the American Native Church was the ingestion of enough peyote to induce a hallucinatory state. It interpreted the *Woody* decision as weighing two values: the importance of preventing the use of peyote, and the necessity of its use in the exercise of a bona fide religion. The court found that the defendant in the instant case had not made a sufficiently strong case for the religious importance of marijuana as far as he was concerned.

In a unanimous decision the Appellate Division of the New York Supreme Court upheld a judgment of contempt against an appellant who refused to testify in a criminal case on the ground that it would violate her religious beliefs to harm one of her co-religionists.[6] The appellate court assumed that the appellant was sincere in her beliefs and found that to compel testimony from her would impose some degree of restriction on her freedom to worship. Nonetheless, it concluded that the interest of society in obtaining information for the enforcement of criminal laws was more important because of the paramount interest of the state to maintain peace and order.

The wife of a mental patient in a state institution sought to avoid liability for his care and treatment on the ground that such charges would discriminatorily burden her religious liberty. Her theory was that since her religion obliged her to refrain from divorce, even though she had grounds for one, she was saddled with financial burdens not imposed on women who divorced their hospitalized husbands. Remarking that her claim was "clearly without merit," the

[4] People v. Mitchell, 52 Cal. Rptr. 884 (1966).
[5] People v. Woody, 61 Cal. 2d 716, 394 P.2d 813 (1964).
[6] People v. Woodruff, 26 A.D. 236, 272 N.Y.S.2d 786 (2d Dept.) *affirming*, 270 N.Y.S.2d 838 (Sup.Ct. 1966); see 4 RELIGION AND THE PUBLIC ORDER 292 (1968).

Illinois Supreme Court reversed a judgment which had excused the wife from liability on this theory.[7] The court held that a person could not be excused from valid, equally-imposed obligations attaching to a legal status freely chosen and continued by the defendant. It noted that grant of such immunity would constitute a religious preference.

The claim by a restaurateur to a constitutional right not to serve Negroes because it would violate his religious beliefs was summarily brushed aside by a federal district court in a suit brought under the Civil Rights Act of 1964.[8] The court said that the defendant did not have the absolute right to practice his religious beliefs in "utter disregard of the clear constitutional rights of other citizens."

A trial court in New York dismissed the petition of a would-be candidate for Congress who was seeking on religious grounds to extend the time period during which he could collect signatures necessary for placing his name on the ballot. The petitioner was an Orthodox Jew, and he and his campaign workers refrained from obtaining signatures for a total of eight days because of the Jewish Sabbath and religious holidays. Noting that the petitioner had had 42 days in which to collect signatures, and parenthetically observing that he had only collected 99 of the 3000 required names in the days remaining after exclusion of the religious holidays, the court concluded that the request for additional time was specious.[9]

A city ordinance prohibiting the dissemination of publications that subject religious or racial groups to ridicule and contempt, or promote social hatred and religious bigotry, was struck down as contrary to the First Amendment by the Court of Appeals of Ohio.[10] Although the court praised the purpose of the legislation to achieve brotherhood, it condemned the means adopted, which it characterized as "thought control." The court implied that only the United States Supreme Court's decision in *Beauharnais v. Illinois* [11] raised an arguable basis

[7] Department of Mental Health v. Warmbir, 37 Ill.2d 267, 226 N.E.2d 4 (1967).

[8] Newman v. Piggie Park Enterprises, Inc., 256 F.Supp. 941 (D. S.C. 1966).

[9] Moskowitz v. Board of Elections, 51 Misc.2d 827, 274 N.Y.S.2d 93 (Sup.Ct., Sp.T. 1966).

[10] City of Cincinnati v. Black, 8 Ohio App.2d 143, 220 N.E.2d 821 (1966).

[11] 343 U.S. 250 (1952).

for supporting the ordinance in question. The *Beauharnais* case upheld a group libel law prohibiting the distribution or exhibition of
publications that defame the members of any race or religion or hold
them up to contempt or derision. After noting that the *Beauharnais*
case had been decided by a sharply divided court and that it had
been subjected to very serious criticism, the court in effect concluded
that it no longer represented good law. It did, however, offer a "technical distinction" for those who required it. It pointed out that the
Beauharnais case dealt with an alleged clear and present danger to
the peace and welfare of the community and related to activities carried on in public. The court found neither element present in the instant case, which involved the discovery of racist and religiously
bigoted material in the office of the National States Rights Party.

A federal district court enjoined the American Nazi Party from
holding proposed marches and demonstrations in Jewish neighbor-
hoods during the Jewish High Holy Days in September 1966.[12] It was
alleged that the line of march would be near Jewish synagogues and
that placards would be carried inscribed with vicious and vulgar language. The court granted the injunction because at trial the defendants had not given any evidence indicating that they would cease to
discriminate against and harass Jews. Finding nothing constructive
in defendants' scurrilous activities, the court rejected the argument
that they were protected by the free speech guarantee of the First
Amendment. Instead the court found that the plaintiffs had the legal
right to assemble for worship and to practice their religion safely,
peacefully, and with dignity.

Encouraged by a 1964 decision of the Supreme Court, *Cooper v.
Pate*,[13] a number of Black Muslim cases have been started and others
already commenced have been persistently litigated, with mixed success. In the *Cooper* case the Supreme Court held that a Black Muslim
prisoner stated a claim upon which judicial relief could be granted
when he alleged that solely because of his religious beliefs he was de-

---

[12] Jewish War Veterans v. American Nazi Party, 260 F.Supp. 452 (N.D. Ill.
1966).
[13] 378 U.S. 546 (1964).

nied privileges extended to members of other religious faiths, such as permission to purchase certain religious publications, to meet and correspond with ministers of his faith, and to attend religious services.

On remand of the *Cooper* case the Seventh Circuit relied on both the clear and present danger doctrine and the rule of equal treatment in religious matters to hold that Black Muslims were entitled to certain religious rights.[14] The court held that without a clear and present danger to prison security, the denial of visitation and correspondence rights to Black Muslims comparable to those extended to prisoners of other religious faiths was unconstitutional. Similarly, the court held that Black Muslims could not be denied the opportunity to hold religious services while such a privilege was granted to other inmates. However, the court noted that it was within the discretion of prison authorities to select the time and place of the services and to establish whatever conditions might be necessary to maintain order, for example, limiting the number in attendance or requiring the presence of guards. But the Seventh Circuit did uphold the ban on certain newspapers because there were findings by the trial judge that the publications were not religious in nature and their strongly racist tones justified censorship. Also upheld was a denial of petitioner's request for Arabian and Swahili grammars; the court was of the opinion that such books were necessary for instruction in a foreign language rather than for the free exercise of religion.

Despite the usual rule of judicial noninterference in matters of prison discipline, the Court of Appeals for the Fourth Circuit ordered a Black Muslim prisoner to be released from a maximum security ward of a state prison in order to protect his religious rights.[15] He had been placed in the ward after requesting religious services for Muslim inmates, but refusing to divulge the names of the other prisoners for whom he spoke. Petitioner claimed that he was fearful retaliatory action would be taken against his co-religionists. The prison authorities argued that the petitioner was not being punished for his views, but

[14] 382 F.2d 518 (7th Cir. 1967).
[15] Howard v. Smith, 365 F.2d 428 (4th Cir. 1966).

was being segregated from his co-religionists to deprive them of his leadership and thereby to prevent the development of disorder and riots.

Judge Sobeloff, writing for the court, rejected the notion that the segregation was not punishment since it would deprive the petitioner of use of the prison library, educational and recreational facilities, reduce the number of his meals, and automatically exclude him from parole. Observing that ordinarily a court would not intervene in matters of prison discipline, he considered the instant case as an exceptional one because it involved an arbitrary and serious sanction directed against conduct bearing a close relationship to First Amendment freedoms. He pointed out that a Protestant inmate would not have been subjected to similar treatment and that the prison authorities could have required disclosure of the identity of inmates desiring the services as a condition for granting them permission to attend.

In other cases Black Muslims were not as successful. A federal district court dismissed the complaint of Black Muslim plaintiffs claiming that they were discriminated against in the Lewisburg Penitentiary because they were only allowed to worship in a small room rather than the penitentiary chapel, were not given a Muslim chaplain, were forbidden to write to Elijah Mohammad, their religious leader, to have him send them a minister, and were denied the opportunity to receive certain religious literature.[16] The court found that the needs of prison security and discipline, as well as other legitimate institutional interests, supported the treatment allegedly extended the Black Muslim prisoners. The court found that the prison officials could in their discretion limit worship meetings to small rooms in the case of a sect with a small following in the prison, and this had been done for other religions as well as the Black Muslims. Similarly, the prison did not have to supply every small sect with a chaplain. As to writing to their religious leader, the court pointed out that the prison authorities did not permit any inmate to correspond with the head of his religious group. With regard to the prohibition of religious literature, the

16 Long v. Katzenback, 258 F.Supp. 89 (M.D. Pa. 1966).

court found that the only clear and specific allegations in the complaint referred to literature subject to legitimate prison censorship because it contained "highly inflammatory material." The court found that the book *The Message to the Black Man* by Elijah Mohammad was not "legitimate Islamic literature." As proof that the prison censorship was not based on religious grounds the court noted that prisoners were permitted to receive certain religious literature, such as a book titled *Muslim Daily Prayers* and the *Holy Quran* by A. Yusuf Ali.

The plaintiffs had also alleged that a "list" of Black Muslim prisoners was maintained and that only those on the list were permitted to attend worship services. When other inmates attempted to attend the services, they were allegedly "locked up" for investigation and Black Muslim literature in their possession was confiscated. The court found that "lists" of religious affiliations were maintained for all religious sects in order to avoid proselytizing among the inmates and other activities that might create agitation, physical violence, and disruption of rehabilitation. However, whereas "recorded" Black Muslims could attend Christian services, "recorded" Christians could not attend Black Muslim services. The court could find no reasonable basis for this difference in treatment set out in the papers filed for a summary judgment, and it carried the case forward for trial on this issue. Thereupon, the Lewisburg Penitentiary issued a policy statement regarding Black Muslims which included provisions for allowing change of religious affiliation in prison. When the court was informed that the one "recorded" Christian plaintiff barred from Black Muslim services had changed his religious affiliation, it dismissed the case as moot.

The Eighth Circuit took the position that the religious freedom of prisoners may be restricted more sharply in the area of proselytization because such efforts have a tendency to disrupt prison discipline and order.[17] It denied a petition for habeas corpus filed by a Black Muslim prisoner who alleged that he was discriminatorily punished for discussing his religion freely with others. Prison authorities claimed that the punishment was given for causing unrest. The court

17 Evans v. Ciccone, 377 F.2d 4 (8th Cir. 1967).

noted that Black Muslims were provided with religious literature and were given opportunities to correspond with Elijah Mohammad and to have a Black Muslim minister conduct services for them.

Two other cases decided in the federal courts took rather restrictive stands on the religious rights of prisoners. In one the court dismissed a complaint alleging a denial of opportunity to attend religious services on the ground that federal courts should not interfere with prison regulations necessary to maintain order and discipline.[18] In the other case the court treated a complaint by a Black Muslim prisoner alleging discrimination as an attempt to harass prison officials because of disciplinary actions taken for reasons other than hostile religious discrimination.[19]

There were a number of cases involving conscientious objectors to the military draft. Most of the defendants who refused to submit to induction on the ground that they had been improperly denied exemptions as conscientious objectors were found guilty.[20] In such cases the rule followed by the courts is that the denial of exemption will not be reversed unless there is "no basis in fact" for the refusal of the Selective Service System to grant the exemption. Pursuant to this test the Ninth Circuit upheld the classification of a registrant as a conscientious objector to combatant service only, rather than to all military service, primarily because of his employment in making Minuteman missiles for the Defense Department.[21] Although the defendant had resigned from his job after receiving notice of the Department of Justice's recommendation that he be classified only as an objector against combatant service, the court concluded that the timing of his change of mind could properly be taken into account on the question of his sincerity.

In contrast to the deference courts grant the Selective Service Sys-

---

[18] Johnson v. District of Southern Missouri Commissioners, 258 F.Supp. 669 (W.D. Mo. 1966).

[19] Fulwood v. Alexander, 267 F.Supp. 92 (M.D. Pa. 1967).

[20] E.g., Storey v. United States, 370 F.2d 255 (9th Cir. 1967); Salamy v. United States, 379 F.2d 838 (10th Cir. 1967); Parrott v. United States, 370 F.2d 388 (9th Cir. 1966).

[21] Storey v. United States, 370 F.2d 255 (9th Cir. 1967).

tem's denials of religious exemptions when challenged on the merits, they are often very strict in requiring draft boards to observe all the procedural safeguards available to registrants. As instances of such a judicial attitude, convictions were overturned where the registrant was denied an opportunity to have a hearing on his claim for exemption [22] and in cases where the local draft board or the appeal board had not made specific findings on critical issues of fact.[23]

The *Geary* case involved the issue of specific findings.[24] The defendant first claimed conscientious objector status after receiving his notice of induction. Under Selective Service regulations a registrant will not be reclassified after receiving his induction order unless the local board "first specifically finds there has been a change in registrant's status resulting from circumstances over which the registrant had no control." [25] Although there is general agreement that this regulation is designed to obviate dilatory tactics and precludes a registrant who had conscientious objections at the time of his initial classification from raising them after receipt of the induction order, there is a split of authority as to whether it also precludes reclassification on the basis of conscientious objections that mature after receipt of the induction order.[26] In the *Geary* case the Second Circuit held that, in view of the strong congressional policy exempting religious conscientious objectors, exemption was meant to reach even those whose claims ripen only when they confront the actuality that they may be conscripted into a situation requiring the taking of another's life. The court also held that when a local draft board refuses to reopen the classification of one belatedly claiming exemption it must make a specific finding that there was no basis for a change in status in the facts alleged by the registrant. The court indicated that a finding as

[22] *See* nn. 24 and 30 *infra.*   [23] *See* nn. 31 and 32 *infra.*
[24] United States v. Geary, 368 F.2d 144 (2d Cir. 1966).
[25] 32 C.F.R. § 1625.2 (b).
[26] *Compare* Boyd v. United States, 269 F.2d 607, 610 (9th Cir. 1959); United States v. Porter, 314 F.2d 833, 836 (7th Cir. 1963) *with* United States v. Keene, 266 F.2d 378, 384 (10th Cir. 1959). During the period surveyed the Fourth Circuit joined those courts denying reclassification for conscientious objections maturing after the induction order. United States v. Al-Majud-Muhammad, 364 F.2d 223 (4th Cir. 1966). See text at n. 36 *infra.*

to whether the registrant's conscientious belief matured before or after receipt of the induction notice might be critical in determining whether reopening was appropriate.

The case was remanded and a trial was held to determine what had been the exact findings of the trial board that had refused to reopen the defendant's classification.[27] Members of the board testified concerning what they had meant when they refused to reopen on the ground that the registrant "did not qualify to be a genuine c.o." The registrant in the case was a young Roman Catholic who over a period of six years had received various student deferments and had first raised his claim to conscientious objection one month after receiving his induction notice. In his letter requesting exemption the registrant had stated: "Once I had resolved the problem of claiming conscientious objector status in my own mind, I refrained from notifying the board because I felt quite secure in my status as a student." Because of this statement, the trial judge was prepared to conclude that whatever objections the defendant had to military service had ripened prior to notice of induction. However, this conclusion was superfluous. The members of the local draft board testified that they had not believed the defendant to be a sincere conscientious objector either before or after receiving the induction notice. The trial judge reinstated the defendant's conviction, observing that the volunteer members of the draft board were "honest, sincere" men "without a trace of prejudice," whose only fault was that they did not speak with the "pristine clarity" of judges or professional witnesses.

The case was again appealed on a number of grounds, including the argument that a board must reopen a classification when presented with new information of a nonfrivolous nature.[28] This argument was summarily rejected with the observation that a registrant must make out a prima facie case of being entitled to reclassification before a local board is required to reopen, at least where reclassification is sought for a change of status after receiving an induction notice. Appellant complained that the local board had not made a specific finding as to when his belief had matured, but the court pointed

[27] 266 F.Supp. 161 (S.D. N.Y. 1967).
[28] 379 F.2d 915 (2d Cir. 1967).

out that its previous decision had not indicated that such a finding was always necessary, and it was hardly necessary when the board found no sincere belief either before or after the induction notice.

Defendant also argued that the draft board members had erroneously considered his belief in the use of force to defend himself and his loved ones when determining his sincerity. The appellate court indicated that willingness to resort to self-defense was irrelevant in the case of a registrant whose opposition to participation in war was uncontroverted. However, the court refused to reverse the conviction in the instant case because the record contained other information casting doubt on the sincerity of the defendant's position.

The Supreme Court's decision in the *Seeger* case,[29] which held that a conscientious objector need not believe in God in order to qualify for an exemption, has led to the necessity of more precisely stated findings. In one case [30] the trial court found inadequate a Department of Justice hearing officer's finding which stated that defendant's "objection ... (was) not on religious training and belief but upon personal and moral belief." Concerned that the appeal board might interpret this language erroneously and reject the defendant's claim to exemption because it was not based on an orthodox belief in God, the court acquitted the defendant, but it did so without prejudice to new proceedings for reclassification and possible reinduction.

Two cases emphasized the necessity of fully informing a claimant for exemption as a conscientious objector of his right to a hearing, one court even suggesting that constitutional due process requires it before a claimant for exemption may be convicted for refusal to submit to induction. To assure that such a hearing is granted, a federal district court held in effect that when a registrant in some way reveals to his draft board that he has conscientious objections to war, local officials must acquaint the defendant with his right to an exemption and inform him of the procedures available to establish it.[31] Failure to do so prevented conviction of the defendant in the case at bar without any inquiry into whether he could have established his claim

---

[29] United States v. Seeger, 380 U.S. 163 (1965).

[30] United States v. Englander, 271 F.Supp. 182 (S.D. N.Y. 1967).

[31] United States v. Sobczak, 264 F.Supp. 752 (N.D. Ga. 1966).

to exemption at the time of induction. The court held that under the circumstances the defendant's refusal to submit to induction was not "wilful," as is required by the Universal Military Training and Service Act.

In another case a Jehovah's Witness who had claimed exemption as a conscientious objector was acquitted because his draft board had not extended a full hearing to him.[32] The defendant had claimed both a ministerial and a conscientious objector exemption. The clerk in his draft board had discouraged him from appealing his 1-A classification because the registrant did not engage in sufficient ministerial activity to qualify for exemption as a clergyman. The court emphasized the importance of a personal appearance by the registrant to establish his sincerity and depth of religious feeling with regard to the conscientious objector claim. Therefore the court found that defendant had been deprived of due process when his claim was rejected without a truly adequate opportunity of presenting himself to the board.

When a soldier already in service claims conscientious objector status, the courts do not appear to grant him the same procedural safeguards. The federal district court for New Jersey held that a soldier claiming such an exemption need not be given a hearing even though a registrant must be given one.[33] It rejected the claim that such a difference in treatment violated the equal protection of the laws. It found that the need of the armed services to order and control men provided a sufficiently rational basis to distinguish between pre-recruits and those already in training. The court also refused to review the papers on record with the Army to determine whether the denial of reclassification in the case was arbitrary and without any basis in fact. It decided that it would be too disruptive of the internal affairs of the military services to have such questions unsettled for the period of time necessary to complete review in the courts.

In another case involving a soldier already in service, the court revealed a predisposition to interpret findings on the issue of conscientious objection in favor of the government.[34] The soldier, seeking relief

32 United States v. Bryan, 263 F.Supp. 895 (N.D. Ga. 1967).
33 Brown v. McNamara, 263 F.Supp. 686 (D. N.J. 1967).
34 Gilliam v. Reaves, 263 F.Supp. 378 (W.D. La. 1966).

by way of habeas corpus, alleged that exemption had been improperly denied him because he was not a member of a church. The directive of the Adjutant General denying the exemption mentioned that the petitioner was not a member of a religious sect or organization. The court interpreted the entire directive in the context of the record as indicating that the motivating reason for the denial was the petitioner's lack of sincerity in his religious claim rather than his lack of church membership.

In opposition to the Second Circuit's decision in the *Geary* case,[35] the Fourth Circuit has held that the fruition of conscientious objections to military service is a circumstance within the control of the registrant and therefore cannot be the basis for reclassification after receipt of an induction notice.[36] The court also observed that in the case before it reclassification should have been denied on the merits in any event, because the defendant's refusal to fight for the United States until it gave the Black Muslims their own territory was a political rather than a religious objection.

A federal district court refused to enjoin the third court martial of a serviceman who disobeyed the orders of his superior because he had conscientious objections to military service.[37] The plaintiff had voluntarily enlisted in the armed services and had only developed his objections once in the Army. The court refused to take jurisdiction over the case on the ground that it had no authority to interfere with court martial proceedings. In the course of its opinion, the court noted that the plaintiff could not assert the statutory exemption granted to conscientious objectors because of his enlistment. Unlike the conscientious objectors who do not wish to enter the military service he had entered into a "contract," which altered his "status." He could not now "throw off the garments he . . . once put on."

Following established authority, the Fifth Circuit rejected the appeal of a conscientious objector who refused to perform civilian duties on the ground that it violated his religious beliefs.[38] The court held

35 See text at nn. 24–27.
36 United States v. Al-Majud-Muhammad, 364 F.2d 223 (4th Cir. 1966).
37 Chavez v. Ferguson, 266 F.Supp. 879 (N.D. Cal. 1967).
38 O'Moore v. United States, 370 F.2d 916 (5th Cir. 1967).

that a "knowing and wilful" refusal to comply with the requirements of the draft laws could not be excused even though the defendant had bona-fide religious objections to compliance.

Overruling one of its prior decisions, the Ninth Circuit held that a conscientious objector who refuses to report for civilian service on the ground that he should have been given a ministerial exemption from both military and alternative civilian service may raise the issue of improper classification in a criminal prosecution for refusal to report for service.[39] A registrant who claims improper classification must report for induction before asserting his refusal to serve, on the theory that Congress did not authorize judicial interference with the selective service process until the process of drafting the registrant had been completed. The court distinguished the case of a registrant who is ordered to civilian service on two grounds. First, he is not subject to military discipline or authority, as is the inductee. Second, and more important, the order to report for civilian service is final as far as the governmental process is concerned. The registrant's subsequent activities involve his relationship with a civilian employer pursuant to the government order.

Registrants who refuse to submit to induction on the ground that they are entitled to a ministerial exemption face the same limited standard of review in criminal prosecutions as do claimants to a conscientious objector exemption. They must demonstrate that there is "no basis in fact" for the denial of exemption. A number of Jehovah's Witnesses [40] and a Black Muslim [41] failed to overturn findings denying them ministerial exemptions and were convicted of refusal to submit to induction.

Religious Oaths

Maryland courts had to contend with clarifying the implications of the *Schowgurow* [42] case, which in 1965 had set aside the convictions

---

[39] Daniels v. United States, 372 F.2d 407 (9th Cir. 1967).

[40] *E.g.*, Wood v. United States, 373 F.2d 894 (5th Cir. 1967); United States v. Jackson, 369 F.2d 936 (4th Cir. 1966); United States v. Kushmer, 365 F.2d 153 (7th Cir. 1966).

[41] Muhammad Ali v. Connolly, 266 F.Supp. 345 (S.D. Tex. 1967).

[42] Schowgurow v. State, 240 Md. 121, 213 A.2d 475 (1965); *see* 4 RELIGION AND THE PUBLIC ORDER 294–95 (1968).

and indictments returned by juries that had been required to declare a belief in God. In the *Schowgurow* case itself the Maryland Court of Appeals announced it would apply the rule retroactively only to those criminal cases that had not become final at the date of the decision. However, it refused to grant even this limited retroactivity in civil cases.[43] This raised the question of how to treat pending appeals in civil commitment cases, such as juvenile delinquency proceedings. Although recognizing the similarity between a criminal conviction and a civil commitment, the Maryland Court of Appeals decided against even limited retroactivity in such cases [44] after observing that the Supreme Court of the United States had not applied retroactively the *Miranda* [45] rules limiting police interrogation in criminal cases.

The Maryland high court also refused to make an exception in a capital criminal case [46] so as to apply the rule retroactively to a conviction that had become final before the *Schowgurow* decision. Two cases raised the embarrassing question of how to treat cases heard by judges who had declared a belief in God pursuant to a state constitutional requirement for taking office. In one case, where the objection was directed at the judges who had heard the case, the Maryland Court of Appeals was able to avoid the issue because the conviction had become final prior to the *Schowgurow* decision.[47] Since it found that the declaration of belief taken by the judges had not affected the fair conduct of the trial, the court decided not to reopen a final judgment on this account.

In the second case this avenue of escape was not open.[48] The defendant's objection did not relate to the presiding judge before whom he pleaded guilty, but rather to the committing magistrate who had issued the arrest warrant and the state's attorney who had prosecuted the case, on the ground that Maryland statutory and constitutional provisions required these officers to affirm a belief in God in order to

43 Schiller v. Lefkowitz, 242 Md. 461, 219 A.2d 378 (1966); *see* 4 RELIGION AND THE PUBLIC ORDER 297 (1968).

44 Mastromarino v. Director, 244 Md. 645, 224 A.2d 674 (1966).

45 Miranda v. Arizona, 384 U.S. 436 (1966).

46 Young v. Warden, 245 Md. 76, 224 A.2d 842 (1966).

47 Breeding v. Warden, 244 Md. 716, 224 A.2d 105 (1966).

48 White v. State, 244 Md. 188, 223 A.2d 259 (1966).

take office. The defendant also objected that under the Maryland Declaration of Rights the complaining witness was required to declare a belief in God in order to obtain an arrest warrant. The court gave "short answers" to these objections; the offending provisions of the Maryland Declaration of Rights had been declared unconstitutional by the United States Supreme Court in the *Torcaso* case [49] so that since June 1961, public officials and complaining witnesses could not have been required to declare a belief in God. Then the court noted that the record was silent as to whether any of the officials or the complaining witness had in fact declared a belief in God. If they had voluntarily done so, the court noted, they would simply be exercising their constitutional rights.

A defendant awaiting retrial, who had been reindicted after the *Schowgurow* case, sought to set aside the second indictment on the ground that the offending provision of the Maryland Constitution requiring belief in God as a qualification for jury service had not been formally repealed.[50] The court found the objection entirely without merit on the ground that the holding in the *Schowgurow* case rendered that provision null and void.

The Court of Appeals for the Fourth Circuit upheld lower federal court decisions that refused to set aside Maryland convictions of both believers [51] and nonbelievers.[52] It held that due process does not require the *Schowgurow* case to be applied retroactively because the defect of improper oaths had "not infected the fact finding process or cast doubt upon its integrity."

The *Schowgurow* case apparently has inspired defendants in other jurisdictions to raise similar objections to their convictions. They have been uniformly unsuccessful. In two cases the Pennsylvania Supreme Court summarily rejected as ridiculous objections based on a state law requirement that judges be required to take either an oath or affirmation. In one case the court said that such a rule would "nullify every criminal conviction ever obtained in Pennsylvania and would

[49] Torcaso v. Watkins, 367 U.S. 488 (1961).
[50] Hutchinson v. State, 1 Md. App. 362, 230 A.2d 352 (Ct.Sp.App. 1967).
[51] Smith v. State of Maryland, 362 F.2d 763 (4th Cir. 1966).
[52] Jacobs v. Brough, 375 F.2d 606 (4th Cir. 1967).

make a mockery of every judge and every public official from the President of the United States to a magistrate.[53] In the second Pennsylvania case it was established that both the trial judge and the prosecuting attorney had taken an oath rather than an affirmation. This fact did not lead the court to a different result.[54] In upholding the defendant's conviction Chief Justice Bell went on to cite United States Supreme Court cases for favorable references to prayers in Congress, the military chaplaincy, and other examples of the religious character of our nation.

The Seventh Circuit refused to set aside a conviction where a member of the indicting grand jury had taken an oath referring to God.[55] The court held that even though a member of the grand jury could not constitutionally be required to express a belief in God, it found that such an expression did not necessarily harm the defendant, who therefore had to show actual prejudice in order to quash the indictment. Besides, the court went on to observe, it did not perceive how the traditional grand jury oath amounted to an expression of a belief in God simply because it contained the words "solemnly swear" and "so help me God."

In another case the defendant, an avowed Methodist, sought to have his conviction for grand larceny set aside on the ground that a religious test was injected in the trial by having the witnesses place their left hands on a New Testament when taking the oath.[56] The Oklahoma Court of Criminal Appeals appeared to treat the matter as one of harmless error and upheld the conviction. In Kentucky a defendant objected in advance to the administration of an oath to the jury that contained the words "so help me God." However, none of the jurors objected, and the oath was administered. The conviction was upheld.[57] The Court of Appeals of Kentucky concluded that the oath involved in the case was not a religious test of jurors since they could freely substitute an affirmation. The court was of the opinion that it

[53] Commonwealth *ex.rel.* Brown v. Rundle, 424 Pa. 505, 227 A.2d 895, 896–97 (1967).

[54] Commonwealth v. Alexander, 426 Pa. 360, 231 A.2d 290 (1967).

[55] United States v. Oliver, 363 F.2d 15 (7th Cir. 1966).

[56] Jones v. State, 426 P.2d 377 (Okla. Cr. App. 1967).

[57] Pierce v. Commonwealth, 408 S.W.2d 187 (Ky. 1966).

was constitutionally proper to invoke a juror's belief in God as a guarantee for his reaching a truthful verdict *"if he does believe in God."* [58] The court did not believe that it was necessary to inquire individually whether each juror believed in God before administering the oath since it was a reasonable assumption that an objection would be made by a nonbelieving juror. Finally the court regarded the Maryland constitutional provision invalidated in the *Schowgurow* case as "entirely different" because it required a declaration of belief in the existence of God as a qualification for jury service.

The Appellate Court of Illinois held that state statutes did not require a belief in God as a prerequisite to serving on a grand jury even though a statutory oath was required that made reference to the Deity.[59] The court referred to another statutory provision which permitted substitution of an affirmation by one having conscientious scruples to an oath in all cases where an oath was required by law. In a California case, the defendant, an atheist, sought to set aside his conviction for burglary on the ground that no atheist had served on the jury at his trial and that an oath was administered to a witness.[60] The court rejected both points because under California law no juror could be disqualified on religious grounds, and each had the option to affirm rather than to take an oath, an option also available to witnesses. Therefore, the court held that defendant had no standing to object to the administration of the oath to a willing witness.

Religion in Public Schools

Attempts to circumvent the United States Supreme Court's ban on devotional exercises in the public schools continued to be tested in the courts. The Seventh Circuit held that it was unconstitutional for an elementary school teacher to require the daily recitation of the verse of thanksgiving.[61] The trial court had upheld the practice on the ground that its purpose was the inculcation of good manners and a

[58] *Id.* at 188. (Emphasis in original.)
[59] People v. Fulton, 84 Ill. App. 280, 228 N.E.2d 203 (1967).
[60] People v. Harris, 61 Cal. Rptr. 488 (Ct. App. 1967).
[61] De Spain v. Dekalb County Community School Dist., 384 F.2d 836 (7th Cir. 1967).

spirit of gratefulness to others in the young school children.[62] Prior to the United States Supreme Court's decision outlawing prayers in the school,[63] the teacher involved had included a reference to God in the verses recited. Two clergymen testified that the verses remained prayers even after explicit reference to God was dropped from them in order to comply with the Supreme Court's decision. There was testimony that some students adopted reverential attitudes while reciting the verses, but there was also testimony indicating that the purpose and effect of the practice was to develop good citizenship. The trial court had concluded that the religious elements involved were *de minimis* and incidental to a secular purpose and activity.

Although the Seventh Circuit, in observing that the plaintiffs were forcing the constitutional issue of nonestablishment of religion "to its outer limits," seemed to agree with the *de minimis* assessment of the trial court, it nonetheless concluded that the recitation constituted an act of praising and thanking the Deity and that the secular benefits derived therefrom were "supplemental" and "adjunctive" to this basic religious purpose. Citing the *Everson* school bus case [64] to the effect that the wall of separation must be "kept high and impregnable" without "the slightest breach," the court concluded that even an innocuous prayer had to be declared unconstitutional when required in the public schools.

In an advisory opinion the Supreme Court of New Hampshire held that it would be constitutional for the legislature to require a period of silent meditation at the beginning of the first class each day in the public schools.[65] It also ruled that the recitation of historical masterpieces or singing of songs could be required as part of an opening patriotic or ceremonial exercise. However, it concluded that a statute authorizing the classroom teacher to include the recitation of the Lord's Prayer or readings from the Holy Bible at her discretion would be unconstitutional. The court was also of the opinion that the state

[62] 255 F.Supp. 655 (N.D. Ill. 1966); see 4 RELIGION AND THE PUBLIC ORDER 283–84 (1968).

[63] School Dist. v. Schempp, 374 U.S. 203 (1963).

[64] Everson v. Board of Educ., 330 U.S. 1 (1947).

[65] Opinion of the Justices, 228 A.2d 161 (N.H. 1967).

could require the installation in public school classrooms of plaques bearing the words: "In God We Trust." Since this motto appears on our national currency, on public buildings, and in the national anthem, the court did not see how its presence in a public school classroom could be unconstitutional.

Parents of some New York City school children sought to restrain public school officials and members of parent associations from issuing and distributing to students on school property statements or petitions urging the passage or repeal of legislation.[66] At two schools the parent associations prepared circulars and had them distributed by teachers. Two of the items concerned the area of church-state separation. One circular urged support of legislation that would repeal the recently enacted New York law that makes publicly purchased textbooks available for use by private and parochial school children. A petition was also circulated at these schools urging delegates to the New York Constitutional Convention to retain the so-called Blaine Amendment, which prohibits the state legislature from using public money directly or indirectly for any school partly or wholly under the control or direction of any religious denomination. Children were asked to return signed copies of the petition to be collected during regular class hours.

Petitioners claimed that their children had been compelled to carry partisan political petitions and information in violation of their political beliefs and religious convictions. Coercion was also alleged because, in the eyes of the pupils, the board of education would appear to put the stamp of approval on certain positions and cause the children of parents with contrary views to be treated as outcasts despised by society. The court rejected the notion of coercion on the ground that it would disable the government from ever acting in a controversial area. It also rejected the argument that either the petitioners' right of privacy or of freedom of religious belief had been violated. As to privacy, the court concluded that such a right did not embrace freedom from partisan political propaganda. As to infringement of religious beliefs, the court held that the circulars only supported the

[66] Pare v. Donovan, 54 Misc.2d 194, 281 N.Y.S.2d 884 (Sup. Ct. 1967).

principle of separation of church and state, an existing constitutional doctrine.

A New York trial court upheld the leasing of church properties by a local school board for use as public school classrooms.[67] The leases had been attacked on the ground that they involved the use of "religious buildings" in giving instruction to public school students. The court rejected the notion that the buildings were "churches" because no religious services were conducted in them and it also rejected the idea that they were "religious schools" because all the instruction given was concededly secular. It upheld the leases by applying the secular purpose and effect test. Since the leases had been negotiated to meet overcrowding in the public school buildings, their purpose was clearly secular. Since all religious symbols had been removed from the leased premises, the court found no religious effect. Petitioners had stressed the proximity of clearly religious buildings and symbols because in one instance the school was adjacent to a Roman Catholic church and in the other it was a wing of a synagogue. The court ridiculed the notion that separation of church and state required keeping school children in complete ignorance of religion and requiring public schools to be built out of sight and beyond earshot of churches and other religious structures.

State Aid to Religious Institutions

Suits were commenced in state and federal courts challenging the constitutionality of the 1965 Elementary and Secondary Education Act on the ground that it extended unconstitutional aid to religion. Title I of the Act requires that federal funds granted to local boards be used in part to provide educational services to students attending private and parochial schools.[68] Title II of the Act provides for the purchase of text books to be loaned to students attending private and parochial schools.[69] Two cases [70] in the federal courts were dismissed on the ground that the plaintiff taxpayers had no standing to sue.

[67] Brown v. Heller, 51 Misc.2d 660, 273 N.Y.S.2d 713 (Sup. Ct. 1966).

[68] 20 U.S.C. §§ 236–44 (Supp. II 1967).

[69] 20 U.S.C. §§ 821–27 (Supp. II 1967).

[70] Flast v. Gardner, 271 F.Supp. 1 (S.D. N.Y. 1967); Protestants and Other Americans v. United States, 266 F.Supp. 473 (S.D. Ohio 1967).

Both courts relied on the authority of *Frothingham v. Mellon,* [71] a Supreme Court decision holding that a taxpayer does not have standing to challenge the constitutionality of federal spending programs.

One of these cases,[72] which was heard by a three-judge court in the southern district of New York, was appealed to the Supreme Court of the United States. In dismissing the case, the lower court felt compelled to distinguish cases like *Everson v. Board of Education,*[73] in which the Supreme Court took jurisdiction to review a taxpayer's challenge of state and local expenditures to finance busing of parochial school students, and like *School District of Abington Township v. Schempp,*[74] in which a federal court enjoined local officials from conducting devotional services in the public schools. It distinguished *Everson* on the ground that a local taxpayer had a direct economic interest in local expenditures, a point noted in the *Frothingham* case itself. It distinguished *Abington* and similar cases on the ground that they were brought by children attending public schools, or their parents, persons having an immediate interest in the practices involved.

Judge Frankel filed a long and vigorous dissent arguing that there were compelling reasons why the court should take judicial review in a case involving expenditures challenged under the establishment clause and that *Frothingham* could be distinguished on these grounds. Starting with the premise that the prohibition of public expenditures to support religion was a central concern of the establishment clause, the dissent went on to observe that even the "slightest breach" of the wall of separation of church and state was considered a serious infringement of nonestablishment by the authors of the First Amendment, notably Madison and Jefferson. Therefore the dissent concluded that taxation of a citizen to support the religion of another involved a "vivid, vital, intimate and grave hurt" which would provide the concrete adverseness necessary for a case and controversy. The dissent also took the position that interpretation of the establishment clause raised the kind of constitutional issue traditionally determined by the courts, unlike such political issues as the propriety of

[71] 262 U.S. 447 (1923).
[72] Flast v. Gardner, 271 F.Supp. 1 (S.D. N.Y. 1967).
[73] 330 U.S. 1 (1947).   [74] 374 U.S. 203 (1963).

nuclear testing, and that if taxpayers were denied standing to sue there would be no one to challenge public expenditures contrary to the establishment clause. Finally, Judge Frankel contrasted the instant plaintiff's interest in maintaining separation of church and state, a nonestablishment concern, with Mrs. Frothingham's interest in trying to limit federal expenditures, an issue involving distribution of governmental powers in a federal system.

The Supreme Court reversed the lower court's decision in the closing days of the 1967 Term.[75] It held that a taxpayer could challenge federal expenditures when two conditions were met: first, that the expenditures are part of a federal "spending" program rather than incidents of a "regulatory" program, and second, that the challenged expenditures allegedly violate specific constitutional limitations. The plaintiffs' challenge of certain federal aids to education on the ground that they violated the establishment clause met the twofold test.

On the state level the highest courts in Pennsylvania and New York upheld expenditures of public funds that aided students attending parochial schools, despite state constitutional bans on aid to sectarian schools, while the Missouri Supreme Court blocked all efforts to extend public educational services to children who regularly attended parochial schools. The Pennsylvania Supreme Court upheld a state statute requiring local school districts to provide free bus transportation for pupils who attend nonprofit, nonpublic elementary or secondary schools whenever such transportation is provided for students in public schools.[76] The law was challenged under the establishment clause of the First Amendment as well as under several provisions of the Pennsylvania Constitution, including one specifically prohibiting the use of public school funds "for the support of any sectarian school." Stressing the health and safety aspects of the legislation, the court concluded on the authority of the *Everson* case that such busing was clearly valid when tested by the First Amendment. Justice Musmanno, writing for the court, ridiculed the notion that state subsidy of a school bus, which he characterized to be a "place of gaiety, levity and juvenile frivolity," would amount to the public support of

[75] 392 U.S. 83 (1968).
[76] Rhoades v. School Dist., 424 Pa. 202, 226 A.2d 53 (1967).

a place of worship contrary to a provision of the Pennsylvania Constitution. Again relying on the health and safety features of busing children to schools, he held that such services should be extended to all
children, regardless of their religious beliefs and practices, just as various health services were offered to all children of the state. None of
these health services had been regarded as unlawful support of a
sectarian school. Noting that the nonpublic school children were to
be transported on established bus routes, the court anticipated that
there would be a mingling of public and parochial school children, a
"salubrious and educational" development in the eyes of the court.
Justice Roberts concurred, finding the legislation to be a welfare measure for the secular benefit of the children attending all schools. However he would add yet another requirement, that the aid given the
students be indisputably marked off from the religious function because he found the teaching of all subjects in parochial schools to be
"infused with religious significance."

Chief Justice Bell dissented, although he agreed that on the authority of the *Everson* case the legislation did not offend the First
Amendment of the federal Constitution. He nonetheless concluded
that public school busing of parochial school children violated those
provisions of the Pennsylvania Constitution prohibiting the application of public funds to sectarian institutions. Since children attending
private schools operating for profit were excluded from the benefits of
the law, Justice Bell concluded that students attending nonprofit sectarian schools were singled out for special benefits in order to support
the schools they attend. In another dissent Justice Cohen questioned
the continuing vitality of the *Everson* case and then took the unusual
position of urging that the statute be struck down so that the Supreme
Court would be provided with an occasion to reconsider the *Everson*
decision. He also rejected the idea that the child benefit theory was
being applied in the case because children attending private schools
operated for profit were not included in the benefits of the law.

A case involving textbooks for students attending parochial schools,
as well as other nonprivate schools, briskly made its way up through
the New York courts to culminate in an appeal to the United States
Supreme Court during the period surveyed. The suit was brought by

two local school boards to restrain the Commissioner of Education from complying with legislation requiring them to loan textbooks designated for use in public schools or approved by public school authorities to students attending parochial schools in grades 7 through 12. The trial court granted summary judgment to the plaintiffs on the ground that the legislation violated both the establishment clause of the First Amendment and Section 3, Article 11 of the New York Constitution which forbids the state "directly or indirectly" to aid any school under the control or direction of a religious denomination.[77] Relying on earlier precedents, including *Judd v. Board of Education*,[78] in which the New York Court of Appeals found that publicly financed busing of parochial school students was an indirect aid to sectarian schools, the court concluded that the "pupil benefit theory" had been rejected as inapplicable under the state constitution. Since textbooks in history and social studies would be provided, the trial court foresaw religious influences improperly affecting the selection of textbooks in the public school. It also envisioned that private religious schools would adopt secular textbooks somewhat offensive to them for the sole purpose of obtaining state financing. The Commissioner sought to have the case dismissed on the ground that local school boards, being public bodies, could not challenge the legality of legislation under which they were directed to act. The trial court held that an exception was to be made to such a rule in the case of a local board of education, most especially when it sought to challenge an expenditure of public funds in contravention of a basic civil right.

On appeal to the Appellate Division, the third department reversed on the ground that creatures of the state could not question the authority extended to them at the discretion of the state legislature.[79] There was a concurring opinion by Judge Staley which went to the merits. He believed that the local school board officials should have standing to challenge the constitutionality of legislation directing them to take certain action because failure to comply with it could

[77] Board of Educ. v. Allen, 51 Misc.2d 297, 273 N.Y.S.2d 238 (Sup.Ct., Sp.T. 1966).
[78] 278 N.Y. 200, 15 N.E.2d 576 (1938).
[79] 27 A.D. 69, 276 N.Y.S.2d 234 (3d Dept. 1966).

result in removal from office. Judge Staley concluded that school officials who have sworn to uphold the state constitution should not be
compelled to choose between risking their jobs or participating silently
in what they regarded to be an unconstitutional program. He then
went on to conclude that the textbook legislation was intended and
operated as an aid to the child rather than an indirect aid to the
school. He implied that the "child benefit principle" had received
such widespread recognition in the courts as to indicate a needed departure from the reasoning and holding of the *Judd* case. He was
also of the opinion that educational textbook aids could be readily
justified under the establishment clause as interpreted in the *Schempp*
case because of their primary secular purpose and effect.

The Court of Appeals affirmed the dismissal, but on the merits.[80]
A majority of the court held that the local board of education had
standing without discussing the matter in detail. It then went on to
overrule the *Judd* case, holding that Article 11 was not meant to prohibit all aids that might remotely benefit sectarian institutions. The
court said that the words "direct and indirect" in Article 11 "relate
solely to the means of attaining the prohibited end of aiding religion
as such." As to the challenge under the establishment clause, the court
disposed of it briefly by observing that it was linguistically impossible to conclude that loans of secular textbooks to all school children,
regardless of their religion or school affiliations, constituted an establishment of religion.

Three judges dissented on the ground that the *Judd* case required
the prohibition of indirect school aids under Article 11 despite the
child benefit theory. Writing for the dissenters, Judge Van Voorhis
also questioned the constitutionality of textbook aids under the First
Amendment. Because of Mr. Justice Douglas's self-proclaimed change
of heart about his vote in the *Everson* case, doubt was expressed as to
the continuing vitality of that case as a precedent. Judge Van Voorhis
also specified two evils inconsistent with the principle of separation of
church and state that might follow from textbook aid. First, he feared
there would be religious pressures in choosing books to be used in the

---

[80] 20 N.Y.2d 109, 281 N.Y.S.2d 799, 228 N.E.2d 791 (1967).

public schools in order that they might also be available for parochial school students; and second, he questioned the power of the state to buy necessaries for parochial schools since it resulted in liberating funds for strictly religious objectives.

The Supreme Court subsequently affirmed the New York Court on the ground that the purpose of the legislation was the advancement of secular education and no evidence had been introduced to show that it had the primary effect of improperly aiding religion.[81]

The Missouri Supreme Court held that a special school district for the education of handicapped children could not send teachers of speech therapy into parochial schools.[82] The trial court [83] had declared the practice to be invalid under sections of the Missouri constitution prohibiting aid to religion, but the supreme court's holding was based on those constitutional provisions that restricted expenditure of public school funds to the maintenance of public schools. In the same case the issue was raised as to whether speech therapy services could be made available to parochial school students at public schools. The special district had undertaken this practice when it had been denied reimbursement by the state board of education for sending teachers into the parochial schools. The board again refused reimbursement and was upheld by the trial court. The supreme court affirmed on the ground that under the Missouri Education Law the student must attend a single school for the entire school day, and the public school authorities could not violate that requirement. It was pointed out in passing that any change in the law that would permit parochial school students to attend public schools raised issues under the religion provisions of the Missouri Constitution which prohibit aid to sectarian institutions.

There was a dissent which maintained that the compulsory education law was ambiguous and that its requirement of attendance "at some day school, public, private, parochial, or parish" could be interpreted to mean attendance at some "schools." The dissent argued that the ambiguity should be resolved in favor of plural attendance be-

---

[81] 392 U.S. 236 (1968).
[82] Special Dist. v. Wheeler, 408 S.W.2d 60 (Mo. 1966).
[83] *See* 4 RELIGION AND THE PUBLIC ORDER 276 (1968).

cause such an interpretation best comported with the legislative intent of securing a minimum education for children and prohibiting child labor during school hours. In addition, the dissent argued that the interpretation of the majority would invalidate desirable dual enrollment programs currently involving arrangements between more than one public school. The attorney general then moved for rehearing on the ground that the court's interpretation of the compulsory education law discriminated against nonpublic school students because they were deprived of dual enrollment opportunities while public school students were not. This motion was summarily dismissed on the ground that the application of the compulsory education law to public schools was not before the court.

In New Jersey the interpretation and application of the school busing law with regard to parochial school children resulted in litigation. Special bus routes were established by a local school board for the purpose of transporting children to and from parochial schools.[84] These routes were declared invalid by a New Jersey lower court on the ground that their formulation was beyond the statutory power of the local board. The applicable statute provides in its first paragraph that local school boards may provide bus transportation for students attending both public and nonprofit schools. In its second paragraph it provides that where transportation is provided for public school students, the local board shall also supply transportation to students attending nonprofit private schools from any point along "established" public-school bus routes to any other point on such routes. The court rejected an interpretation of the statute that would permit the creation of parochial-school bus routes as a discretionary matter under the first paragraph and require transportation of parochial school students along established routes as a mandatory matter pursuant to the second paragraph. Conceding that the statute was ambiguous and open to this interpretation, the court turned to legislative history and past expressions of judicial opinion to conclude that the legislation only authorized transportation along established routes. Plaintiffs had also challenged the statute under the establishment clause even though it

[84] Fox v. Board of Educ., 93 N.J. Super. 544, 226 A.2d 471 (1967).

was the very one upheld in the *Everson* case. After expressing the opinion that the statute would be declared invalid if again reviewed by the Supreme Court at the present time, the trial judge felt compelled to follow existing precedent until it was expressly overruled.

A taxpayer brought suit to invalidate the auction sale of realty by New York City to Brooklyn Law School.[85] Pursuant to city ordinance the bidding on the realty was limited to nonprofit corporations organized for educational and other purposes. A ground advanced in opposition to the sale was that church-related corporations might benefit from the statute since many of them fell within the class favored. The court dismissed this objection on the ground that it was irrelevant in a case involving a sale to a nonsectarian educational institution.

Tax Exemption

In several cases tax exempt status was denied religious organizations with regard to activities considered to be secular. Two cases involved exemption from the federal income tax. In one of these [86] a Roman Catholic publishing house seeking to promote the ends of Catholic Action claimed that its entire publishing effort was religious and educational because it was directed to the ends of Catholic Action. Accordingly, it purported to qualify as an organization "organized and operated exclusively for religious, . . . or educational purposes." A federal district court held that its activities, the sale of books at a profit, was clearly a business activity and therefore its operations were not exclusively religious or educational. The court distinguished other cases where substantial commercial activities, such as the sale of books, did not subject the religious or educational organization to taxation because such activities were ancillary to and directly supportive of other significant and clearly exempt activities of the organization. Since the publishing house was an independent corporation, it could not be considered an integral part of the educational activities of either the local diocese or neighboring University of Notre Dame.

In the second case the Eighth Circuit upheld a finding of the Tax

---

[85] Hama Realty Co. v. City of New York, 52 Misc.2d 192, 274 N.Y.S.2d 392 (Sup.Ct. Sp.T. 1966).

[86] Fides Publishers Ass'n. v. United States, 263 F.Supp. 924 (N.D. Ind. 1967).

Court that an organization involved in extensive publishing activities
of a commercial character, the Foundation for Divine Meditation
(F.D.M.), was not exempt even though the substance of its publications bore some relationship to the ultimately religious purposes of the
organization.[87] The taxpayer had raised two objections to the Tax
Court's findings that its purposes were not exclusively religious: first,
it maintained that the statutory power granted to the federal taxing
authorities to determine whether a religious organization is entitled
to an income tax exemption because of its activities violates the free
exercise clause; and second, it argued that the only test for the income
of a religious organization is the destination of the revenues involved.
It claimed exemption under the second point because profits of the
organization were retained in the treasury of F.D.M., an allegedly religious organization.

The court rejected both points. On the religious liberty point it referred to various state court cases holding that the income of a religious organization may be taxed. It then went on to hold that exemptions could be withheld from some religiously organized organizations
as long as this was done on a reasonable, nondiscriminatory basis that
did not involve an inquiry into questions of religious doctrine. Denial
of the tax exemption because F.D.M. had a substantial nonreligious
purpose was just such a legitimate basis for distinction. In finding
F.D.M. to have a substantial nonreligious purpose the court noted
that it put out three kinds of publications, most of which appear to
have been the products of F.D.M.'s founder and director for life, Dr.
Merle Parker. The first class of publications encompassed works on
metaphysics, faith healing, philosophy, physical and psychological development, and dietary practices. The second comprised works designed to permit readers to increase their financial income, such as
outlining F.D.M. projects in which prospective subscribers (referred
to as customers by the court) would receive ming tree seeds and instructions on how to grow $1,000 worth on a single window sill. Al-
though disavowing an intention to determine what constitutes a religious practice, the court dryly observed that this second category of

---

[87] Parker v. Commissioner, 365 F.2d 792 (8th Cir. 1966).

publications seemed to have little relationship to F.D.M.'s avowed religious activities. A third category of publications related to various crusades undertaken by F.D.M., including Christian healing and anti-cigarette-smoking campaigns. Publications in all categories would be sent to subscribers for payment of a minimum donation, which varied, and which the court believed was "undoubtedly calculated to give F.D.M. profit on the sale."

On the second point, that the profits were retained by F.D.M. for its religious purposes, the petitioner relied on federal cases holding that income from "limited trading" incidental to the religious purposes of an organization did not deprive it of its exemption so long as the funds were definitely used for a religious end. However, the court concluded that on the facts F.D.M.'s commercial activities could be viewed as constituting a substantial nonreligious purpose of the Foundation, a distinct end in themselves. The court found that this conclusion of the Tax Court was supported by the extent and scope of the profit-making publications of F.D.M., the nonreligious subject matter of some of these publications, existence of recurrent annual profits, substantial accumulation of net earnings, and various statements by Dr. Parker in which he described himself as being in the mail-order business.

On the state level two church-related organizations were denied exemptions from the real property tax on the ground that their activities were not exclusively religious. One case involved an incorporated religious shrine at Auriesville, New York, commemorating the death of certain Roman Catholic missionaries to the Indians.[88] Although the local tax assessors had exempted the bulk of the land at the site, they had assessed the cafeteria, a dining hall, hotel facilities for guests and a building for visiting nuns called the Sisters' Convent. The land exempted included shrines, statues, paths, roadways, maintenance shops, restrooms and areas, all used in connection with the religious activities of the corporation, along with a large church, an esplanade, and buildings for teaching and for the living requirements of clergy, students, and employees resident at the shrine.

[88] Shrine of Our Lady v. Board of Assessors, 54 Misc.2d 145, 281 N.Y.S.2d 544 (Sup.Ct. 1967).

The petitioner corporation urged that the feeding and housing of persons who visit the shrine were necessary and incidental to its clearly exempt purposes. New York law exempts "real property owned by a corporation . . . organized exclusively for . . . religious . . . missionary . . . educational [and] historical purposes . . . or for two or more such purposes, and used exclusively for carrying out thereupon one or more of such purposes." The petitioner's corporate purposes included missionary activities on behalf of the Roman Catholic church, dissemination of knowledge concerning the first Catholic mission to the Indians at Auriesville and its converts, as well as the organization and conduct of pilgrimages to the shrine. The court conceded that as a general rule a tax exemption would be appropriate in the case of a commercial, profitable use that was associated with and supportive of exempt purposes. However, the court did not regard the shrine's claim for total exemption as coming within this rule because its dining and hotel facilities were open to and advertised to the public and because their patrons regarded the shrine as a pleasant tourist attraction. It also noted that, since restaurants and hotels were both available in the vicinity, it was not necessary for the shrine to provide accommodations for its guests. The Sisters' Convent was held to be exempt because it was found to be used exclusively for a purpose incidental to the work of the shrine.

In the second case the Supreme Court of Florida upheld the denial of tax exemption in the case of a nonprofit home for retired elderly people operated and controlled by the state synod of the Presbyterian Church in the United States.[89] Since the home charged most of its inmates for "full maintenance" and required a heavy "founders fee" of those able to pay, the court concluded that the property was not being held exclusively for charitable purposes and rejected the argument that it was held for a combination of religious and charitable purposes.

There were two vigorous dissents, both emphasizing the church affiliation of the home and its religious purpose in seeking to create a

---

[89] Presbyterian Homes v. City of Bradenton, 190 So.2d 771 (Fla. 1966).

Christian atmosphere. Both dissents noted the growing need for homes to care for the elderly. They pointed out that such homes were generally not self-sufficient and that the state synod and some of its agencies contributed in part to such homes. One dissent also pointed out that the "founders fees" were being used to amass capital to establish the home initially, and that once under way, it was hoped that greater subsidies would be made available to it. The other dissent observed that many exempt charitable institutions, such as hospitals, required their beneficiaries to pay for at least part of their services and that exempt educational institutions also charged fees as a rule. However, the emphasis on the religious factor in both opinions implied that this element was most important in the eyes of the dissenters for recognizing the claim of exemption in the case of a home for the elderly.

A somewhat different result was reached by the Nebraska Supreme Court, which upheld the tax exemption of a nonprofit nursing home owned and operated by a church-related organization.[90] The home charged inmates or their relatives for services rendered, and in the case of indigents received payments from the county welfare department. Although daily and weekly religious services were conducted on the premises on a voluntary basis, the court concluded that the dominant use and purpose of the property involved was not religious. Nonetheless, the exemption was upheld on the basis that caring for the aged and the infirm constituted an exclusively charitable purpose and use notwithstanding the requirement of payment. The court noted that the word charitable had come to include more than eleemosynary activities and included certain services for the good of humanity even when rendered at a moderate cost to the beneficiary, as in the case of nonprofit hospitals. One judge dissented on the ground that every nursing home in the state could now claim exemption by incorporating as a nonprofit corporation while draining off all profit in substantial salaries and expenses.

[90] Evangelical Lutheran Good Samaritan Soc'y v. County of Gage, 181 Neb. 831, 151 N.W.2d 446 (1967).

Tort Immunity and Other Privileges

In several cases the decision to reject or limit further the doctrine of charitable immunity for negligent torts of servants was first taken or reaffirmed. The Supreme Court of Idaho, which had previously restricted the doctrine of charitable immunity to claims by nonpaying beneficiaries of a charity for negligent injury, decided to follow the trend of current decisions and go all the way and abrogate the doctrine completely.[91] Therefore, it permitted suit to be brought against the governing body of a group of churches for injuries suffered by a minor while on a supervised church outing.

The Iowa Supreme Court reaffirmed an earlier precedent holding that charitable organizations, including churches, could be held liable for negligence.[92] It also clarified the scope of an earlier precedent by announcing that the immunity was removed for both paying and nonpaying beneficiaries. The Supreme Court of Pennsylvania extended the scope of a previous decision that had abrogated charitable immunity where a paying patient had sued a hospital for negligent treatment; it permitted a suit against a synagogue for personal injuries suffered as the result of a fall on the sidewalk fronting the building.[93]

The North Carolina Supreme Court prospectively overruled the doctrine of charitable immunity insofar as it applied to hospitals that charged for services.[94] In the case at bar it permitted recovery against the defendant hospital, which rendered services to indigent patients regardless of ability to pay but which obtained substantial payment from the county welfare department for part of the cost involved. The court held that such a hospital had lost its status as a charitable institution because a true charity does not require any payment from its beneficiaries. The court expressly stated that its decision did not reach true charities such as churches, orphanages, rescue missions, transient homes for the indigent, and other similar institutions.

The Wisconsin Supreme Court reaffirmed its decision to abrogate

91 Bell v. Presbytery of Boise, 421 P.2d 745 (Ida. 1966).
92 Sullivan v. First Presbyterian Church, 152 N.W.2d 628 (Ia. 1967).
93 Nolan v. Tifereth Israel Synagogue, 425 Pa. 106, 227 A.2d 675 (1967).
94 Rabon v. Rowan Memorial Hosp., 269 N.C. 1, 152 S.E.2d 485 (1967).

charitable immunity only prospectively in a case involving an injury that had occurred prior to its decision setting aside charitable immunity.[95] The defendant church was covered by an insurance policy for public liability, but the court refused to grant recovery on this ground because there had been no showing that the policy expressly provided for the waiver of charitable immunity. The case involved injuries sustained by a parochial school student while cleaning votive candle holders at the request of a religious instructor. The court dismissed the argument that the furnishing of the votive candles was a commercial, nonimmune activity because it produced income. The court found that the use of votive candles was an integral part of the religious ceremonies of the Roman Catholic Church and had been for centuries.

Contrary to the current trend, the Colorado court reaffirmed its limited doctrine of charitable immunity which prohibits the satisfaction of a judgment against a charitable institution out of its trust funds in cases involving the negligence of its servants.[96]

The claim that members of a religious sect have an absolute privilege to engage in conduct designed to alienate the affections of a spouse was rejected by the Supreme Court of Washington.[97] The action was brought by a husband who alleged and offered proof that the pastor and leading members of a religious sect caused his wife to remain away from home for unreasonable periods of time, that on one occasion they had concealed her whereabouts when she had moved out of the family home, that on another occasion the defendant pastor had accused the husband of being "full of the devil" in the presence of the latter's wife and children, and finally that some of the other defendants had advised the wife to divorce the plaintiff. The proof at trial indicated that the animosity of the defendants increased after the plaintiff sought to have his wife withdraw from the sect. It also revealed that at meetings of the sect the leadership took the position that several homes in the church should be broken up and that death

---

[95] Wojtanowski v. Franciscan Fathers, 34 Wisc.2d 1, 148 N.W.2d 54 (1967).
[96] Hemenway v. The Presbyterian Hospital Ass'n., 419 P.2d 312 (Colo. 1966).
[97] Carrieri v. Bush, 419 P.2d 132 (Wash. 1966).

would pursue those who did not adhere to church discipline. The trial court dismissed the case at the conclusion of the plaintiff's presentation of evidence.

On appeal the defendants contended that they had an absolute privilege to interfere in the appellant's marriage on religious grounds. The court ruled that ordinarily ill will or a reckless recommendation of separation was not necessary to establish a case of alienation of affection where an intermeddling stranger engaged in disruptive conduct without justification. But such allegations and proof of malice or recklessness would be necessary in the case of a personally or professionally interested person, such as a relative or a marriage counselor, who could reasonably and in good faith intervene in the domestic affairs of a married couple. The court would grant only such a qualified privilege of intervention on religious grounds. It said: "[O]ne does not, under the guise of exercising religious beliefs, acquire a license to wrongfully interfere with family relationships." Because the plaintiff had presented enough evidence to raise the issue of ill will and recklessness, the appellate court reversed for a new trial.

The Supreme Court of Alabama rejected the argument that confidential communications to a clergyman carry with them an absolute privilege against suits for libel.[98] Consequently, it held that when defendant was being sued for libel based on a letter written to his priest in which he charged his wife, the plaintiff, with adultery, the defendant could not seek to dismiss the complaint. At best, he had a conditional privilege which he would have to plead specially and accompany with a denial of actual malice.

Ministers called to testify in judicial proceedings were unsuccessful in claiming the privilege of confidential communication in two cases. In a suit for alienation of affections the plaintiff successfully compelled the production of certain letters written by the plaintiff's wife to the defendant even though these letters had been turned over by the defendant's wife to her minister for safe keeping.[99] The issue raised was whether the letters were privileged because held by the

98 Tonsmeire v. Tonsmeire, 199 So.2d 645 (Ala. 1967).
99 Allen v. Lindeman, 148 N.W.2d 610 (Ia. 1967).

clergyman. The governing Iowa statute affords a privilege to clergymen covering "any confidential communication properly entrusted to him in his professional capacity, and necessary and proper to enable him to discharge the function of his office according to the usual course of practice or discipline." The Iowa court recognized that the privilege had been construed broadly, but held that it could not reach an independent document that was not privileged in the hands of the person who had entrusted it to the minister. Otherwise, the court noted, relevant unprivileged evidence could be placed beyond judicial process by the simple expedient of depositing it with an attorney, a clergyman, or any other person who could be the recipient of a privileged communication under the statute.

In a criminal prosecution for rape, a minister who was called as a witness by both parties refused to testify at all in the proceedings on the ground that it would interfere with his religious obligations.[100] The judge presiding at the trial found him in contempt of court. Under the state statute making confidential communications with clergymen privileged, the layman communicant has the right to waive the privilege. Since the communicant waived his privilege, the minister sought to set aside his conviction of contempt by relying on his right to religious liberty under the First Amendment. The North Carolina Supreme Court rejected this argument, noting that if a clergyman could urge a broad privilege dependent on his personal religious views, so could any layman. It held that recognition of such a broad right would prove disruptive of the administration of justice and that therefore a compelling state interest took precedence over individual religious claims in this area. The court distinguished the Minnesota case of *In Re Jenison*,[101] in which a juror was excused from service on account of religious scruples. It pointed out that alternative jury service could be obtained from other persons without religious objections but that quite often the religionist who refuses to testify might be the only witness available.

---

[100] *In re* Williams, 269 N.C. 68, 152 S.E.2d 317 (1967).
[101] 125 N.W.2d 588 (1964).

Zoning and Related Cases

The religious liberty argument was advanced in a few zoning cases with mixed success. A New York trial court ruled that under governing state precedents a municipality could prescribe special restrictions as to height, length, set-back, and parking for religious buildings erected in residential zones, the free exercsie clause of the First Amendment notwithstanding.[102] Petitioner's site plan for an addition to an existing building had already been approved by the Planning Commission and the building plans had been forwarded to the Building Inspector and the Board of Architectural Review when an ordinance was passed requiring the Planning Commission to specify certain restrictions applying to nonresidential buildings in residential areas. After receiving approval from the Board of Architectural Review the petitioner refused to apply again for approval from the Planning Commission, arguing in part that the ordinance violated the First and Fourteenth Amendments of the United States. The trial judge recognized that petitioner could not be entirely excluded from a residential neighborhood nor unreasonably restricted in order to protect property values, prevent noise, or other inconveniences. However, it recognized that reasonable restrictions relating to public health, safety, and welfare could be appropriately imposed.

In an Illinois case the court referred to religious liberty to reinforce its judgment upholding a grant to a synagogue of a special use exception in a commercial zone.[103] Neighboring property owners appealed from a zoning board decision that permitted this use, advancing the argument that the synagogue would destroy the commercial continuity of the neighborhood and thereby lessen its attractiveness to pedestrian customers. They also argued that the use would cause traffic congestion, particularly since the proposed building would not provide for off-street parking. The zoning board of appeals had concluded that there would be no traffic problem because the members of the synagogue are prohibited from using motor vehicles on the Sabbath

---

[102] Westchester Reform Temple v. Griffin, 52 Misc.2d 726, 276 N.Y.S.2d 737 (Sup. Ct. 1966).

[103] Wolbach v. Zoning Bd. of Appeals, 82 Ill. App. 288, 226 N.E.2d 679 (1967).

and on high religious holidays. The appellants challenged this finding of the board as lacking substantial evidence because it did not take into account weekday use of the synagogue nor the likelihood that such use would increase with an expanding congregation. The appellate court met this point with the rule that the findings of fact by an administrative agency in Illinois will be upheld unless "an opposite conclusion be clearly evident." The court did go on to note, however, that if the increased traffic argument by appellants were adopted as sound it would be sufficient to bar all buildings for religious worship from the commercial areas of Chicago, a result "not consonant with the constitutional guarantees of religion."

In other cases religious organizations were freed from restrictions on the use of their property without any reliance on the free exercise principle. One case involved an order enjoining a Jewish congregation from using a building as a synagogue because the land was subject to private covenants restricting it to residential use.[104] When defendant bought the synagogue it had been used as a chapel and religious administration office by a congregation of Seventh Day Adventists for eighteen years, continuously and openly, without any objection from neighboring property owners. Relying on equitable principles alone and ignoring the religious factor entirely, the Court of Appeals of New York reversed and refused to enforce the covenants where delay had become "unconscionable" and had caused the party against whom the covenants were now asserted to act in reliance on the long established use.

In another New York case a lower court interpreted a village zoning ordinance in a way that granted parochial schools preferred treatment as compared with nonprofit private schools.[105] Petitioner had been denied a permit to construct a church and an affiliated school on a twelve acre plot of land because a local ordinance required "a nonprofit private school to have 60 acres of land." That ordinance made no mention of parochial schools. However, the ordinance permitting

---

[104] Zaccaro v. Congregation Tifereth Israel, 20 N.Y.2d 77, 281 N.Y.S.2d 773 (1967).

[105] Greater New York Corp. of Seventh Day Adventists v. Miller, 54 Misc.2d 268, 282 N.Y.S.2d 390 (Sup. Ct. 1967).

special exception uses in residential zones included "parochial schools" specifically and made no mention of minimum acreage requirements. Accordingly, petitioner argued that it was entitled to a special use permit on twelve acres of land. The village board of appeals denied the special exception use on the ground that the words "parochial schools" in the ordinance did not include schools which gave full-time instruction in secular subjects as well as religious instruction. In reversing, the court interpreted the ordinance in light of the widespread use of the word "parochial schools" to include full-time schools operated under religious auspices. In doing so, it noted that a zoning ordinance is to be strictly construed in favor of the owner.

The problem of accessory uses with regard to churches and church-related schools raises some difficult problems. This is particularly so with regard to the residence of members of a religious order serving as teachers in a parochial school. In a Missouri case an appellate court upheld an injunction preventing the construction of a residence for nine to eleven teaching nuns of a parochial school because it violated private restrictive covenants limiting the use of the land to "detached single family dwellings." [106] Although the court's opinion noted that the internal living arrangements and relationships between the nuns had familial characteristics, it held that most people would not describe the nuns living together in such a building as a "family" nor the residence as a "single family dwelling."

A contrary result obtained in a Florida case where the appellate court refused to interpret the word "family" according to common parlance when it was used in a zoning ordinance that defined a "family" as "one or more persons occupying premises and living as a single housekeeping unit" and distinguished a family residence from a "boarding house, a lodging house or hotel." [107] Since the ordinance clearly went beyond the common concept of family based on consanguinity or affinity, the court concluded that a building in a district zoned for "single family residences" could be used by a small group of religious novices who would live on the premises under the direction

---

[106] Cash v. Catholic Diocese, 414 S.W.2d 346 (Mo. K.C. Ct. App. 1967).
[107] Carrol v. City of Miami Beach, 198 So.2d 643 (Fla. Ct. App. 1967).

of a Mother Superior. There was a strong dissent urging that the word "family" be given its common meaning because that would best achieve the legislative purpose of the ordinance. The dissent argued that the interpretation of the majority would permit college sorority and fraternity houses to qualify as single family residences, a result believed to be clearly at odds with the purpose of the ordinance.

Participation by a church-related institution in an urban renewal project was attacked as an unconstitutional aid to religion in one case.[108] The owner of property condemned as part of a federally subsidized urban renewal project brought suit in the federal district court to enjoin the City of Grand Rapids from proceeding with the program. Among other things, he alleged that a private sectarian hospital located in the area would probably be the successful bidder and become the principal redeveloper. It was argued that the benefits flowing from such participation would violate the First and Fourteenth Amendments.

In upholding the project the court pointed out that although the sectarian institution would benefit from being able to purchase the property at a lower price from the city than from its current owners, this benefit would be one generally available to all members of the public who might qualify to participate in urban renewal programs. The redevelopment plan would achieve the public purpose of removing an area of blight and any subsequent uses consistent with the plan would be incidental or ancillary to that purpose. The court quoted from the Supreme Court's decision in the *Berman* case,[109] which had upheld the constitutionality of urban redevelopment programs, to illustrate that churches were expected to be included in urban renewal projects. A second, even more conclusive reason for upholding participation was advanced by the court; the proposed uses in the redevelopment plan would be for a conspicuously public secular purpose, the erection and maintenance of a medical center. A number of state court opinions were cited to indicate that the hospital care provided by a private sectarian, nonprofit institution constitutes a secular function which can be directly aided by the state because of

[108] Ellis v. City of Grand Rapids, 257 F.Supp. 564 (W.D. Mich. 1966).
[109] Berman v. Parker, 348 U.S. 26 (1954).

the latter's paramount interest in health. Finally, if a hospital were denied the right to participate only because of its religious affiliation, serious questions of violation of equal protection and religious liberty would be raised.

The religious factor was injected into an eminent domain proceeding for the purpose of increasing the value of land held by certain kinds of religious organizations. The case involved condemnation of land owned by the Roman Catholic Diocese of Buffalo for cemetery purposes.[110] In testifying concerning the rate of return for purposes of capitalizing the value of a cemetery, a witness for the diocese urged that cemetery land held for nonprofit purposes should be valued more than similar parcels held for profit and that "consecrated land" should be valued more highly than nonconsecrated land simply "dedicated" to cemetery purposes. The witness testified that in some religious denominations, notably the Roman Catholic, religious beliefs require members to be buried in sacred ground. This testimony was apparently ignored by the lower court in arriving at a rate of return.

On appeal to the New York Court of Appeals, Judge Van Voorhis, dissenting on other grounds, commented on this testimony. He argued that under no rational system of valuation could the value of the land depend on who owned it rather than its potential use. He could not understand how land could be transformed in value simply by its transfer into the hands of a nonprofit organization. Similarly, he rejected the notion that the same cemetery land would have a different value when held by different sects, allowing those who require their constituents to be buried in consecrated ground to claim greater value for their property because of their religious beliefs.

In reviewing the grant of a license to a private club located near a Methodist church, the Superior Court of Delaware directed the Alcoholic Beverage Control Commission to take and consider evidence related to the tenets of the Methodist Church concerning consumption of alcohol.[111] The court concluded that such evidence should be taken

---

[110] Diocese of Buffalo v. State, 18 N.Y.2d 41, 271 N.Y.S.2d 670, 218 N.E.2d 544 (1966).

[111] Application of X-Chequer Inn, 229 A.2d 22 (Del. Super. Ct. 1967).

into account by the Commission in balancing the interest of the church against the club's interest in the proposed liquor license.

Intra-Church Property Disputes

In the nineteenth century case of *Watson v. Jones* [112] the Supreme Court of the United States held that federal courts should determine the use and control of church property in accordance with the rules and practices of the denomination involved. Accordingly, in the case of a church with a congregational structure the right to control the use of the property lies with a majority of its members, and in a church with an hierarchial one the use should be determined by the persons vested with such authority under the rules and practices of the church. The question has been raised whether the rule of the *Watson* case is required by constitutional law,[113] particularly in light of the Supreme Court's decisions in the *Kedroff* [114] and *Kreshik* [115] cases, which held that it was unconstitutional for the state of New York to transfer property held by a Soviet-sponsored church in the United States to a rebellious local faction.

A federal district court in Alabama has ruled that at least part of the *Watson* rule is constitutionally required.[116] The court struck down the Dumas Act of Alabama, which attempted to transfer the control of church property in Protestant denominations to local congregations regardless of contrary internal church regulations. The Act, which was passed in 1959, provided that where 65 percent or more of a local congregation declares itself in disagreement with the laws, discipline, social creeds, and jurisdictional system of its parent church, the majority may sever its connection with the latter and retain the possession of church property. After finding themselves in basic disagreement over the social policies of the Methodist Church, over 65 percent of

---

[112] 80 U.S. (13 Wall.) 679 (1872).

[113] *E.g.* Note, *Judicial Intervention in Disputes over the Use of Church Property,* 75 HARV. L. REV. 1142 (1962).

[114] Kedroff v. St. Nicholas Cathedral, 344 U.S. 94 (1952).

[115] Kreshik v. St. Nicholas Cathedral, 363 U.S. 190 (1960).

[116] Goodson v. Northside Bible Church, 261 F.Supp. 99 (S.D. Ala. 1966), *aff'd.* 387 F.2d 534 (1968).

the congregation of Trinity Methodist Church of Mobile separated themselves from the parent church and took over control of the church property pursuant to procedures of the Dumas Act. Plaintiff, representing the Methodist Church, brought an action to recover the property on the ground that the Dumas Act violated the First and Fourteenth Amendments of the Constitution.

The trial court found that the statute violated the free exercise clause of the First Amendment because it interfered with the constitutionally protected freedom of the Methodist Church to select and assign itinerant ministers to local congregations. The court was of the opinion that the holding of the *Watson* case that the hierarchial bodies of a connectional church should determine property disputes within their ecclesiastical jurisdiction was now constitutionally required. Since the General Conference of the Methodist Church is vested with ultimate control over the appointment of ministers, the court found that the statutory transfer of this power to a majority of the congregation violated the constitution of the church. The court also concluded that the Dumas Act violated the basic principle of separation of church and state embodied in the First Amendment because it singled out only Protestant churches for its special treatment and because it expressed a preference for a congregational church structure.

In determining intra-church property disputes, many state courts qualify the dictum in the *Watson* case concerning majority control of property in congregational-type churches. They hold that a majority cannot divert church property to another denomination or to the support of doctrines radically and fundamentally opposed to the traditional ones of the church. Because of this qualification, the merger of the Evangelical and Reformed Church with a number of assenting churches of the Congregational Christian Churches of United States into the United Church of Christ in 1951 is still open to legal challenge over fifteen years later. In 1953, the New York Court of Appeals upheld the merger when it was challenged by a Congregational church that objected to the union. In that case, the *Cadman* case,[117] the plaintiff church had attempted to block the General Council of

---

[117] Cadman Memorial v. Kenyon, 306 N.Y. 151, 116 N.E.2d 481 (1953).

the Congregational Churches from participating in the merger in order to prevent the properties and funds held by the various boards and agencies of the General Council from passing to the merged church. These boards and agencies had been formed to carry on specific functions in areas of joint concern of the individual Congregational churches. The New York court denied recovery in that case on the ground that each individual Congregational church had made absolute gifts to the boards and agencies of the General Council, so that they had no property interests giving them standing to object to the change in ecclesiastical affiliation of the agencies. However, the New York court did go on to observe that the proposed union would "in no way change the historical pattern of the individual Congregational Church." It based this conclusion on certain concessions in the case to the effect that the merger would not subject any Congregational church to the United Church of Christ as far as ecclesiastical affairs were concerned; also it was clear that no individual Congregational church could be compelled to join the proposed merger contrary to the wishes of the majority of its congregation.

The *Cadman* case, a class action, was successfully relied on to bar subsequent lawsuits seeking to challenge various aspects of the merger.[118] However, the Supreme Court of Michigan rejected this approach during the period surveyed in a case brought by the dissenting minority of an individual Congregational church that had decided to merge.[119] The plaintiffs sought to recall the local church from the merger on the ground that participation in the union violated the basic autonomy of Congregational churches as to matters of doctrine and thereby brought about a substantial departure from basic Congregational tenets. The trial judge had dismissed the case on a motion for summary judgment without going into the question of substantial departure because he found that this issue had been decided against the plaintiffs in the *Cadman* case. His judgment was affirmed by the Michigan Court of Appeals.

---

[118] *E.g.*, First Congregational Church v. Evangelical and Reformed Church, 305 F.2d 724 (2d Cir. 1962); *see* 1963 RELIGION AND THE PUBLIC ORDER 277 (1964).
[119] Berkaw v. Mayflower Congregational Church, 378 Mich. 239, 144 N.W.2d 444 (1966).

The State Supreme Court reversed on the ground that the *Cadman* case had not in fact passed on the question of substantial departure. The Michigan court sought to restrict the language of the New York court suggesting that there had been no departure from basic Congregational doctrines to the context of a suit brought by a *nonassenting* church objecting to the merger, as was the case in *Cadman*. It pointed out that such a church would have none of its proprety interests affected in such a merger. Therefore there had been no civil issue before the New York court to decide in *Cadman*. The Michigan court concluded that the New York Court of Appeals had been "keenly aware of its own jurisdictional limitations and thus did not consciously take up any ecclesiastical questions, any idle phrases suggesting such to the contrary notwithstanding." The case at bar was remanded by the Michigan Supreme Court for a trial on the issue of whether the majority of the local had in fact violated basic Congregational doctrines by joining in the merger.

There were other state cases applying the limitation that a majority may not depart from fundamental doctrine and continue to control church property, but in none of them was the fact of substantial departure established.[120] The Supreme Court of Virginia found that a dispute in a local congregation of the Christian Church did not involve matters of fundamental doctrine.[121] The local dispute mirrored a more general one that had arisen in 1955 concerning the proper degree of cooperation among individual churches of the denomination. A group of the churches, generally known as the Disciples of Christ, preach Christian unity and support missionary societies. In 1963 the majority of the local congregation voted to sever its connection with the Virginia Christian Missionary Society and generally to adopt a more independent stand. A minority of the congregation challenged this change in policy as a departure from fundamental doctrine.

The court held that there was no such departure. It found that all Christian Churches, even those which cooperate through missionary societies, remain essentially independent, autonomous parties. There-

---

[120] *E.g.,* Church at Seattle v. Hendrix, 422 P.2d 482 (Wash. 1967). Other examples are cited in nn. 121–124.
[121] Baber v. Caldwell, 207 Va. 694, 152 S.E.2d 23 (1967).

fore, even if the local congregation had been "inter-related" with other Christian churches and had cooperated with them prior to 1953, its change of policy in this regard was not a basic one.

An interpleader action was brought in the Missouri courts to determine which of two contending factions of a small church, the Pentacostal Tabernacle, was entitled to surplus funds from a forced sale of church property subject to a mortgage.[122] For a number of years the congregation met in rented quarters. Throughout this period the church was entirely self-governing and had no formal structure. When the property in question was purchased, three trustees were appointed for the purpose of holding it. Two of the trustees, constituting one faction in litigation, formulated a set of by-laws for the church, which were rejected. As interpreted by the court, these rules would have ousted the incumbent pastor. The remaining trustee and the pastor headed up the second faction. They subsequently called a meeting of the congregation, which unanimously voted to affiliate with a nationally organized body, the Church of God. The trial court awarded the surplus proceeds to the Church of God faction.

The two trustees appealed from the decision on two grounds. First, they claimed that the meeting held to determine affiliation with the Church of God was void because they had not received sufficient notice. At the trial both factions alleged that the other side had "withdrawn" from the local congregation when the proposed by-laws were rejected. Since the trial court had apparently found that the two trustees were the ones who had withdrawn, they were not entitled to notice of the subsequent meeting to affiliate. The second ground of attack alleged that affiliation with the Church of God involved departure from basic doctrines of the Pentacostal Tabernacle. The court found no evidence on the record of any conflict between the theological beliefs of the two churches. The two trustees challenging the affiliation relied primarily on the fact that the Pentacostal Tabernacle did not have any formalized government whereas the Church of God was highly organized, with national headquarters, and with state and district superintendents. The court held that in a congregational-type

122 Lewis v. Wolfe, 413 S.W.2d 314 (Mo. Ct.App. 1967).

church the minority could only prevail by showing a "real and substantial departure from the *essential theological doctrine of the church.*" It went on to say that "changes which affect only the business management or temporal control, or the mere form of worship" were not within the scope of a basic departure from doctrine.

In a litigation to determine which of two companies would be able to use certain property under conflicting oil and gas leases, the Kentucky Court of Appeals concluded that the decision depended upon whether the founders of the Regular Baptist Church at Flat Creek, the record owner of the property, believed in absolute predestination or limited predestination.[123] The founders of the church had believed in limited predestination. But there was a schism at the turn of the century and the believers in "absolute predestination" expelled the other faction, which merged with the Salem Primitive Baptist Church. The lower court also found that in 1957 the congregation of the Flat Creek church merged with the Salem church. Adherents to the doctrine of "absolute predestination" apparently did not recognize the merger. However, the property involved had been used only as a cemetery for some time prior to the merger, and the county clerk had appointed trustees for the property to convey an oil lease to defendant. Plaintiff, the Salem Baptist Church, brought suit to quiet title and confirm the rights that they had granted on an oil lease to a second company. The trial court found for the plaintiff because of the 1957 merger, and the Court of Appeals affirmed. The latter apparently concluded that the 1957 merger with the Salem Church was valid because the affiliation with believers in the doctrine of "limited predestination" actually involved a return to the views of the church's founders.

The North Carolina Supreme Court attempted to dispose finally of a dispute between two factions of the Davis Original Free Will Baptist Church in a matter that had several times appeared before the court during the preceding years.[124] The court found that the schism in the local church mirrored disagreements between the North Carolina association of Free Will Baptist Churches and the national asso-

[123] Volger v. Salem Primitive Baptist Church, 415 S.W.2d 72 (Ky. 1967).
[124] Paul v. Piner, 271 N.C. 123, 155 S.E.2d 526 (1967).

ciation. There was no evidence in the record that the disagreement turned on fundamental matters of doctrine. Proceeding from the general rule that church property should remain in the control of a faction faithful to the doctrines of the church, the state supreme court upheld a judgment for the defendant, the party controlling the property, simply because the plaintiffs had failed to show any departure from fundamental doctrines.

The New York Court of Appeals upheld a decision concerning an expenditure of church funds because it had been made in accordance with the appropriate ecclesiastical authorities.[125] The court, without delivering an opinion, upheld the dismissal of a complaint that sought to enjoin the Presbytery of Western New York from expending funds on any organization linked to the Industrial Areas Foundation of Saul Alinsky, a community organizer, on the ground that the expenditure was not for religious purposes. The appellate division had decided that a trial need not be held to determine whether the proposed use of church funds was foreign to the discipline, rules, and usages of the Presbyterian Church.[126] It had found that the expenditures were lawful because the General Assembly of the United Presbyterian Church had approved a statement of policy in support of community organization.

When a Seventh Day Adventist church became defunct, a trial court in Texas set aside a transfer made by minority members of the congregation to a named trustee, but refused to transfer the property to one of eight self-styled successors to the church. Instead, the court appointed a receiver to hold the property in trust for certain intervening parties in the litigation who had made contributions to the church in order to establish a fund for care in their old age. In previous years these persons had made "Second Tithes" to the church. The "First Tithe" was for gospel work. The successor congregation that had initiated the litigation sought to have the trial court's order set aside on two grounds. First, it contended that there was no evidence to support the conclusion that the church property involved in the

---

[125] Knight v. The Presbytery of Western New York, 18 N.Y.2d 868, 276 N.Y.S.2d 120, 222 N.E.2d 738 (1967).
[126] 26 A.D. 19, 270 N.Y.S.2d 218 (1966).

case had been purchased with "Second Tithe Funds." The appellate court found the point irrelevant because even if the church had mingled "First Tithe" and "Second Tithe" funds, then both would be held subject to the trust for the care of "Second Tithe" contributors in their old age. Second, the appellants urged that under Texas statutes the property of the defendant's church passed to it as successor. The court held that the statutes relied on were inapplicable because of the special trust impressed on the funds.[127]

A Texas congregation sought to recover property conveyed to a former pastor by a warranty deed that had been executed pursuant to a church resolution directing the pastor to build a parsonage on the land when feasible and also granting the church an option to repurchase the equity in the property when it was financially able to do so. The deed itself made no mention of the parsonage or the option to repurchase. Since the property never was improved, the church sought to recover it by reimbursing the pastor for the taxes he had paid on it. He claimed that his equity was much larger and included the value of numerous services that he had rendered to the congregation gratuitously.

The court did not have to determine the extent of the pastor's equity because it found that the option to repurchase was void as a restraint on alienation.[128] It refused even to consider enforcement of an alleged promise by the pastor to reconvey the land to the church because the statute of limitations on contract actions had passed. It refused to impose a constructive trust on the property because such relief would have required the plaintiff church to allege and prove fraud on the pastor's part, such as an intention never to perform the promise when he took the property. No such allegation or proof was offered.

In deciding between conflicting claims of title to property, the Maryland Court of Appeals decided in favor of a church even though there was a gap in the succession of trustees holding the property for

[127] General Ass'n of Davidian Seventh Day Adventists, Inc. v. General Ass'n, 410 S.W.2d 256 (Civ. App. Tex. 1966).
[128] Trustees of Casa View Assembly v. Williams, 414 S.W.2d 697 (Tex. Civ. App. 1967).

the church in the 1890's.[129] The gap was bridged when new trustees were subsequently elected in accordance with the ritual and discipline of the Methodist Episcopal Church in the United States of America.

The Michigan Court of Appeals held that church members who object to church purchase of property constitute a class under Michigan law that could bring a suit to enjoin the proposed acquisition and to demand an accounting of church funds.[130]

A New York trial court enjoined the deacon and trustees of a Baptist church from holding a meeting to vote on the dismissal of the pastor because the notice of the meeting had not been given in strict accordance with Section 133 of the New York Religious Corporation Law.[131] Since Hiscox's *New Directory of Baptist Churches* did not make any reference to formalities for calling a meeting and since there was no evidence of a custom or usage concerning the matter in the church involved, the court decided to require compliance with Section 133.

Testamentary Disposition

A party contesting a will in California unsuccessfully attempted to use the court as a forum in which to try some of the doctrines of the Roman Catholic religion. The testator of the estate left the bulk of it to various persons and groups affiliated with the Roman Catholic church. The will was attacked on the grounds of fraud and undue influence. The plaintiff alleged that defendant had been educated by Roman Catholic agencies, which had instilled in him a belief in heaven, hell, and purgatory and had led him to believe that, as a reward for gifts to the Roman Catholic church and its agencies, prayers and ceremonials would be said to help him gain heaven or to shorten his stay in purgatory. The Roman Catholic legatees answered the complaint by admitting the Church's teaching about heaven, hell and purgatory and that salvation could be obtained by means of faith, supplemented by good works, including gifts to the church; but they

---

[129] Smith v. Washington, 245 Md. 300, 226 A.2d 335 (1967).

[130] Miller v. McClung, 4 Mich. App. 714, 145 N.W.2d 473 (1966).

[131] Hayes v. Brantley, 53 Misc.2d 1040, 280 N.Y.S.2d 291 (Sup.Ct. 1967).

denied that, as a reward for such gifts, the church would recite prayers or perform ceremonials to avoid hell, or to escape more quickly from purgatory.

The trial court granted summary judgment and this was upheld by the court of appeal.[132] The latter relied on the Supreme Court's decision in the *Ballard* case [133] which held that the First Amendment prohibited judicial inquiry into the truth or falsity of the religious doctrines of any church. At most the court would inquire into the sincerity with which those beliefs were held by individual persons. The will could only be attacked by alleging and proving lack of belief on the part of those who had advanced the teachings. Since the complaint did not allege that the persons who had taught the testator had been insincere, it was dismissed.

Sunday Closing Laws

Sunday closing laws have been challenged under the Fourteenth Amendment of the federal constitution on three grounds; first, that they constitute an establishment of religion contrary to the First Amendment; second, that they usually contain discriminatory exemptions that violate the equal protection and due process clauses; and third, that they are enforced in a discriminatory fashion. During the period surveyed, North Dakota's Sunday closing laws were attacked on all three grounds. They were attacked as an establishment of religion because their language revealed religious concerns by making references to "Sabbath breaking" and by expressing the purpose of setting aside the first day of the week "for rest and religious uses." The North Dakota Supreme Court [134] recognized that the laws had a religious basis historically, but concluded that, like the Maryland Sunday closing law upheld by the Supreme Court in the *McGowan* case,[135] they had come to serve secular ends. Current exemptions from the laws for certain recreational activities indicated to the court that they

---

[132] *In re* Estate of Supple, 55 Cal. Rptr. 542 (1967).
[133] United States v. Ballard, 322 U.S. 78 (1944).
[134] State v. Gamble Skogmo Inc., 144 N.W.2d 749 (N.D. 1966).
[135] McGowan v. Maryland, 366 U.S. 420 (1961).

had the secular purpose of providing a common day of rest and recreation rather than one of religious observance.

The laws were also attacked on the ground that they provided for an arbitrary pattern of exemptions, which was exemplified by permission to sell fruit on Sunday whereas the sale of bread was prohibited. The court, again relying on the reasoning and result in the *McGowan* case which had upheld the constitutionality of diverse exemptions, concluded that the state had to be granted wide discretion in formulating Sunday closing laws. Noting the complexity of the interests involved in achieving a common day of rest on the one hand while providing sufficient opportunity for recreational pursuits and the availability of necessary commodities on the other, the state court followed the Supreme Court in concluding that only invidious discrimination resting on irrational grounds would constitute a constitutional infirmity.

Finally, the defendant, a large discount store, alleged discriminatory enforcement of the law in that certain nonexempt activities, such as Sunday radio and television broadcasting as well as the sale of food and merchandise on the midways of fairgrounds, had not been prosecuted. The court held that only purposeful and intentional discrimination in the enforcement of the law against certain classes of offenders constituted such discrimination. The court required the defendant to demonstrate a pattern of nonenforcement against other sellers in the same category as itself.

In three cases violators of Sunday closing laws were able to resist criminal convictions on the ground that the law was being discriminatorily enforced. In two of the cases commercial establishments selling goods in competition with the complaining offenders were involved. A large discount house was able to enjoin prosecution of the Sunday laws as long as "drug stores," "groceries," and "supermarkets" were permitted to remain open on Sunday to sell competing merchandise.[136] The injunction was upheld by the Kentucky Court of Appeals on the ground that the prohibited discrimination violated the equal protection clause of the Fourteenth Amendment.

---

[136] City of Ashland v. Heck's, Inc., 407 S.W.2d 421 (Ky. 1966).

In the second case, involving the enforcement of an Atlanta, Georgia municipal ordinance, the court found pursuant to a stipulation that drug stores were not only selling drugs on Sunday, an item of necessity exempted from the statute, but that they were also selling merchandise such as television sets and lawn mowers, in competition with the petitioners seeking to enjoin enforcement of the statute.[137] Television repairmen also were able to work on Sunday without interference. The court, however, did not enjoin all enforcement of the ordinance; it limited its decree to the restraint of discriminatory enforcement.

The third case did not appear to involve discrimination among competitors. In it the Municipal Court of Akron, Ohio refused to convict thirty-seven employees of the Grant Tiger Store because it found that the Sunday closing ordinance was not being enforced against men working on construction projects.[138] Although they were aware that the construction workers were laboring on Sunday, the village police took no action. When employees of the Grant Tiger Store filed affidavits charging these other violations, they were dismissed in the Mayor's Court for lack of evidence after the defendant construction workers pleaded "no contest." On these facts the municipal court found that the law enforcement officials of the village of Fairlawn were consciously and intentionally discriminating against the Grant Tiger Store. For this reason it dismissed the prosecutions with prejudice.

The Supreme Court of New Hampshire delivered an advisory opinion upholding the constitutionality of certain proposed revisions of that state's Sunday closing law.[139] It held that businesses could be exempted from coverage under the act on the basis of smallness in store size or of number of regular employees. However, the court noted that while an exemption limited to all stores smaller than 5000 square feet was a reasonable classification, one encompassing all stores under 9000 sq. ft. was not. The latter exemption would be unconstitutional

---

[137] Zayre v. City of Atlanta, 276 F.Supp. 892 (N.D. Ga. 1967).
[138] Village of Fairlawn v. Fuller, 221 N.E.2d 851 (Ohio, Mun. Ct. Akron 1966).
[139] Opinion of the Justices, 229 A.2d 188 (N.H. 1967).

because of "arbitrary and invidious discrimination between stores of a competitive nature."

An opinion was simultaneously requested concerning an exemption for any secular place of business under the control of a Sabbatarian who causes all the places of business over which he has control in New Hampshire to close down during the 24-hour period of his Sabbath. The court concluded that such an exemption would not violate the establishment clause. Indeed, the court noted in passing that there was opinion to the effect that the Supreme Court's decision in the *Braunfeld* case [140] might be overruled and such Sabbatarian exemptions might become constitutionally required under the free exercise clause.

A New York City judge refused to apply the state's Sunday closing law to outlaw commercial practices that had been going on for almost a century.[141] Until March 1967, the city's fresh foodstuff market had been located at the downtown Washington Market. The practice had been to close down Saturday afternoon and reopen Sunday in the afternoon, at which time produce would be removed from freight cars while fresh fruits and vegetables would be rebagged for distribution. As a result of urban renewal the market was forced to move to the Bronx, and the local police precincts in charge of the area initiated the prosecution through the legal bureau of the New York City Police Department.

Defendant successfully argued that its activities came within the statutory exemption for "works of necessity." The trial judge expressed his intention to interpret the law in a way best suited to the needs of modern life. He found that one of those needs was the requirement of the public to have fresh fruits and vegetables in its diet. Accordingly, after observing that the New York courts had ruled that "painting one's mother-in-law's house on Sunday [could not be considered] anything but a work of necessity" the judge decided to include the market activities under that standard.

Two other courts declined to interpret Sunday closing laws in such

140 Braunfeld v. Brown, 366 U.S. 599 (1961).
141 People v. Spinelli, 54 Misc.2d 485, 282 N.Y.S.2d 354 (N.Y.C. Crim. Ct. 1967).

a generous fashion. The city court for Utica, New York, held that the sale of gas-line anti-freeze on Sunday did not come within the statutory exemption for the sale of "gasoline." [142] In response to defendant's argument that the statutory exemption had been interpreted in the past to include radiator anti-freeze because, "like gasoline," it was a by-product of crude petroleum and was important to Sunday travel in cold weather, the court answered that the exemptions should be construed according to their "natural and most obvious sense."

The Ohio Court of Appeals reversed the dismissal of a Sunday closing law prosecution against a retail store employee who had given a customer directions of how to pay by check at the check-out counter.[143] The reason for the trial court's dismissal was the failure by the prosecution to establish that the employee's duties were not intellectual. The appellate court ruled that the statute's prohibition of "common labor" on Sunday covered skilled labor.

The Supreme Court of North Carolina refused to permit judicial examination of the motives of city officials in enacting a Sunday closing ordinance.[144] The owner of a general retail store sought to have the ordinance declared invalid on the ground that it was the product of a conspiracy between local officials and merchants who wanted to close on Sunday and yet did not want the plaintiff to enjoy a competitive advantage. The court affirmed a dismissal of the complaint on the ground that the courts could do no more than examine whether the local authorities had power to enact the ordinance.

In what appeared to be a case of first impression, the Maryland Court of Appeals held that a contract for the sale of land was unenforceable when executed on Sunday in violation of the state's Sunday closing law.[145] The court read the statutory prohibition of "work" and "bodily labor" on Sunday as meant to cover the operations of real estate agents.

---

[142] People v. Berkowitz, 54 Misc.2d 156, 281 N.Y.S.2d 156 (City Ct. Utica 1967).

[143] State v. Heaton, 10 Ohio App.2d 44, 225 N.E.2d 608 (1967).

[144] Clark's Greenville, Inc. v. West, 268 N.C. 527, 151 S.E.2d 5 (1966).

[145] Patton v. Graves, 244 Md. 528, 224 A.2d 411 (1966).

Domestic Relations

In a child custody case turning entirely on the religious beliefs and practices of the mother, the California Court of Appeal ruled that she should be awarded custody of the child even though there was a substantial risk that her religious attitudes might create an environment not in the best interests of the child.[146] As part of a divorce decree the trial judge had awarded custody of a two-year-old child to the father. Both parents were members of the Plymouth Brethren. After their marriage a schism developed in their local religious community which led to a schism in the marriage. The wife, at her father's prompting, joined the Plymouth faction which believes in "separation." This doctrine rejects such worldly activities as listening to the radio, watching television, and playing social games. It also requires that those who adhere to these beliefs live apart from others engaged in worldly activities, and most particularly that the true believer not take meals in common with the "unclean." Because of her beliefs, the wife quarreled with her husband concerning the operation of radio and television sets in the home and refused to take her meals with him, although she would prepare his food. These activities on her part led to the divorce.

The mother testified that she would bring up the child in her father's house and inculcate in him respect for the doctrine of separation. She admitted that this would imply that the child should no longer visit with his father, but she agreed to abide by the court's decree and observe any visitation rights extended to him. The trial judge found that both parents were of good moral character but awarded custody to the father on the ground that it would be best for the mental health of the child. The judge found that constant exposure to the doctrine of separation would tend to alienate the child from his father. He found that it would also alienate him from his classmates at school, diminish his interest in secular learning, and keep him from participating in many valuable social organizations, such as the Boy Scouts.

The court of appeal reversed, rejecting the trial judge's argument of "spiritual and intellectual impoverishment." The court pointed out

[146] Quiner v. Quiner, 59 Cal. Rptr. 503 (Ct. App. 1967).

that under California law custody was to be granted to the mother, all other matters being equal. Since the trial judge had found both parents equally qualified except for the religious factor, the appellate court regarded the award to the father as a penalty for the mother's religious beliefs. In its opinion, the trial court's finding that the child's mental health would be endangered was inextricably bound up with an evaluation of the mother's religious beliefs. The court of appeal seemed to suggest that the trial court had rejected the spiritual doctrine of separation because of its deviation from the accepted norm of the community. But, as long as the deviation did not involve conduct that was secularly immoral, unlawful, or contrary to public policy, the appellate court would not condemn it simply because it departed from what was considered socially desirable by most of the community.

The court concluded that religious teachings could only be a basis for the award when there was evidence that they had actually impaired the child's mental health. Short of such a demonstration the court would not take any action that would interfere with religiously motivated behavior patterns. The court noted that one of the reasons why courts did not take religious beliefs into account in awarding custody was because of their incompetence to know what was best in such matters. It observed that no court would dare remove a child from the custody of his parents when both subscribed to the Plymouth doctrine of separation. In addition, the court noted that certain social divisiveness was a necessary condition of achieving religious liberty in a pluralistic society and it cited parochial schools as a case in point.

The court was somewhat more concerned because the doctrine of separation threatened to produce a substantial cleavage between the child and his father. However, the court was not sure that the doctrine would "take" with the child, who would be with the father during liberal visitation periods. Even if it did "take," the court held that it would not necessarily mean that the child would no longer love and respect his father simply because he rejected the latter's way of life. Finally, with regard to protecting the child's mental health generally as well as his relationship to his father, the court noted that if the father could demonstrate that evil effects were in fact being caused by the mother's religious teachings, the decree could be altered in the future. Absent such a showing, the court refused to depart from the usual rule of giving the mother custody.

There was a vigorous dissent which rejected the idea that both parents were equally qualified to care for the child when the home life that the mother proposed to provide was "dismally narrow and dull." It refused to regard the denial of custody as a "penalty" for the mother's religious beliefs. If deprivation of custody were to be construed as a penalty, the dissent argued that it should be properly imposed on the mother because it was her conduct in rejecting the father as "unclean" that caused the disruption of the family. The dissent heaped scorn on the majority's contradictory propositions that the son could be taught to reject his father as "unclean" on the one hand and continue to respect and love him on the other. It was particularly concerned with the imposition of a marked environmental change on the now four-year-old child who had been in the father's custody for the previous two years following the trial court's award. The dissent was not very much consoled with the assurance that the decree could be changed upon demonstration of actual ill effects because "a lifetime of remedial care often fails to correct traumas sustained in childhood."

In Connecticut a wife who had obtained a legal separation from her husband on the ground of adultery unsuccessfully sought to bar him from obtaining a final divorce; [147] her objection was that divorce was contrary to her religious beliefs as a Roman Catholic. In granting the divorce, the court noted that religious factors were relevant in matrimonial cases, but they could not automatically outweigh contrary social interests. Since the court found neither party to be interested in resuming the marriage relationship, it concluded that there were no social considerations to outweigh the husband's interest in being able to remarry.

In an Arizona case the religious factor was adverted to in deciding the custody of an orphan.[148] The paternal grandparents, who were ill and in their seventies, were vying for custody of their grandchildren

---

[147] Marazita v. Marazita, 27 Conn. Sup. 190, 233 A.2d 145 (1967).
[148] *In re* Anonymous, 4 Ariz. App. 588, 422 P.2d 419 (1967).

with a maternal aunt and uncle, who were healthy, in their forties, and had three other young children. An adoption decree in favor of the aunt and uncle was affirmed by the state court of appeals. One of the factors noted by the court was that the children had been baptized Catholics, like their adoptive parents, whereas the grandparents were Protestant.

The New York constitutional provision stating that a child "shall" be placed in the custody of a person of the same religious persuasion "when practicable" was interpreted to require such placement unless there were some "compelling reason" to do otherwise.[149] Accordingly, the court awarded custody of two children baptized and confirmed as Roman Catholics to their paternal aunt and uncle, who were also Catholics, rather than to their maternal aunt and uncle, who were Episcopalians.

LEGISLATIVE, ADMINISTRATIVE, AND OTHER DEVELOPMENTS

Religion in the Public Schools

Congressional efforts to modify the Supreme Court's decisions prohibiting devotional Bible reading and prayers gradually subsided during the period surveyed. Senator Dirksen's proposed constitutional amendment that would have permitted "students or others" to engage in voluntary prayers in public schools reached the Senate floor in September 1966 but was defeated 49–37. Senator Dirksen again introduced his amendment in the opening days of the Ninetieth Congress but no action was taken on it.

Some local school districts continued to permit individual public school teachers to recite prayers or read from the Bible on their own initiative despite the Supreme Court's decisions. Such an approach was considered proper by Attorney General Blankenship of Oklahoma in February 1967. In doing so, he withdrew an opinion rendered several months before by his predecessor, Attorney General Nesbit, that all religious exercises in the public schools were unconstitutional. Attorney General Blankenship was of the opinion that dicta of the Su-

---

[149] Starr v. DeRocco, 29 A.D. 662, 286 N.Y.S.2d 313 (2d Dept. 1967).

preme Court in the *Schempp* and *Murray* cases contrary to the "clear language" of the First Amendment need not be followed. Since the First Amendment prohibits a "law respecting the establishment of religion," he concluded that it only reaches official "law making." Similarly he concluded that since the *Murray* and *Schempp* decisions involved devotional exercises prescribed by local authorities they were not controlling where "voluntary" exercises undertaken by the individual teachers were concerned.

The attorney general of Minnesota ruled that baccalaureate services in the public schools were unconstitutional even when attendance was voluntary. Because of the secular cultural significance of the Christmas season the attorney general of Wisconsin ruled that Christmas pageants could be presented in public schools when they were directed to nonreligious purposes.

The attorney general of Oregon rendered an opinion that it would be unconstitutional for a school board to permit a "student body chaplain" to give an invocation at student body council meetings and student body assemblies. Although the attorney general recognized that technically the student body organization is separate from the school, nonetheless its activities receive the implicit approval and support of the state because it is subject to the direction and guidance of school officials, uses school property during school hours, and must adhere to administrative rules.

In New Mexico the attorney general ruled that it would violate both the state and federal constitutions for the public schools to grant credit to their pupils for Bible study or other religious instruction received at church Sunday schools. The opinion treated the granting of credit for such study as tantamount to incorporating the religious courses into the public school program. The attorney general concluded that such incorporation was clearly prohibited by the *Engel* and *Schempp* cases.

Interest in the "objective teaching about religion" continues. The Pennsylvania Department of Public Instruction, in conjunction with the Pennsylvania State University, developed a religious literature course that includes study of the Bible; it is an optional course offered on the secondary school level. The attorney general of Wisconsin delivered an opinion that academic study "about" religion is proper in state-supported institutions of higher learning.

State Aid to Church-Related Institutions

Senator Ervin continued his efforts to pass legislation designed to give federal courts jurisdiction over taxpayer suits challenging federal expenditures under programs such as the 1964 Economic Opportunity Act and the 1965 Elementary and Secondary Education Act when grants are made to church-related institutions. The proposed legislation was passed twice by the Senate, in July 1966 and in April 1967. It was designed to reverse the rule of the *Frothingham* case barring taxpayer suits in federal courts by specifically authorizing suits challenging federal expenditures under the establishment clause of the First Amendment. Before the bill was acted on by the House, the Supreme Court decided to hear the appeal from a taxpayer suit challenging the 1965 education law, which had been dismissed by the Second Circuit on the basis of the *Frothingham* case. The Court subsequently reversed the lower court and held that taxpayers could challenge federal "spending" programs that violate specific constitutional limitations, such as the prohibition in the establishment clause. This decision permits cases initiated in federal courts in Ohio, Pennsylvania, and New York to proceed to a decision on the merits in their challenges to various aspects of and grants under the 1964 and 1965 Acts.

On the state level there were few developments of new state aid to students attending nonpublic schools. Most notable, perhaps, was the enactment in Ohio of legislation providing for a wide range of auxiliary aids to students attending nonpublic schools. Specifically listed are guidance, testing, and counseling programs; services for the deaf, blind, emotionally disturbed, crippled or physically handicapped; audio-visual aids, speech and hearing services; and programs for improving the educational and cultural status of disadvantaged pupils. Finally, the state is to provide services in a category apparently designed as a catch-all to include all supplementary aids apart from aid to the standard curriculum: it covers programs of "nonreligious instruction other than basic classroom instruction." All such supplementary services are to be provided to students in nonpublic schools on the same basis as provided to students in public schools.

In New Jersey expanded bus aid to students attending parochial schools was enacted. Under previous law local school boards could only transport such pupils along bus routes established for the public schools. Under the new law this limitation was removed and transportation had to be provided by local boards to any nonprofit school in the state when such transportation was supplied to public school students. The school must be "remote" from the home of the student seeking the state aid but no farther than 20 miles distant. Under the new law payments have been made to parents who drive their own children to nonprofit schools when the students are eligible for state aid under the new law.

In the November 1966 election Wisconsin voters approved a proposed amendment to the state constitution which would authorize public provision of transportation to nonpublic schools, including parochial schools. In Nebraska the voters voted down a similar amendment to their state constitution. Bus bills introduced into both the Minnesota and Iowa legislatures were not enacted. But the Iowa legislature did authorize a study of the private school transportation issue. In Indiana the state senate voted down an amendment to the state's busing law which would have made provision of transportation of pupils in nonpublic schools mandatory where such services are now discretionary with local boards.

A constitutional convention was convened in New York during 1967 to revise the state constitution. Among the extensive changes recommended by the Convention was the removal of the so-called Blaine Amendment to the New York Constitution, which prohibits direct or indirect state aid to schools under the direction or control of religious denominations or orders. In its place it was recommended that a more general prohibition against establishment of religion, similar to that in the First Amendment, be adopted. Many Roman Catholic officials urged the voters to approve of the proposed constitutional revision in the November 1967 elections because it included the elimination of the Amendment. Groups traditionally opposed to state aid to sectarian schools urged defeat of the referendum, which was also opposed by other groups on other grounds. The voters rejected the proposed changes.

The existing New York constitutional provision was invoked by Attorney General Lefkowitz in declaring unconstitutional a $100,000 grant made to establish and support an Albert Schweitzer Chair in the Humanities at Fordham University. The State Board of Regents had entered into two one-year contracts renewable annually in order to award Professor Marshall McLuhan such a chair at Fordham. The first contract was with the University and provided that the state would pay up to $70,000 for facilities, equipment, supplies, and professional and clerical assistants to support Professor McLuhan in his research and work. Attorney General Lefkowitz found such benefits to constitute direct aid to a sectarian institution. Even though he conceded that the grant did not involve a "gain to the strictly religious posture" of Fordham, he concluded that the school's general reputation would be enhanced by the award and its ability to attract scholars and develop graduate studies would be strengthened. The second contract was between the Regents and McLuhan. It provided that he would be paid $30,000 to fill the chair. Since the second contract was made in reliance of the first invalid contract, the attorney general concluded it was dependent on the first and equally invalid.

In New Jersey the legislature authorized a special study to determine how the state could aid private educational programs.

The attorney general of Oregon ruled that Hill-Burton funds administered by the state board of health can be applied to construction at church-related hospitals without violating the state constitution's prohibition against aid to sectarian institutions. The state board allocates the funds made available to Oregon by the federal government among nonprofit hospitals which apply for grants. Disbursements are made by the state treasurer out of a special Medical Facilities Construction Account. Despite state involvement, the attorney general concluded that the funds remained federal funds. He apparently based this conclusion on the degree of control exercised by the Surgeon General over the disbursement of the funds. While the work is in progress, the Surgeon General transmits funds to the state treasurer to cover that part of the construction certified by the state board of health to be already completed. The recipient of the grant then receives the money from the special account by presenting a voucher. The opinion noted that no state funds were expended "on a reimbursement basis or otherwise."

Finally, the attorney general concluded that even if the funds were to be regarded as state funds, expenditures for hospital construction were not unconstitutional merely because the institution benefited was sectarian. He held that the nature of the function undertaken by the institution, rather than the character of its affiliation, determined whether the aid improperly aided sectarian institutions.

Religious Pressures and Tensions over Public Issues

Mounting pressure to change the abortion laws created the greatest amount of controversy concerning moral issues in public matters. Support grows for the Model Penal Code's proposed revision of current abortion laws. The proposed changes would permit terminations of pregnancies in three situations not now recognized by most laws, which allow destruction of the fetus only to preserve the life of the mother. The three additional justifications relate to pregnancies that endanger the health of the mother, ones that have resulted from rape or incest, and ones that are likely to lead to the birth of a defective child.

During the period surveyed both Colorado and North Carolina revised their laws to permit abortion in the three kinds of cases suggested by the Model Penal Code. California law underwent a more restricted revision; only two of the three recommendations were adopted. Because of vigorous opposition from Governor Reagan and the threat of a veto, the legislature dropped the justification for abortion in cases where defective births were a risk. The California law is also more restrictive as to when a pregnancy can be legitimately terminated under the two new justifications. Such operations must be performed within the first twenty weeks of gestation. The North Carolina and Colorado laws, like the Model Penal Code recommendation, place no time limit on terminating a pregnancy generally, although the Colorado law does require the operation to be performed in the first four months of pregnancy when justification is based on rape.

Similar legislation was introduced in over twenty states, including New York, New Jersey, Pennsylvania, Maine, Maryland, Florida, New Mexico, Rhode Island, Arizona, Virginia, Texas, and Minnesota. Most of the bills were sidetracked when they encountered heavy opposition, notably from members of the Roman Catholic community. Nonetheless, laws patterned on the Model Penal Code were passed in Georgia and Maryland after the period surveyed had ended.

Donald A. Giannella

Date Due

AP 30 '75			
AP 7 '76			
MY 5 '76			

Demco 38-297